More Than Counting

STANDARDS EDITION

More Than COUNTING

Standards-Based Math Activities for Young Thinkers in Preschool and Kindergarten

SALLY MOOMAW and BRENDA HIERONYMUS

Redleaf Press®
www.redleafpress.org
800-423-8309

Published by Redleaf Press
10 Yorkton Court
St. Paul, MN 55117
www.redleafpress.org

First edition 2011
Cover design by James Handrigan
Cover photographs by Heather L. Guthridge
Interior typeset in Archer and designed by Percolator
Interior photos by David C. Baxter and Heather L. Guthridge
Printed in the United States of America
17 16 15 14 13 12 11 10   1 2 3 4 5 6 7 8

Library of Congress Cataloging-in-Publication Data
Moomaw, Sally, 1948–
    More than counting : math activities for preschool and kindergarten / Sally Moomaw and Brenda Hieronymus. — Standards ed.
        p. cm. — (More than . . . series)
    Includes bibliographical references.
    ISBN 978-1-60554-029-0 (alk. paper)
    1. Mathematics—Study and teaching (Preschool) 2. Mathematics—Study and teaching—Activity programs. I. Hieronymus, Brenda, 1945- II. Title.
QA135.6.M688 2011
372.7—dc22
                                                            2010029804

Printed on acid-free paper

Contents

Chapter 3 THE NUMBER AND OPERATIONS STANDARD—ARITHMETIC OPERATIONS

Teachers' Questions

Math Activities and Standards—Arithmetic Operations

Chapter 6 THE MEASUREMENT STANDARD

Chapter 7 THE DATA ANALYSIS AND PROBABILITY STANDARD

CHAPTER 1

Understanding and Applying Mathematics Standards for Young Children

Ian, age four years ten months, seemed to be lagging in the formation of basic math concepts, such as one-to-one correspondence, that were part of the number sense standard for preschool and kindergarten in his state. He showed little sustained interest in math materials. His teaching team discussed their concerns and decided they needed to embed mathematical curriculum in the areas where Ian typically played rather than continuing to try to direct Ian to areas with specific math materials. Because Ian liked dramatic play, his teachers decided to plan specific one-to-one correspondence activities for the dramatic play area. They used colored tape to divide a cookie sheet into boxes and introduced cookie magnets that fit into the boxes. Ian was excited when he saw the new materials. Soon he was carefully placing one cookie into each box on the cookie sheet. Shortly thereafter, he began using one-to-one correspondence to play math quantification games.

A crowd of children gathered every day at the farmers' market in the dramatic play area of a preschool classroom. The large basket of fruits and vegetables was constantly dumped on the floor. The teacher was disappointed with the quality of play in the center. Her director suggested that individual baskets for each type of food might alleviate the dumping problem. After the teacher made this small change, she noticed an entirely different type of play emerging. Children started sorting the food into categories.

They began counting how many of each type of food they had and comparing the quantities. Some children attempted to apportion the food so that each child had the same amount. Both the teacher and the director were delighted. The director brought a copy of the state's mathematics standards to the next planning session. "Look," she said, pointing to a page in the booklet. "The sorting that the children are doing in the farmers' market is part of the algebra standard. And look at the number sense standard on this page. Counting, comparing quantities, and dividing materials are all part of that standard. I think you've become a math teacher!"

• • •

For years, skillful preschool and kindergarten teachers have planned intentionally for their students based on the interests and developmental levels of individual children, as well as the group. More recently, this planning has been guided in part by national and state standards that have been developed for specific curricular areas, including mathematics. Teachers of even the youngest children must now translate these standards into effective and appropriate programs.

Fortunately, as the above scenarios illustrate, mathematics standards align well with a rich, play-based curriculum that is planned and implemented by reflective, knowledgeable teachers. Children construct important mathematical concepts when they encounter situations that encourage mathematical thinking. In fact, the National Council of Teachers of Mathematics (NCTM) states, "Adults support young children's diligence and mathematical development when they direct attention to the mathematics children use in their play, challenge them to solve problems, and encourage their persistence" (NCTM 2000). As early childhood educators, our charge is to understand the mathematics standards so we can continue to design curricular activities that best support learning.

Teachers' Questions

What are national mathematics standards?

National mathematics standards generally refer to standards drafted by NCTM, which was the first national organization to respond to the call for national standards in education. NCTM's Curriculum and Evaluation Standards for School Mathematics sets specific goals for educators to improve mathematics education and focuses heavily on thinking and problem-solving skills (NCTM 1989). This document was followed by *Principles and Standards for School Mathematics*, which integrates curriculum, teaching, and evaluation (NCTM 2000). The NCTM standards have been widely modeled by states across the nation and extend down to preschool.

The NCTM standards are divided into five content standards, or broad areas of mathematical learning, and five process standards, which comprise the strategies and methods individuals use to develop and understand mathematical concepts. Although content and process standards are of necessity closely connected, they are discussed separately for ease of understanding. The standards themselves span the broad educational period of preschool through twelfth grade and maintain their content area designations throughout. They are further organized across grade bands, starting with pre-kindergarten through grade 2. Therefore, the same standards address varying content based on the developmental levels of students.

What are the mathematics content standards?

The five NCTM content standards are briefly described in table 1. This book is organized around those standards, with each chapter devoted to a specific standard. The exception is the Number and Operations standard, which encompasses the largest amount of material in the early years and has therefore been separated into two chapters. Assessment is covered in chapter 8.

What are the mathematics process standards?

The five NCTM process standards are described in table 2. The process standards are highlighted under each activity throughout this book along with appropriate questions to encourage their application.

How do state standards differ from national standards in mathematics?

Most states have closely based their mathematics standards on the NCTM model, particularly with regard to the content standards. Nevertheless, in many states, standards-based education does not begin until kindergarten. Preschool teachers in those states can consult the kindergarten standards to gain an idea of the expected tracks in mathematics. While content remains similar across states, the language used to describe the standards may differ from that used by NCTM. For example, Florida identifies preschool and kindergarten standards under the following headings: Number

Sense, Number and Operations, Patterns and Seriation, Geometry, Spatial Relations, and Measurement (Florida Dept. of Education 2007). Notice Florida has divided the NCTM Number and Operations standard into two separate standards; similarly, the NCTM Geometry standard has been split into Geometry and Spatial Sense. Florida's Patterns and Seriation would correspond to the Algebra standard in NCTM, and Data Analysis and Probability has been omitted as a category but may be encompassed under Number and Operations. By looking closely at the definitions in table 1, teachers will be able to align their own state standards to the appropriate national standards in most cases.

Which standards are most important?

Early childhood mathematics experts differ somewhat with regard to their recommendations for early childhood educators. For example, the National Mathematics Advisory Panel recommends that all early mathematics instruction lead toward the development of algebra concepts (National Mathematics Advisory Panel 2008). On the other hand, the National Research Council (NRS) and NCTM *Curriculum Focal Points* focus on number, geometry, and measurement during the early years (NRS 2009; NCTM 2006). While the findings may appear at odds, closer examina-

Table 1: NCTM Content Standards in Mathematics

Content Standard and Highlighted Chapter(s)	Description
Number and Operations Chapters 2 and 3	This broad standard focuses on the development of a deep understanding of number, including the relationships among numbers and arithmetic operations.
Algebra Chapter 4	The algebra standard encompasses an understanding of patterns and relationships and includes the analyzing, representation, and modeling of mathematical situations.
Geometry Chapter 5	Geometry involves an understanding of spatial relationships as well as the properties of two- and three-dimensional objects.
Measurement Chapter 6	The measurement standard encompasses the measurable attributes of objects, appropriate units of measure, and the application of number to measurement.
Data Analysis and Probability Chapter 7	This standard includes organizing and interpreting data and determining the likelihood that certain events or relationships will occur.

tion shows the National Mathematics Advisory Panel acknowledges that fluency with whole numbers and fractions (number sense) and certain aspects of geometry and measurement are important foundations for later algebra. Similarly, NCTM closely connects algebra and data analysis to their *Curriculum Focal Points*. All five content standards are important and complement one another. The relationships among standards are highlighted for each activity throughout this book.

Why is "math talk" important in the early years?

Research has shown that the amount of math-related talking teachers engage in with young children is significantly related to the mathematical learning of the children over the school year (Klibanoff et al. 2006, 59–69). Intentional teachers can integrate math talk into the numerous conversations they have with children throughout the day, whether during play, snack or lunch, circle time, or actual math activities. For example, while interacting with children in the block area, the teacher might model one-to-one correspondence for those who skip over objects when counting. The teacher might say, "Help me count the cars on my train. I want to make sure I don't miss any."

Teachers can also use leading questions to encourage children to think mathematically. When children encounter a mathematical problem, the teacher can serve as a facilitator. Careful choice of questions can move

Table 2: NCTM Process Standards in Mathematics

Process Standard	Description
Problem Solving	Problem solving involves drawing upon previous knowledge to solve a unique problem. It is a primary means by which children develop mathematical understanding.
Reasoning and Proof	Reasoning and proof encompasses developing and evaluating mathematical arguments.
Communication	The communication standard encourages children to formulate and express their mathematical thinking.
Connections	The connections standard includes interconnections among various areas of mathematics, as well as the relationship between mathematics and other curricular areas.
Representation	Representation encompasses the variety of methods that children use to model and communicate mathematical concepts.

children forward in their thinking. The following are examples of leading questions that encourage children to think harder or change the direction of their thinking:

- How can we tell which row has more?

- Is there another way to find out if you both have the same amount?

- If two more friends come to our party, will we have enough cups?

- How many ice balls do you think will fit into this cup?

Should mathematics be considered a specific curriculum in preschool and kindergarten?

Absolutely. Although mathematics can and should be integrated throughout the classroom, designating it as a specific course of study encourages teachers to focus on mathematics curriculum, learning, and outcomes. Current expectations for preschool and kindergarten teachers include alignment of curriculum to mathematics content and process standards as well as documentation of learning. Focusing on the content areas of mathematics and incorporating teaching strategies that intentionally encourage children to think and communicate mathematically require that mathematics be designated as a specific curriculum starting in preschool and kindergarten.

Why is it important to integrate mathematics throughout the curriculum?

Each area of the classroom presents unique opportunities for children to encounter real math problems to solve through their play. From dividing eggs equitably in the dramatic play area to finding enough triangular-shaped blocks for the entire perimeter of the roof of a block structure, children must deal with real math problems throughout their day. Teachers can increase the possibilities for children to engage in mathematical thinking by embedding opportunities for mathematical reasoning in their plans for each area of the classroom.

There is another important reason for integrating mathematics throughout the classroom. Some children avoid even the most inviting mathematics materials because they feel insecure in the mathematics area or fear failure. By introducing the same concepts in areas of the classroom in which particular children feel most comfortable, teachers allow children to think about mathematical possibilities within a secure, supportive environment. A child who may not want to join a group at the mathematics game table may be very interested in finding enough plastic worms for each of his friends' fishing poles in the dramatic play area. Later, when he has become more confident, he may apply the same concepts used in quantifying the fishing bait to a game in the math center, especially if it's a fishing game.

What is universal design, and how does it apply to mathematics?

The concept of universal design originated in architecture to designate designs that accommodated the broadest spectrum of possible users. The term has become widely adopted in education to refer to inclusive learning environments that support all learners, including those with specific disabilities, as full participants (Salend 2008, 328–31). Universal design for learning (often referred to as UDL) adheres to three important principles:

1. Instruction should provide multiple ways for students to acquire knowledge.

2. Students should have many different means to demonstrate what they know.

3. Educators should employ many different methods to engage learners.

In preschool and kindergarten classrooms, well-designed math activities are often open-ended, so they already accommodate a wide range of developmental levels. For example, a game in which children roll a die to determine how many counters to take supports children at three distinct levels of thinking: (1) *global,* in which children know that they need to take some counters and may distinguish between a few and a lot; (2) *one-to-one correspondence,* in which children align one counter with each dot on the die; and (3) *counting,* in which children count the dots to determine how many counters to take. Other children might play the game with two dice and add the quantities. The important point is the material itself is designed to accommodate this range of students.

Integrating mathematics throughout the classroom provides further support for UDL principles. Children can engage in mathematical learning and communicate what they understand through art, music, building, and other play activities.

Dramatic Play Area

Cookie Sheets and Cookie Magnets

DESCRIPTION

Many teachers include a bakery in the dramatic play area. For this activity, colored tape is used to divide cookie sheets into boxes, and magnetic cookies fit into the grid spaces. Children are encouraged to put objects into a one-to-one correspondence relationship as they seek one cookie for each box on the cookie sheet.

MATERIALS

☐ cookie sheets divided into a grid with colored tape

☐ cookie magnets made from plastic cookies and magnetic tape or commercially available

CHILD'S LEVEL

This activity is designed for children who are working on one-to-one correspondence; however, the materials are self-leveling, so children with more advanced skills may use them as tools for counting, addition, and subtraction.

WHAT TO LOOK FOR

- Many children will place one cookie into each box on the cookie sheets in a one-to-one correspondence relationship.

- Some children will count the cookies.

- Some children will compare the quantities of cookies on two cookie sheets.

MORE >

- Children may add extra cookies to their sheet and re-count to find the total.
- Some children will count the empty spaces to find out how many more cookies they need to fill the cookie sheet.
- Children may subtract as they give away some cookies and then count how many they have left.

MODIFICATIONS FOR SPECIAL NEEDS OR SITUATIONS

No specific modifications are anticipated for children with special needs. Teachers could add order forms to the area for more advanced children or suggest that they make price tags.

MATHEMATICS CONTENT STANDARD CONNECTIONS

This activity aligns primarily with Number and Operations. It incorporates concepts of one-to-one correspondence, counting, set comparisons, addition, and subtraction. Because the activity also allows children to model a mathematical problem, it aligns to the Algebra standard.

COMMENTS AND QUESTIONS RELATED TO MATHEMATICS PROCESS STANDARDS

Problem Solving: Do we have enough chocolate cookies to fill your cookie sheet?

Reasoning and Proof: Troy says there are more chocolate chip cookies than chocolate cookies. How do you know, Troy?

Communication: Tell me how many cookies to bake so we can each have two.

Connections: Can you write down my order please? I want two chocolate cookies and one chocolate chip. (Connects to Literacy)

Representation: What will my order look like if I add two more chocolate chip cookies?

Sensory Table

Frogs on Lily Pads

DESCRIPTION

In this activity, small plastic frogs and pretend lily pads placed in the class water table provide the incentive for children to think about one-to-one correspondence and quantification. Many children quickly decide that one frog should sit on each lily pad—a one-to-one correspondence alignment. Teacher's questions can further direct children's thinking along those lines, as well as create additional mathematical situations for children to model. For example, the teacher might ask how many lily pads are needed if two frogs sit on each lily pad.

MATERIALS

☐ approximately 12 small plastic frogs

☐ green plastic coasters or lids (approximately 3 inches in diameter) to use as lily pads (1 per frog)

☐ sensory table or plastic dish pans with water

☐ fishing nets (optional)

CHILD'S LEVEL

This activity is appropriate for many levels. Younger children may focus on one-to-one correspondence and put one frog on each lily pad. Older children may use the frogs for addition, subtraction, multiplication, or division.

WHAT TO LOOK FOR

• Many children will put one frog on each lily pad in a one-to-one correspondence relationship.

• Some children will add additional frogs to the lily pads.

MORE >

- Children may put the same number of frogs on several lily pads and quantify the results (multiplication).

- Children may devise strategies to divide the frogs equitably.

- Some frogs vary by color, size, or design. Children may sort frogs by their various attributes.

MODIFICATIONS FOR SPECIAL NEEDS OR SITUATIONS

To help children focus on one-to-one correspondence, use lily pads that are about the same size as the frogs. This will encourage children to pair one frog with each lily pad. For older or more advanced children, use larger lily pads and more frogs. This will encourage addition and multiplication as children put varying quantities of frogs on the lily pads.

MATHEMATICS CONTENT STANDARD CONNECTIONS

This activity aligns directly with Number and Operations. It focuses on the mathematical concepts of one-to-one correspondence, quantification, and the arithmetic operations (addition, subtraction, multiplication, and division). Because children will use the frogs to model various mathematical relationships, it can also be considered part of the Algebra standard. Sorting the frogs or creating patterns with them would be a further alignment to algebra.

COMMENTS AND QUESTIONS RELATED TO MATHEMATICS PROCESS STANDARDS

Problem Solving: How many frogs do you need in order to put one on each lily pad?

Reasoning and Proof: How can you tell which lily pad has the most frogs?

Communication: Tell Barry why you think he has too many frogs.

Connections: You've sorted the frogs by color. Let's line them up by color on this tray and find out which color has the most. (Connects to Data Analysis)

Representation: What would it look like if each lily pad had two frogs on it?

Snack

Goldfish Cracker Story

DESCRIPTION

The following story, or a similar one created by the teacher or a child, can encourage children to think mathematically as they reenact the story with their snack crackers.

> Once four goldfish were swimming in a pond.

> **Can you show what that would look like?**

> A little girl and her friend were fishing in the pond, and they each caught a goldfish.

> **How many fish were left?**

> The girls felt sorry for the fish, so they threw them back into the pond. Soon another fish joined the group.

> **How many fish were there now?**

> A hungry turtle ate one of the fish.

> **How many fish were left?**

> Then a man caught two fish and put them in a bowl to take home.

> **How many fish were left?**

> What do you think happened next?

MATERIALS

☐ goldfish crackers

☐ napkins (preferably blue)

CHILD'S LEVEL

Both preschool and kindergarten children find this activity challenging and interesting. The teacher can vary the difficulty of questions in the story based on the level of the children.

MORE >

WHAT TO LOOK FOR

- Children will use the goldfish crackers to act out the story.
- Some children will only respond to one mathematical operation if there are two questions.
- Children will add and subtract fish as they model the story.
- Some children will extend the story or make up their own stories.
- Some children will decide what to do by watching other children.

MODIFICATIONS FOR SPECIAL NEEDS OR SITUATIONS

Start with fewer crackers (two or three) and simplify the directions for children who are younger or less advanced. Use more goldfish with children who are more experienced with quantification. In kindergarten, teachers can create stories that emphasize particular number combinations children may be working on.

MATHEMATICS CONTENT STANDARD CONNECTIONS

Because the emphasis in this activity is on modeling mathematical problems, it aligns with the Algebra standard. It connects equally well to Number and Operations with its emphasis on quantification, addition, and subtraction.

COMMENTS AND QUESTIONS RELATED TO MATHEMATICS PROCESS STANDARDS

Problem Solving: Each question in the story emphasizes problem solving.

Reasoning and Proof: How did you figure out how many fish would be left?

Communication: Tell Christina why you think she should have five fish now instead of four.

Connections: Is there a way to make a pattern with the fish? (Connects to Algebra)

Representation: Can you draw a picture of this story?

Wood Block Sound Patterns

Some instruments are made of wood.

DESCRIPTION

Music is one of the first activities through which children begin to perceive, imitate, and create patterns. Clapping patterns and repeating melodies in songs are examples. This activity allows children to experiment with two hollow wood blocks that are identical except in size and, therefore, pitch. As children quickly discover, the larger wood block has a lower sound than the smaller wood block. Children often create alternating high-low patterns with the wood blocks.

MATERIALS

☐ 2 wood blocks that differ in size, commercially available or constructed as follows:

1. From a piece of wood approximately 3½ inches wide and 1½ inches thick (commonly called a "two by four"), cut two lengths of wood, one 5 inches long and the other 3 inches long, to form the base of each wood block.

2. From a piece of wood approximately 3½ inches wide and ¾ inches thick (commonly called a "one by four"), cut two lengths of wood, one 5 inches long and the other 3 inches long, to form the top of each wood block.

3. From a strip of wood approximately ½ inch wide and ¼ inch thick, cut 6 strips of wood to fit evenly along three edges of each of the 2 wood block bases.

MORE >

4. Sand the wood pieces. Glue the thin strips of wood to the bases of the two wood blocks with wood glue. Then glue the tops into place.

5. To make mallets for the wood blocks, glue a large macramé bead onto a 7-inch dowel that fits firmly through the hole in the bead. (Be certain the bead cannot be pulled off the dowel so it does not pose a potential choking threat.)

CHILD'S LEVEL

This activity is appropriate for all children. It is designed for children to experiment with beginning patterns; however, older children may create more complex patterns.

WHAT TO LOOK FOR

- Children will experiment with the wood blocks and notice that they differ in sound.
- Many children will alternate between the two wood blocks, creating an A-B pattern.
- Some children will create longer and more complex patterns.
- Some children will copy patterns created by the teacher or other children.

MODIFICATIONS FOR SPECIAL NEEDS OR SITUATIONS

No modifications for this activity are anticipated.

MATHEMATICS CONTENT STANDARD CONNECTIONS

This activity aligns with the Algebra standard because of its focus on patterning. It also connects to the Measurement standard because children will compare sizes of wood blocks.

COMMENTS AND QUESTIONS RELATED TO MATHEMATICS PROCESS STANDARDS

Problem Solving: How would it sound if you played two times on each wood block?

Reasoning and Proof: How can you tell that your pattern is the same as Ethan's?

Communication: What do I need to do to play your pattern?

Connections: How many times did I tap the big wood block? Did I tap the small block the same number of times? (Connects to Number and Operations)

Representation: How could we make a high-low pattern with our hands?

Pumpkin Growing Prediction Chart

How do you think pumpkins grow?

on a tree	on a bush	under ground	on a vine
Sarah			
Steven		Patty	
Chad		Ronnie	
Mark	Robin	Jimmy	
Amanda	Ruby	Trey	Audrey
Jeff	Eric	Barb	Peter

DESCRIPTION

This graph is used prior to a field trip to a pumpkin farm. It encourages children to engage in scientific inquiry, including forming a prediction, collecting data, and checking their hypothesis. Children predict whether pumpkins grow on a tree (like apples), on a bush (like berries), under the ground (like carrots), or on a vine (like grapes). On the field trip, children can verify whether their predictions were correct or not.

MATERIALS

☐ posterboard or paper, 12 × 18 inches

☐ illustrations of a pumpkin growing on a tree, a bush, under the ground, or on a vine to place at the bottom of each column

☐ a name tag to record each child's prediction

☐ tape to attach the name tags to the chart

MORE >

CHILD'S LEVEL

This graph is most appropriate for older preschool and kindergarten children as it involves making predictions. Nevertheless, all children in the class will be interested in participating.

WHAT TO LOOK FOR

• Some children have not seen pumpkins growing and, therefore, have to guess based on their experiences with other things that grow.

• Many children will be able to tell which columns have the most and the fewest votes by comparing the heights of the columns.

• Some children will accurately count the votes in each column.

• Some children will accurately determine how many more votes one column has than another, particularly if the columns are adjacent.

MODIFICATIONS FOR SPECIAL NEEDS OR SITUATIONS

For children with visual acuity problems, use a larger chart with strong contrast between the background and the print on the name tags. Younger children and children with cognitive delays may benefit from strong pointing gestures by the teacher as the votes are counted and the columns compared.

This activity can be easily adapted to be used with field trips to apple orchards and other types of farms.

MATHEMATICS CONTENT STANDARD CONNECTIONS

This activity aligns to the Data Analysis and Probability standard because children are organizing data (their votes) on a graph and using the graph to assess their predictions. Because children are also quantifying the number of votes in each category and comparing them, the activity also aligns strongly with Number and Operations.

COMMENTS AND QUESTIONS RELATED TO MATHEMATICS PROCESS STANDARDS

Problem Solving: Which column has the fewest (or most) votes? Are any columns tied?

Reasoning and Proof: How do you know that this column has the most votes?

Communication: Steve and Sammy aren't here today. What will happen to the graph if they both think pumpkins grow on trees?

Connections: What shape(s) do you think the pumpkins will be? Do you think the pumpkins at the farm will all be the same size? (Connects to Geometry and Measurement)

Representation: We're going to make a class book about our field trip. Help me write down what the graph tells us about our predictions.

Art Area

Surfaces, Edges, and Points

DESCRIPTION

Three components of geometric solids are surfaces (sides), edges (places where two surfaces connect), and points (places where three or more surfaces connect). In this activity, children dip various parts of three-dimensional solids into paint and create imprints on paper. The imprints enable children to better visualize and talk about the shapes of the surfaces, the lines that form the edges, and the points created by multiple surfaces coming together, as in the point at the top of a steeple.

MATERIALS

☐ geometric solids, commercially available or teacher found/created

☐ tempera paint placed in a dish lined with a sponge to absorb the excess paint

☐ paper

Materials Note: Plastic or foam geometric solids work best for this activity because the paint easily washes off. Teachers who do not have access to commercial materials can use a small ball for a sphere, small boxes for cubes

MORE >

and rectangular solids, and a can for a cylinder. Other shapes can be created with plastic or foam material from craft stores.

CHILD'S LEVEL

This activity is suitable for children of all ages. Older preschool and kindergarten children can be expected to pay more attention to edges and points (if so directed by the teacher), while younger children may focus more on the shapes of the surfaces.

WHAT TO LOOK FOR

- Children will compare the shapes created by the various surfaces.

- Some children will be surprised at the shapes created. For example, the base of the pyramid is square while the sides are triangles.

- Most children will not explore the edges and points unless directed by the teacher.

MODIFICATIONS FOR SPECIAL NEEDS OR SITUATIONS

For younger children or children with cognitive delays, teachers can reduce the number of geometric solids to two or three. This makes comparisons and discussion easier. Children with visual impairments can use paint mixed with sand so that they can feel the imprints after they have dried and compare them to the original objects.

MATHEMATICS CONTENT STANDARD CONNECTIONS

This activity connects directly to the Geometry standard. Some children may sort and classify the shapes, which would connect to the Algebra standard.

COMMENTS AND QUESTIONS RELATED TO MATHEMATICS PROCESS STANDARDS

Problem Solving: How can we figure out how many sides of this prism are rectangles and how many sides are triangles?

Reasoning and Proof: How do you know that all of the sides of the cube are the same shape?

Communication: Tell David how you made that X on your paper. I don't see any shapes with an X. (Note: An X can be made with the edges of geometric forms.)

Connections: Are there more shapes with edges or without edges? (Connects to Algebra through the use of sorting and to Number and Operations because of set comparison)

Representation: Tomorrow we'll use these shapes with the playdough and see if we can create the same lines and shapes that you made with the paint.

Block Area

Blocks and Mirrors

DESCRIPTION

Mirrors allow children to observe symmetrical images of their own creations, such as block structures or drawings. In this activity, children build with colored table blocks in front of a nonbreakable mirror. Children quickly notice that the back of their structure appears to be the front in the mirror image.

MATERIALS

☐ colored table blocks or other small building materials

☐ nonbreakable mirror to place behind the building area

☐ additional small, nonbreakable mirrors to create reflections of various angles of the block structure (optional)

CHILD'S LEVEL

Children of all ages are interested in mirror images. Older preschool and kindergarten children are more likely to focus on the symmetrical aspect of the images.

WHAT TO LOOK FOR

• Children will marvel at the symmetrical image of their work created by the mirror.

• Children will eventually realize that the image in the mirror is the back of their actual structure rather than the front.

• Children will see geometric shapes from many different angles, particularly if several mirrors are used.

MORE >

MODIFICATIONS FOR SPECIAL NEEDS OR SITUATIONS

Younger children, or children with cognitive delays, may benefit from using fewer but larger blocks, such as fabric-covered blocks. Blocks that have designs drawn on them allow children to see an image in the mirror that they may not be able to see from the front, thereby making the effect of the mirror more noticeable.

MATHEMATICS CONTENT STANDARD CONNECTIONS

Because this activity involves shapes, positional terms, and symmetrical images, it aligns to the Geometry standard. Symmetry is a specific type of pattern; therefore, this activity also connects to the Algebra standard.

COMMENTS AND QUESTIONS RELATED TO MATHEMATICS PROCESS STANDARDS

Problem Solving: Where should I put this toy person so that I can see him only in the mirror?

Reasoning and Proof: How do you know it's the back side of the building you're seeing in the mirror?

Communication: I want to make a tower like yours. What shapes do I need and where should they go?

Connections: Are there enough rectangular blocks left for me to make a tower like yours? (Connects to Number and Operations)

Representation: How can we remember how this structure looks in case we want to build it again? What ideas do you have?

Gross-Motor Area

Forward and Back

DESCRIPTION

This game is similar to the short path games found in chapter 2. Carpet squares are arranged to form three straight paths of ten mats each that lead to a finish line. One child can hop along each path at a time. Children take turns drawing from a jumbo deck of cards that show how many spaces to hop forward or backward.

MATERIALS

☐ 30 carpet squares

☐ tape for the finish line

☐ jumbo card deck made from 8½ × 11 inch white construction paper with from 1 to 4 circle stickers and the words "Go forward" or "Go back" on each card

CHILD'S LEVEL

This game is most appropriate for older preschool and kindergarten children because it involves more complicated directions than many of the other games; however, younger children will likely simplify it to meet their own developmental needs, such as by always hopping forward.

WHAT TO LOOK FOR

• Many of the older children will follow the directions on the cards and move a corresponding number of spaces forward or backward along the path.

• Some children will only move forward along the path.

MORE >

- Some children may disregard the cards and hop along the path in a one-to-one correspondence fashion, with one hop per carpet square.

MODIFICATIONS FOR SPECIAL NEEDS OR SITUATIONS

For younger children or children with cognitive delays, remove the words from the cards and reduce the number of dots to one or two per card.

MATHEMATICS CONTENT STANDARD CONNECTIONS

This game simulates a number line, which strongly aligns to the Number and Operations standard. Children can move forward and backward along the path, simulating addition and subtraction along a number line.

COMMENTS AND QUESTIONS RELATED TO MATHEMATICS PROCESS STANDARDS

Problem Solving: You hopped four spaces on your first turn, and now you have to go back two spaces. How many spaces along the path will that be?

Reasoning and Proof: How can you tell that you're ahead of Ja'quez on the path?

Communication: Can you explain to Rosalie why you think she went in the wrong direction?

Connections: Who is farther along the path so far? (Connects to Measurement)

Representation: Show me how many times this card says to hop.

Baby Stroller Game

DESCRIPTION

For this game, lines are drawn on a sidewalk to create a path similar to that in a board game. Children with doll strollers are the movers. The children roll a giant dot die to determine how many spaces to push their strollers along the path. When they reach the end, they can select a toy for their dolls.

MATERIALS

☐ tempera paint or chalk used to draw path lines on the sidewalk

☐ 1–6 die made from a large, stuffed fabric cube with from 1 to 6 dots painted on each side

☐ doll strollers and dolls

☐ baby toys (optional)

CHILD'S LEVEL

This activity is appropriate for either preschool or kindergarten children. The path simulates a number line.

WHAT TO LOOK FOR

• Children will roll the die and move a corresponding number of spaces along the path.

• Children will use various strategies (global, one-to-one correspondence, or counting) to determine how many spaces to move.

• Children may correct one another when they feel a mistake has been made.

• Some children will play the game repeatedly to collect more toys for their dolls.

MORE >

MODIFICATIONS FOR SPECIAL NEEDS OR SITUATIONS

For children who are just beginning to quantify, use a 1–3 die rather than a 1–6 die.

MATHEMATICS CONTENT STANDARD CONNECTIONS

Like activity 1.8, this game connects to the Number and Operations standard. Children have many opportunities to practice quantification skills and also to gain a feel for moving along a number line.

COMMENTS AND QUESTIONS RELATED TO MATHEMATICS PROCESS STANDARDS

Problem Solving: How much do you need to roll on the die to get to the end of the path?

Reasoning and Proof: Colin thinks you moved too many spaces. Can you explain why you think you moved the right number of spaces?

Communication: How did you decide how many spaces to move?

Connections: How many spaces long is our path? Are all of the spaces the same size? (Connects to Measurement)

Representation: Can you draw a picture of this path so that we can play the game inside with the tiny baby strollers? How many spaces do we need for the path?

Science Area

Seed Race

DESCRIPTION

Science and mathematics are often interconnected. This activity connects biology and measurement. Children plant three types of seeds that are selected because they grow at different rates and to different heights. A piece of Plexiglas placed on one side of the container allows children to measure daily growth of the various plants without restricting sunlight. Children can record daily the height of each plant by marking directly on the Plexiglas with permanent markers.

If desired, the Plexiglas can be periodically removed from the container and the lengths of the marks be measured with standard or nonstandard measuring tools.

MATERIALS

☐ 3 types of seeds (sunflower, green bean, and carrot are suggested)

☐ container that is long enough to spread out the seeds, such as an inexpensive window box or plastic dish pan

MORE >

- ☐ potting soil
- ☐ Plexiglas pane to place in the back of the container
- ☐ permanent markers
- ☐ standard or nonstandard measuring tools, such as rulers or paper clips (optional)

CHILD'S LEVEL

This activity is suitable for children of a wide developmental range. Young preschoolers can visually judge the heights of the plants and use comparison terms, such as *tall* or *little*. Older children can compare growth daily, make predictions about future growth, and record growth using a variety of measurement tools.

WHAT TO LOOK FOR

- Children will use the marks on the Plexiglas to monitor growth daily.
- Children will begin to use comparison terms, such as "growing faster" and "taller."
- Some children will be interested in using tools to translate growth into measurement units.

MODIFICATIONS FOR SPECIAL NEEDS OR SITUATIONS

All children can participate at some level in this activity. Children with visual disabilities can use puffy paint to mark plant growth daily. On subsequent days, they can feel the previous marks.

MATHEMATICS CONTENT STANDARD CONNECTIONS

This activity directly aligns with the Measurement standard. Because children are creating a mathematical model on the Plexiglas, it is also connected to Algebra. Children who measure plant growth may also employ Number and Operations as they quantify the units.

COMMENTS AND QUESTIONS RELATED TO MATHEMATICS PROCESS STANDARDS

Problem Solving: How can we tell how much the sunflower has grown compared to yesterday?

Reasoning and Proof: How do you know the bean grew more than the carrot?

Communication: We're going to make a book about our plants. What should we say about the sunflowers today?

Connections: Are all of the sunflowers taller than the carrots? (Connects to Life Science)

Representation: What's another way to show how tall each plant is?

CHAPTER 2

The Number and Operations Standard—Quantification

Hiroki eagerly played an elephant stacking game with his teacher. Each time he rolled the dice, he counted the dots and then stacked an equivalent number of small blocks on the back of a plastic elephant. The tower of blocks grew higher and higher. A crowd of spectators gathered around the math table. Whenever the teacher or Hiroki rolled the dice, the watchful children squealed with delight as they, too, computed how many more blocks would be stacked on the tower. One child yelled excitedly, "Stop! No more blocks. You already have more than twenty." Another one said, "Hope for two dots, so you won't knock down the tower. Roll just one die, not two." When the tower fell, the teacher told the children that the game began with forty blocks in the basket and asked Hiroki to make sure all of them were still there. Hiroki counted the blocks, saying the counting words in sequence; he skipped some numbers and double counted others. Jamie, who had been quietly watching, lined up the blocks in several rows and accurately counted them.

· · ·

Math games such as this one provide opportunities for children to repeatedly think about Number and Operations as they respond to the play challenges posed by the materials. Frequently, other children are drawn to the excitement of the games, and collective negotiation and problem solving emerge. Children are challenged to broaden their thinking as they listen to the ideas of their peers and discuss the ramifications of each roll of the dice. Teachers gather important assessment data during interactions with math materials. They observe thinking strategies and errors in thinking. They are careful to avoid *immediately* correcting errors, such as when Hiroki skipped some blocks and double counted others. They make notes about their observations. Their assessment notes help them use intentional teaching strategies at another time to model organizing materials for counting. Sometimes a peer, like Jamie, models a more logical way of solving the problem. Everyone benefits from the experience, including the teacher who now has assessment data for both Hiroki and Jamie.

Teachers' Questions

How does the Number and Operations standard apply to young children?

Young children are developing the foundation for the broad mathematical area of Number and Operations. These foundational concepts include developing quantification strategies, understanding and applying counting principles, and comparing sets. For this reason, the Number and Operations standard is regarded as the most important content standard for young children and the most all-encompassing (NCTM 2006).

The Number and Operations standard focuses on the development of a deep understanding of number, often referred to as *number sense,* which includes the ability to decompose numbers and use them as referents. If this sounds overly complicated for young children, recall that even very young children learn that two can be decomposed as "one for me and one for you." Just as children memorize the alphabet song, many young children begin to learn the sequence of the words used for counting and repeat them in their play—although the sequence may not yet be the conventional one. Teachers often overhear conversations about who has more or less, observe children holding up three fingers to indicate how old they are, or help mediate an intense discussion about how many days until the next field trip. All of these instances demonstrate an understanding of number concepts.

What are the developmental stages of quantification?

Teachers will observe children progressing through three stages of quantification: global, one-to-one correspondence, and counting (Kamii 1982, 35). This was already mentioned in chapter 1. An understanding of these levels of thinking is critical to the development of appropriate curriculum for young children. As adults, we often think of counting as the only way to quantify, but children begin to solve mathematical problems long before they are able to understand and employ counting as their strategy for quantifying. Quantification is the concept of determining "how many." Although the age at which children enter the three quantification stages will vary, as will the length of time they spend in each stage, the order of the stages is progressive and reflects shifts in children's logical thinking as they develop.

Global: Young children are initially guided by their perceptions when quantifying, and this is reflected in the global stage of quantification. At this level, children make a visual approximation of the quantity they are attempting to match. For example, if a child wants to take as many crackers as another child and it looks like the other child has a lot of crackers, the first child may take a handful as her method of producing an equivalent amount. If asked to take as many teddy bears as dots on a card, a child may make a pile of bears that visually appear to be the same amount as the dots on the card.

One-to-One Correspondence: At this stage, children continue to use their visual or tactile perceptions as a guide for quantifying but in a much more logical manner. When attempting to take an equivalent amount for a given set, children in the one-to-one correspondence stage align or match one new item for each object in the original set. When asked to get enough plates for everyone at the table, the child may place one plate in front of each chair to create an equivalent set. If asked if he has as many baby bear counters as mama bear counters, the child may match each mama bear counter with a baby bear counter by aligning them in rows across from each other—one mama bear for each baby bear.

Counting: At this stage, children quantify by counting the number of objects in the original set and then counting an equivalent number of pieces for their new set. While children may make errors in their counting, selecting counting as the strategy for solving quantification problems shows they have advanced in their mathematical thinking.

What important counting principles must young children learn?

Three important counting principles for young children to understand are the stable order principle, one-to-one correspondence, and cardinality (Gelman and Gallistel 1978). To accurately use counting to quantify, children must realize there is a particular order to saying the counting words (stable order principle). This is sometimes called rote counting. Children must also realize they can count each object once and only once and must therefore say only one number for each object counted (one-to-one correspondence). Children choose counting as the strategy for quantifying or creating an equivalent set when they understand that the last item they count represents the total (cardinality).

Do children make errors in thinking at the counting stage of quantification?

Children make errors in their understanding of stable order and one-to-one correspondence. Children typically remember the counting words in sequence up to a point and then may repeat some counting words or say them in random order. This demonstrates an error in stable order. With age and experience, children gradually remember more and more of the correct sequence of the counting words. When counting objects, children often double count objects or skip objects to be counted. They do not yet realize the importance of accurately counting each object once and only once. In other words, children do not apply the concept of one-to-one correspondence to counting. This concept develops with age and experience as more logical thought develops.

Is there a specific order in which children construct counting concepts?

Although many children learn to say the counting words in sequence at an early age, there is not a specific hierarchy to constructing the counting concepts. Children can understand cardinality and make mistakes in stable order counting or count objects more than once. Children may say the counting words in sequence but skip objects as they attempt to quantify. Children often make more errors when the quantification problem is more challenging. A child may accurately quantify ten objects configured in a row but make errors when attempting to quantify twenty objects in a random configuration.

Do children reach the counting stage of quantification and remain in that stage?

Young children typically choose the quantification strategy that is best for a problem-solving situation. A child may choose to quantify by counting objects less than ten and use one-to-one correspondence to create an equivalent set of objects greater than ten. A child may be able to equally divide ten objects into two rows at the stage of one-to-one correspondence, yet divide thirty objects into two sets using the global strategy by making two piles of objects that visually look like they contain the same amount of objects.

How can teachers support children's construction of quantification?

Teachers can model alternative methods of quantification without judging or correcting children on the strategies they are using. It is important for teachers to continually assess children's level of quantification so that when teachers choose to enter play situations they can model quantification at or slightly above the level of the children. For example, the teacher might model cardinality for children who do not yet realize the last number counted represents the total. While playing in the block area, the teacher might say, "I wonder how many chairs I need for my people. Let's see—one, two, three, four. I have four people, so I need four chairs. Can you help me find four chairs?" A teacher who observes children double counting objects, might say, "I am going to line up my cars and count them." This models the strategy of organizing objects for more accurate quantification. If the teacher models a strategy that is too far above the level of the children, the children will not be able to reflect on the experience in a meaningful way. This is why the teacher's understanding of what stage of quantification the children are in is so important.

Teachers can also create interesting math games that encourage children to create and compare sets and count. Many examples are included in this chapter, as well as in chapter 3.

What types of math games should teachers use with young children?

Math manipulative games that include a die or spinner and interesting objects to quantify help children construct quantification concepts. Other types of quantification games include a grid or bingo type of card to hold the counters or a path to move them along.

Math manipulative games are important because they encourage children to create sets with movable objects. Children can use game pieces to create many mathematical relations. For example, children form one-to-one correspondence relationships when they learn to align one object with each dot on a die or to say one counting word each time they take an object. As children decide how many counters to take in a game, they must constantly quantify a set of dots on the die or spinner and create an equivalent set of objects. Children eventually begin to roll two dice and discover they can get the total by counting all the dots. In this way, addition concepts begin to emerge. Games that encourage children to take away counters foster the construction of subtraction concepts.

Math grid games are similar to manipulative games, but they provide a bingo type of board with designated spaces to set the counters. This supports one-to-one correspondence concepts, because children must typically place one object on each space to win the game. The grid spaces allow children to visualize how many more objects they need to cover the total number of spaces, which provides an addition or subtraction problem like they will encounter in other forms later in school.

Path games also encourage children to create and compare sets, but instead of forming sets with concrete objects, children move a specific number of spaces along a path equivalent to the set of dots they roll on a die. This is more abstract than simply taking objects that match a number of dots. As the child moves his or her mover, the spaces that have been counted are not represented with a concrete material, such as a cover-up piece. Path games are important because they introduce the concept of a number line, with each step along the path one more than the previous space. The easiest path games are called **short path games** because they have approximately 10 spaces, which is many fewer than their counterparts, **long path games.** There are two other differences between these two types of path games. To make them less confusing for children who are transitioning from grid to path games, the short path games provide a separate path for each player and the path is straight. In contrast, the long path games have one curved path for all players. While the short path games are more difficult than grid games, they are considerably less difficult than long path games.

How does assessment guide planning?

Teachers who carefully record observations of children can use these informal assessments to guide their planning for the class as well as for an individual child. For example, if a teacher has a group of children who are largely at the global stage of quantification, she may include more opportunities throughout the classroom for children to explore one-to-one correspondence, such as asking a child to get one cup for each person at the snack table or one paintbrush for each paint container. This may encourage children to move forward to a new level in their thinking, perhaps at a faster pace than if they had fewer opportunities to think about one-to-one relationships. Likewise, the teacher might create additional opportunities in the classroom to model counting as a quantification strategy if she feels children are ready for more of this type of experience.

How can teachers help children develop number sense concepts?

Teachers should use intentional teaching strategies in the classroom to model number sense concepts. Intentional teaching includes instruction to a child or group of children in the form of modeling or demonstration, prompting, directly teaching or reteaching information, or encouraging children to discuss errors with one another. This may be a brief, natural interaction between the child and teacher in which the teacher focuses on what the child is doing or thinking mathematically and then encourages or provides elaboration. For example, the teacher might comment, "I see one plastic fish in each of your three bowls. How many fish will you have if you put two fish in each bowl?" Intentional teaching is essential to the construction of number sense. While children build on their own experiences and intuitive understanding about number sense concepts, teacher interactions impact learning in significant ways.

How can teachers modify number sense activities for children with disabilities?

Children with disabilities enjoy and benefit from the same curricular materials as children who are developing typically. Simple modifications can make specific activities accessible to all children. Certain number sense activities may need to be modified to best meet the needs of a specific child. For example, children with physical disabilities or impaired motor function may need larger game pieces or a game board taped to the table. While this simple change does not affect the interest in the game or the ability to use the game for children who are typically developing, it is crucial to the successful participation of the child with motor skill challenges.

Children with cognitive disabilities may be moving through developmental stages at a slower rate than children who are developing typically. They may need materials designed for younger children and may also require more time to explore certain materials or concepts. Teachers may notice that children with cognitive delays quantify materials at the global stage for a longer period of time than children who are developing typically. They may also need more opportunities to explore one-to-one correspondence relationships. Some children continue to explore materials sensorially, such as by putting things into their mouths, for longer than other children. Teachers need to make note of these developmental needs when planning materials for number sense activities and make certain that the materials do not pose a choking hazard.

What are some pitfalls teachers should avoid that impede math progress?

Teachers often think of their role as imparting knowledge, but telling children the way to solve math problems or correcting their errors does little to assist in their construction of number sense. Both of these methods discourage children from thinking on their own. Children should feel confident about their own abilities to think and solve problems. When teachers tell children what methods to use to solve problems, they unintentionally teach children to rely on adults rather than develop their own thinking skills. Whenever people, adults or children alike, attempt to solve new problems, errors inevitably result. It is by working through these errors that new ways of thinking emerge. Teachers must remind themselves that children's errors are reflections of their current level of thinking. The mistakes that children make are not permanent and will be resolved as new ways of thinking develop. The more children have to think, the better thinkers they become.

Teachers sometimes refrain from interacting for fear of discouraging thinking, but appropriate questions, comments, and activities designed by the teacher actually facilitate the construction of number sense. While naturally occurring experiences help young children construct number sense, the teacher must capitalize on these opportunities by posing open-ended questions that guide children's thinking (Kamii 1982). In other words, teachers must intentionally bridge mathematical learning for children through their play.

Strawberry Picking Game

DESCRIPTION

Strawberries are a favorite treat for snack. This activity provides an opportunity for children to pretend to collect small cloth or plastic strawberries into baskets as they quantify and compare amounts they each have. Children take turns rolling the die and collecting the strawberries to place into the small baskets.

MATERIALS

☐ 20–30 cloth or plastic strawberries

☐ 2 vegetable baskets or other small baskets

☐ tongs (optional)

☐ 1–3 or 1–6 teacher-made die

CHILD'S LEVEL

This activity meets the needs of a wide range of children, from those just beginning to quantify to those comparing larger sets and beginning to add and subtract small quantities. The use of tongs is interesting to all children and may meet a specific Individualized Education Program (IEP) goal for a child with a disability.

WHAT TO LOOK FOR

- Children often roll the die to decide how many strawberries to take.

- Children playing the game together may compare how many strawberries they each have.

- Some children will count to create a set of strawberries equivalent to the set of dots on the die.

- Some children may use one-to-one correspondence to compare sets of strawberries to dots on the die.

- When two or more children play together, they may compare sets of strawberries

MORE >

by counting the sets or by lining them up and using one-to-one correspondence for quantification.

- Children may subtract as they give away some strawberries and then count how many they have left.

MODIFICATIONS FOR SPECIAL NEEDS OR SITUATIONS

No specific modifications are anticipated for children with disabilities. Teachers could reduce the quantity of strawberries or adapt the type of tongs to meet the needs of a specific child. Teachers can substitute objects of high interest to a specific child in order to attract the child to the game. Teachers should make sure the objects do not fit through a choke tube if children still put things into their mouths. Larger quantities of strawberries or combinations of fruits along with a pair of dice will challenge the mathematical thinking of older, more experienced children.

MATHEMATICS CONTENT STANDARD CONNECTIONS

This activity aligns primarily with Number and Operations. It incorporates concepts of one-to-one correspondence, counting, set comparisons, addition, and subtraction. Because the activity provides opportunities for children to model a mathematical problem, it also incorporates aspects of the Algebra standard.

COMMENTS AND QUESTIONS RELATED TO MATHEMATICS PROCESS STANDARDS

Problem Solving: Do you have enough strawberries for each of you to have ten?

Reasoning and Proof: Claire says that Megan has more strawberries and that it isn't fair. How do you know, Claire?

Communication: How many more strawberries will you need to have ten?

Connections: How many strawberries does it take to cover the bottom of your basket? (Connects to Measurement)

Representation: Is there a way for us to show your parents how many strawberries we each have at the end of the game?

"More" Game

DESCRIPTION

Teachers often find it challenging to help children who have severe language limitations to progress in the formation of mathematical concepts; however, some children who do not use spoken language are able to use signs. The sign language symbol for *more* emerges as children begin to learn sign language. This game piggybacks beginning quantification skills onto the ability to sign for *more*. Children play by spinning a spinner divided in half, with one visual symbol for *more* on one half of the spinner and two symbols for *more* on the other half. Children can select one or two counters (in this case, small dinosaurs) to correspond to the quantity on the spinner. Teachers help by modeling the sign for *more* and pairing it with a dinosaur.

MATERIALS

☐ teacher-made spinner, as pictured and described above

☐ counters that appeal to the child (in this case, dinosaurs)

CHILD'S LEVEL

This activity is appropriate for preschool and kindergarten children with severe language limitations.

WHAT TO LOOK FOR

• Some children with autism spectrum disorders may require many experiences with this and similar games before they begin to construct the relationship between the number of times *more* is signed and the number of objects they can take.

MORE >

- Many children will need adult facilitation to model the sign for *more* appropriately in the context of the game.

MODIFICATIONS FOR SPECIAL NEEDS OR SITUATIONS

If the child is too distracted by the spinner, eliminate it and take turns signing *more* and taking one dinosaur (or other object). Record the cue for *more* on an augmentative language device, if appropriate.

MATHEMATICS CONTENT STANDARD CONNECTIONS

This activity is designed for children at the very beginning level of quantification and communication. It focuses primarily on Number and Operations.

COMMENTS AND QUESTIONS RELATED TO MATHEMATICS PROCESS STANDARDS

Problem Solving: Get enough dinosaurs to have one for each hand.

Reasoning and Proof: Do we each have two?

Communication: Show me how many more you want.

Connections: Use a show of fingers followed by the *more* sign to indicate quantities throughout the classroom, such as when giving the child more carrots at lunch.

Representation: I need one more. Can you give me one more?

Nature Game

DESCRIPTION

Materials from the environment are readily available to teachers, and children enjoy handling small pinecones, nuts, and other natural objects. Ice cube trays are also an inexpensive resource and may have as few as eight holes or as many as fourteen or more. Teachers can select the type of ice cube tray, type and quantity of dice, and the counters to meet the needs of the group and to make connections to other curricular areas or interests.

MATERIALS

☐ 2 ice cube trays

☐ small natural items, such as nuts and pinecones, or 2 types of seed pods or shells (enough of each to fill 1 tray)

☐ 2 tongs (optional)

☐ 1–3 teacher-made die or spinner

CHILD'S LEVEL

Because this game has relatively few pieces, it is a good beginning game for children who are working on one-to-one correspondence or quantification to three. Older, more experienced children might need more spaces and a 1–6 die to increase the complexity of the game.

WHAT TO LOOK FOR

• Children often use the die or spinner to determine how many nuts or pinecones to put into their trays.

• Some children will count to create an equivalent set between the die and the nuts or pinecones; others will use one-to-one correspondence.

• Children may compare the number of nuts one person has with the number of pinecones another person has.

MORE >

- Some children may disregard the die or spinner and put one item into each hole of the tray. They are working on one-to-one correspondence.

MODIFICATIONS FOR SPECIAL NEEDS OR SITUATIONS

Although this game does not need modifications for children with disabilities, teachers should make sure the objects do not fit through a choke tube and adjust the quantity of objects as well as the type of die or spinner to meet developmental levels of the children.

MATHEMATICS CONTENT STANDARD CONNECTIONS

This game relates primarily to Number and Operations and incorporates the concepts of one-to-one correspondence, counting, and comparing sets. Intentional teaching strategies also provide opportunities for children to think about Algebra as they consider patterning using the different materials.

COMMENTS AND QUESTIONS RELATED TO MATHEMATICS PROCESS STANDARDS

Problem Solving: How many more pinecones do you need in order to have as many pinecones as nuts?

Reasoning and Proof: Are there enough pinecones to divide them evenly between the two trays?

Communication: How can we find out if we have the same number of pinecones as nuts?

Connections: Let's make a pattern with the pinecones and nuts. (Connects to Algebra)

Representation: How will your tray look if you have the same amount of pinecones and nuts?

Teddy Bears and Cubes

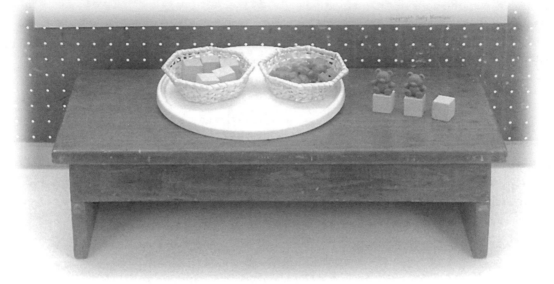

DESCRIPTION

This game encourages young or very inexperienced children to place the bears and cubes in a one-to-one correspondence relationship and to think about quantification of amounts less than ten.

MATERIALS

☐ 8 or more large teddy bear counters (2 of each color)

☐ 8 or more 1-inch cubes in a color different from the bears

☐ 2 baskets, 1 for the bears and 1 for the cubes

☐ tray for displaying the activity

CHILD'S LEVEL

This game is primarily designed for older toddlers or very young preschool children. The game does not include a die or spinner and relies on the interaction between teacher and child.

WHAT TO LOOK FOR

• Many children will place one bear on top of each cube in a one-to-one correspondence relationship.

• Initially, children may stack the cubes on top of one another and not think about a one-to-one relationship between the bears and cubes. Teachers may scaffold learning as they interact with children as a play partner.

• Children may compare the quantities of bears and cubes.

• Some children may play with the bears in a pretend way.

• Some children will count the bears after this has been modeled.

MODIFICATIONS FOR SPECIAL NEEDS OR SITUATIONS

The design of this activity readily meets the needs of some children with cognitive and

MORE >

physical disabilities. The bears and cubes are easy to pick up, and the quantity is not overwhelming. If necessary, the quantities of bears and cubes can be reduced, and teachers can use small stuffed bears and larger blocks in place of the small cubes and teddy bears.

MATHEMATICS CONTENT STANDARD CONNECTIONS

This simple activity focuses on beginning concepts related to Number and Operations. The teacher's use of the language of mathematics enhances the construction of number sense. This activity provides ample opportunity for the teacher to model the sequence of counting words while interacting with a child.

COMMENTS AND QUESTIONS RELATED TO MATHEMATICS PROCESS STANDARDS

Problem Solving: Do you have enough bears and cubes for each bear to sit on a block?

Reasoning and Proof: How do you know you have enough bears to sit on each block?

Communication: What should we do with the bears and blocks?

Connections: Do you have just as many red bears as blue bears? (Connects to Data Analysis)

Representation: I want each bear to sit on a block. What would that look like?

Doghouse Game

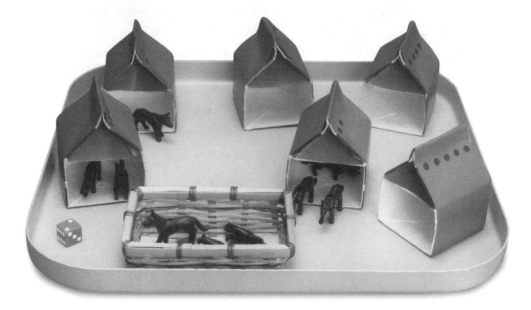

DESCRIPTION

In this game, children must consider how to solve the problem of where to place the dogs. Does one dog go in the house with one dot or the house with six dots? Does the six-dot house get six dogs? Do the doghouses have to be filled in order from one to six, or can they be filled in a random manner? As they ponder these and other questions, children solve mathematical problems through an interesting activity.

MATERIALS

☐ 6 doghouses made from half-pint milk cartons, covered or painted with 1–6 dots on the roofs

☐ 6 or more small plastic dogs

☐ 1–6 die

CHILD'S LEVEL

This game is most appropriate for children quantifying to six. Younger children may use the materials to focus on one-to-one correspondence and counting.

WHAT TO LOOK FOR

• Some children will put one dog into each doghouse.

• Some children may roll the die and put a dog in a doghouse with a corresponding number of dots on the roof (roll five dots on the die and place a dog in the doghouse that has five dots).

• Some children may roll the die and try to put a corresponding number of dogs in the doghouse that has the corresponding number of dots (this may require the teacher to have more dogs available).

MORE >

MODIFICATIONS FOR SPECIAL NEEDS OR SITUATIONS

The doghouses can be made from quart or half-gallon milk cartons and larger dogs can be used. Older, more experienced children may use a pair of dice and twenty-one dogs. The goal of the game might be to place one dog in the doghouse that has one dot, two dogs in the doghouse that has two dots, and so on until each doghouse has the appropriate number of dogs. If teachers use a variety of dogs in different sizes, children may focus on quantity and size of dogs as they place them in the doghouses.

MATHEMATICS CONTENT STANDARD CONNECTIONS

This activity incorporates concepts from both Number and Operations and Algebra. Children quantify and compare sets of dogs and houses (Number and Operations). Children also model a problem using concrete materials (Algebra). If the materials include a variety of sizes of dogs, teachers might ask questions with a focus on Measurement, such as "How many large dogs fit into the doghouse?"

COMMENTS AND QUESTIONS RELATED TO MATHEMATICS PROCESS STANDARDS

Problem Solving: If you roll three dots on the die, where will you place the dogs?

Reasoning and Proof: How will you decide which doghouse to fill first?

Communication: How many dogs can live in this house?

Connections: Do I have just as many big dogs as I do little dogs? (Connects to Measurement)

Representation: Let's keep track of which doghouses you have filled. I have some paper for us to use.

Parking Lot

DESCRIPTION

In this activity, a wooden bench in the block area is turned into a parking lot, and children are encouraged to think about one-to-one correspondence and mathematical problem solving in a high interest activity center. Some children may avoid traditional math materials but be very attracted to block building. This activity takes math into the block area. Colored tape is used to divide the bench into a grid of parking spaces for toy vehicles, which are often used as accessories in the block area.

MATERIALS

☐ wooden bench, wooden plank, or a piece of heavy cardboard

☐ colored tape

☐ small toy vehicles

CHILD'S LEVEL

This activity is most appropriate for preschool children. Kindergarten children working on one-to-one correspondence may also benefit from this activity. The teacher's questioning strategies can encourage children to think about more challenging math problems as well.

WHAT TO LOOK FOR

- Children will put one vehicle into each parking space in a one-to-one correspondence relationship.

- Some children will sort the vehicles by a particular attribute, such as color or type, and park similar vehicles together.

- Children may count empty spaces to see how many more vehicles they can park.

- Children will use various strategies to divide the vehicles among themselves.

MORE >

MODIFICATIONS FOR SPECIAL NEEDS OR SITUATIONS

Larger cars or trucks can be used in a parking lot made with colored tape on a carpet or floor in the classroom or gross-motor area. A child with a physical disability could maneuver larger vehicles into such parking spaces. The number of spaces and vehicles can be adjusted to meet the needs of specific children. Tempera paint can be used in an outside area to make the parking lot, because the paint washes off with water.

To make the game more complex, use different kinds of vehicles and focus questions on quantities of each type.

MATHEMATICS CONTENT STANDARD CONNECTIONS

This activity directly relates to the Number and Operations standard, including counting and one-to-one correspondence. It allows children to model a mathematical problem as they answer their own questions or questions posed by the teacher, and therefore also corresponds to the Algebra standard.

COMMENTS AND QUESTIONS RELATED TO MATHEMATICS PROCESS STANDARDS

Problem Solving: Are there enough parking spaces for all the cars?

Reasoning and Proof: How many more cars do you need to fill the remaining parking spaces?

Communication: Evan wants to put two cars in each parking space. Mary Beth, will you show him how you did that yesterday?

Connections: How many spaces long is the parking lot? (Connects to Measurement)

Representation: If you want to remember which cars you put in each space, is there a way to show me that on paper?

Elephant Stacking

DESCRIPTION

This is an exciting manipulative game for children who are at various developmental levels. Children take turns rolling dice and attempting to stack an equivalent number of small blocks or disks on the back of a toy elephant. Each player tries not to be the one to topple the stack. The game combines the physical challenge of balancing the tallest stack of blocks possible with the math concepts of creating and comparing sets and counting. Older children enjoy predicting the possibility of the blocks toppling on the next turn.

MATERIALS

☐ Duplo elephant, or other toy animal with a flat back

☐ small blocks (¼-inch thick plastic blocks called Rainbow Counters were used in the photo) or disks, such as poker chips for older children

☐ 1–6 die or a pair of dice

CHILD'S LEVEL

This activity is appropriate for both preschool and kindergarten children. The level of difficulty varies by the choice of dice and the quantity and type of items to stack.

WHAT TO LOOK FOR

• Children will try to create the highest possible tower of blocks.

• Children will quantify the amount on the die and try to add an equivalent number of blocks to the stack.

• Some children will stack blocks without regard to the number of dots on the die.

MORE >

- Children will discover that a large number can be a hindrance because it increases the odds of knocking over the tower.
- Some children will roll the pair of dice and add the sets together to get the total.

MODIFICATIONS FOR SPECIAL NEEDS OR SITUATIONS

For children with motor concerns, hook the elephant to a Duplo base plate and switch to one-inch cubes or small jewelry boxes for stacking. For younger children or children with cognitive delays, use a 1–3 die (made from a 1-inch cube and ¼-inch round file folder stickers) and 1-inch cubes for stacking. For older children who can handle larger quantities, use two dice and poker chips for stacking. Poker chips are thin, so many more can be piled on the elephant's back before they fall.

MATHEMATICS CONTENT STANDARD CONNECTIONS

This activity includes many elements of Number and Operations. Children create sets of blocks equal to dots on the dice, compare sets of blocks they each stack, and often count to quantify how many blocks are stacked on the elephant.

COMMENTS AND QUESTIONS RELATED TO MATHEMATICS PROCESS STANDARDS

Problem Solving: You rolled three dots and five dots? How many blocks will you place on the elephant?

Reasoning and Proof: Wes, you say the stack has thirty blocks. How can we find out?

Communication: How many blocks are left in the basket to stack on the elephant?

Connections: How many cubes high is the tower? (Connects to Measurement)

Representation: What would the dice look like if I want ten blocks to stack on the elephant? Is there a different combination of dots that equals ten?

ACTIVITY 2.8

Spiderwebs

DESCRIPTION

Each child has a plastic spiderweb in this manipulative game. Children take turns drawing cards to determine how many spiders to place on their webs.

MATERIALS

☐ 2 plastic spiderwebs

☐ small plastic spiders

☐ spider cards made by affixing from 1 to 6 spider stickers on index cards and laminating them for durability

CHILD'S LEVEL

This activity is appropriate for preschool and kindergarten children.

WHAT TO LOOK FOR

• Some children will quantify the number of spiders on the cards and attempt to take an equivalent number of spiders for their webs.

• Children will select a quantification strategy (global, one-to-one correspondence, or counting) commensurate with their level of thinking.

• Some children will re-quantify the total number of spiders they have each time they add more.

MODIFICATIONS FOR SPECIAL NEEDS OR SITUATIONS

If needed, children can use an augmentative language device, programmed with either

MORE >

visual or auditory cues, to determine how many spiders to place on the web. Increase the number of spiders on the cards from one to ten for experienced children. They will enjoy the challenge of quantifying larger amounts.

MATHEMATICS CONTENT STANDARD CONNECTIONS

As children pick a card and create and compare sets, they engage in mathematical thinking that is the basis for Number and Operations.

COMMENTS AND QUESTIONS RELATED TO MATHEMATICS PROCESS STANDARDS

Problem Solving: How many spiders will you have if you take one more spider?

Reasoning and Proof: How do you know you should take eight spiders?

Communication: Tell Rhiannon how you divided the spiders so you each have the same amount.

Connections: Look at the lines in the spider-web. They make a symmetrical pattern. (Connects to Geometry)

Representation: If one spider crawls away, how many spiders will be left? Show me what that would look like.

Dinosaur Challenge

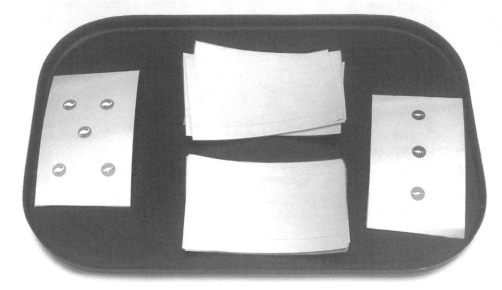

DESCRIPTION

Dinosaur Challenge is a variation of the traditional card game War. The teacher-made playing cards consist of dinosaur stickers on index cards. Each card has one to six dinosaurs on it. Children divide the cards among themselves before beginning the game. All the players turn over a card simultaneously. The player with the largest number of dinosaurs on his or her card takes all cards from that round. Children decide what to do if players turn over cards with an equivalent number of dinosaurs on them. When all cards have been used, children determine how many cards each player has won. This game challenges children to compare sets as they try to determine whose card has the most dinosaurs.

MATERIALS

☐ 40–50 dinosaur playing cards made by placing 1–6 dinosaur stickers on index cards and laminating them for durability

☐ paper and pencils for documenting the score at the end of each round of play

CHILD'S LEVEL

This game is most appropriate for kindergarten children. It is more difficult than most of the die and counter games that use concrete manipulative pieces.

WHAT TO LOOK FOR

- Children will argue and discuss as they decide whose card has the most dinosaurs.
- Children will quantify and compare how many cards they have at the end of the game.
- Children will devise strategies for dividing the cards at the beginning of the game.

MODIFICATIONS FOR SPECIAL NEEDS OR SITUATIONS

To decrease the level of difficulty, this card game can be designed with 1–3 dinosaur

MORE >

stickers per card. Children do not need to keep score using paper and pencils. For children with visual disabilities, the cards can be made using dots made of sandpaper. For older children who have become adept at comparing sets of one to six dinosaurs, introduce additional cards with sets up to ten.

MATHEMATICS CONTENT STANDARD CONNECTIONS

This activity directly aligns with the Number and Operations standard, as children compare sets of dots on the cards. Many children will count the dots by touching each dot and saying the number words in sequence. Some children may think about addition and subtraction as they play.

COMMENTS AND QUESTIONS RELATED TO MATHEMATICS PROCESS STANDARDS

Problem Solving: Whose card has the most dinosaurs?

Reasoning and Proof: Kevin, you said you have seven pairs of cards. How many cards is that altogether?

Communication: How will we know who has the most cards?

Connections: Whose cards make the longest row? (Connects to Measurement)

Representation: How will we remember how many pairs we each had? What will that look like on paper?

Autumn Game Set

This set of three games, at three levels of difficulty, is based on a common topic of interest to many children who observe autumnal changes in the environment. Each game has the potential to be more or less challenging, depending on the number of spaces and type of dice and counters. There are no specific rules for playing each game. They are self-leveling and meet the needs of a diverse group of children. Teachers offer suggestions or model ways to play the game, but they should be open to children's ideas. Kindergarten children may be more interested in making rules for the games than preschool children. The games can be adapted easily for any of the other three seasons.

Autumn Grid Game

MATERIALS

- ☐ 2 grid boards marked into 9 spaces, each space with a squirrel illustration in the middle
- ☐ 18 acorn caps or large marble chips
- ☐ 1–3 teacher-made die
- ☐ lamination for protection and durability of the game

CHILD'S LEVEL

This grid is most appropriate for children who are constructing one-to-one correspondence or quantifying from 1 to 3 using a die.

WHAT TO LOOK FOR

- Children may roll the die and take a corresponding quantity of acorn caps to place one per squirrel. They are quantifying by counting the dots and taking an equivalent quantity of acorn caps.

MORE >

- Some children may roll the die, point to a dot, take an acorn cap, and then point to another dot and take an acorn cap. They are quantifying using one-to-one correspondence.

- Some children may place an acorn cap on each squirrel without rolling the die. They are thinking about one-to-one correspondence but have not created a relationship between the quantity of dots on the die and the quantity of acorn caps needed.

- Some children may compare quantities of acorn caps they each have.

- Children may quantify the acorn caps or squirrels by counting and comparing sets.

MODIFICATIONS FOR SPECIAL NEEDS OR SITUATIONS

Use bottle caps as the counters or pieces for the game. Larger pieces may be easier for some children to control. Use multiple acorns and a 1–6 die for older, more experienced children who may want to give each squirrel more than one acorn.

Autumn Short Path Game

MATERIALS

- ☐ 2 pieces of posterboard, each 6 × 18 inches
- ☐ 20 1-inch circles to form the straight path on each game board
- ☐ 2 small acorn movers (glue an acorn on a wooden spool or disk)
- ☐ illustration of a squirrel at the end of each path
- ☐ print, such as "Take a nut to the squirrel," on each board
- ☐ 1–3 die or spinner
- ☐ lamination for protection and durability of the game

CHILD'S LEVEL

The game is most appropriate for children just beginning to play path games using a 1–3 die or spinner. Each child has a separate game board, and players take turns rolling the die or spinning the spinner. This encourages children to develop the skill of turn taking and offers opportunities for them to observe the teacher or a peer model a strategy different from their own.

WHAT TO LOOK FOR

- Children may advance along the path according to the number on the die or spinner.

MORE >

- Some children will hop along the path without regard to the die or spinner.

- Children may often move the first two spaces when rolling two dots and then move just one more when they roll three on the next turn. They do not yet perceive the sets as different but demonstrate an understanding of the quantity three. This error in thinking changes over time and through peer and teacher modeling.

MODIFICATIONS FOR SPECIAL NEEDS OR SITUATIONS

The path can be made more accessible to children with a visual disability by outlining the circles with puffy paint. Felt or foam circles can be glued on top of laminated board using rubber cement. All children will be attracted to the game, and children who need to can use touch to help distinguish the spaces on the path.

Autumn Long Path Collection Game

MATERIALS

☐ brown posterboard, 15 × 15 inches

☐ 24 or more 1-inch circles to form the path

☐ 5 basket stickers for collection spaces

☐ 25 or more acorns in a basket for collecting on the collection spaces

☐ 2 plastic or flocked squirrels, in 2 colors, as the movers (may need to mount on spool or disk)

☐ 1–6 die or pair of dice

☐ lamination for protection and durability of the game

CHILD'S LEVEL

This game is more complex than the Autumn Short Path Game because it has more spaces, does not have a beginning and ending point, uses a more complex die, and has the added element of collecting acorns each time the player lands on a basket sticker on the path. Teachers encourage children to quantify and compare the acorns they have collected at the end of the game or at any point during the game.

Children may begin on any space along the path and continue moving spaces until the game is complete. Older children may enjoy discussing where to begin or may design

MORE >

guidelines for playing the game. The rules of the game can change each time children play or may be altered based on mathematical interests and understanding of the children involved. Children often make up guidelines more complex than teachers design.

WHAT TO LOOK FOR

- Children may move along the path according to the roll of the die and collect an acorn each time they land on a basket sticker.

- Some children will quantify the acorns by counting.

- Children may quantify the acorns at the end of the game by lining them up in rows and comparing sets.

MODIFICATIONS FOR SPECIAL NEEDS OR SITUATIONS

Board games are designed to meet the needs of children at various levels of mathematical understanding. Teachers encourage children to play the game most suited to their level of thinking by offering to play the game too. Choose the type of game best suited to an individual child.

MATHEMATICS CONTENT STANDARD CONNECTIONS

This game set aligns primarily with Number and Operations. All the games incorporate concepts of one-to-one correspondence, quantification, counting, and set comparisons.

The path games may incorporate concepts of addition and subtraction as children quantify how many spaces they have moved or how many more spaces they need to move along the path. Because the games also allow children to model a mathematical problem, they incorporate aspects of the Algebra standard.

COMMENTS AND QUESTIONS RELATED TO MATHEMATICS PROCESS STANDARDS

Problem Solving: (grid game) How many more acorns do I need to give one to each squirrel? (path games) If I roll three on the die, will I get to the end of the path?

Reasoning and Proof: (grid game) Do we each have the same amount of acorns for our game? (path games) How many spaces until I reach the end of the path? (long path game) What do I have to roll on the die to catch up to your squirrel?

Communication: (grid game) Tell me how many more acorns I need to collect for my squirrels.

(path games) I want to give my squirrel an acorn. How far do I have to go on the path?

Connections: (long path game) Which basket is closer to your mover? (Connects to Measurement)

Representation: (path games) What do I have to roll on the die to get to the squirrel?

Teddy Bear Game Set

Teddy Bears seem to have universal appeal for children. This game set capitalizes on that interest and coordinates with the *Corduroy* books by Don Freeman. The grid, short path, and long path games can be designed to meet the needs of different groups of children by increasing or reducing the number and type of counters, the number of spaces for the long path game, and the inclusion of bonus spaces. See the general instructions for board games in appendix A.

Teddy Bear Grid Game

MATERIALS

☐ 2 light brown posterboard grids, 10 × 5 inches, each with 10 pictures of the bear Corduroy

☐ 20 large buttons in 1 or 2 colors

☐ 2 small baskets for holding the buttons

☐ 1–3 die

☐ lamination for protection and durability of the game

☐ a copy of the book *Corduroy* by Don Freeman (optional)

CHILD'S LEVEL

The grid game is most appropriate for children who are using one-to-one correspondence or counting up to three for quantification. The large buttons fit into the grid space well, emphasizing the one-to-one relationship, and the die has only 1–3 dots on each side.

WHAT TO LOOK FOR

• Children may roll the die, take a corresponding amount of buttons, and place one button per each space on the grid.

MORE >

- Children may place one button per bear but do not use the die. They are thinking about one-to-one correspondence rather than quantifying the amount of dots on the die.
- Children may compare the quantities of buttons they each have.
- Some children will count the buttons, the bears, or both.

MODIFICATIONS FOR SPECIAL NEEDS OR SITUATIONS

For younger children or children with cognitive delays, use milk or juice jug lids made to look like buttons by drawing four dots on the top. These will be easier than buttons for some children to handle. The game can also be played by covering the bears with the jug lids and play the game as a peekaboo game that encourages turn taking and one-to-one correspondence. The die does not have to be used. For children with more mathematical knowledge, use a pair of dice and encourage children to collect several buttons for each bear.

Teddy Bear Short Path Game

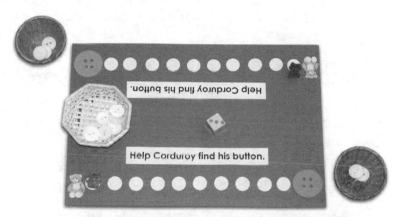

MATERIALS

☐ posterboard, 12 × 18 inches

☐ 20 paw print or circle stickers to form the two separate paths, making 10 spaces for each path

☐ illustrations of teddy bear at the beginning of each path

☐ 2 large (2-inch) buttons glued to the board for the end points of each path

☐ 2 small bears to use as movers

☐ 1–3 die

☐ print, such as "Help Corduroy find his button," written in the middle of the board for each player to read

☐ small container to hold a selection of buttons to collect at the end of the path (optional)

☐ lamination for protection and durability of the game

☐ a copy of the book *Corduroy* by Don Freeman (optional)

CHILD'S LEVEL

This type of path game is best suited for children with experience playing grid games, quantifying to three, and using the die to determine how many spaces to advance on the path.

MORE >

WHAT TO LOOK FOR

- Children will advance along the path according to the quantity of dots on the die.

- Some children will hop to the end of the path without regard for the die. This will decrease with experience and modeling by other children or teachers on their turn.

- Some children will collect a button at the end of the path and return to the beginning to play again. They may quantify how many buttons they have at the end of each game.

- A few children will place the buttons on the spaces of the path in a one-to-one correspondence manner. They may not be ready for the more abstract nature of path games, but teachers can take advantage of opportunities to ask them mathematical questions.

- Some children will re-count the space their mover occupies before advancing on the path.

- Some children will miscount the dots on the die or re-count the spaces on the path.

MODIFICATIONS FOR SPECIAL NEEDS OR SITUATIONS

For children with visual disabilities, outline the path spaces with puffy paint. After the paint has dried, children will be able to feel the spaces. If the game is too complex for children, encourage them to play the Teddy Bear Grid Game with you after you finish. Playing grid games helps children solidify the concepts needed to play more abstract path games. If the game is not challenging for children, encourage them to play the long path game with you or with each other.

Teddy Bear Long Path Game

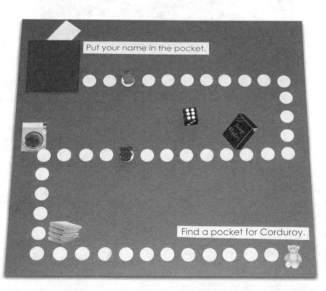

MATERIALS

☐ posterboard, 22 × 22 inches

☐ 25 or more bear paw stickers to form the path

☐ illustration of teddy bear at the beginning of the path with print, such as "Find a pocket for Corduroy"

☐ illustrations of towels, a clothes dryer, and soap flakes to place along the path, following the story line of the book

MORE >

□ a felt pocket at the ending point, glued to the board after lamination

□ paper and pencil for children to write their name and place in the pocket

□ 2 small bear figures, each a different color, to use as the movers

□ 1–6 die

□ lamination for protection and durability of the game

□ a copy of the book *Corduroy* by Don Freeman (optional)

CHILD'S LEVEL

The design of this long path game is appropriate for children quantifying up to five or six who have had experience playing grid games and short path games.

WHAT TO LOOK FOR

• Children will use the die to determine how far to advance on the path by counting the dots.

• Some children will miscount the dots on the die or the spaces on the path.

• Some children will re-count the space their mover occupies before advancing on the path.

MODIFICATIONS FOR SPECIAL NEEDS OR SITUATIONS

If the long path game is too complex, encourage children to play the Teddy Bear Short Path or Grid Game with you when you finish. For children with visual disabilities, use raised felt stickers or puffy paint to make the path tactile.

MATHEMATICS CONTENT STANDARD CONNECTIONS

This game set aligns primarily with Number and Operations. All the games incorporate concepts of one-to-one correspondence, quantification, counting, and set comparisons. The path games may incorporate concepts of addition and subtraction as children quantify how many spaces they have moved or how many more spaces they need to move along the path. Because the games also allow children to model a mathematical problem, they incorporate aspects of the Algebra standard.

COMMENTS AND QUESTIONS RELATED TO MATHEMATICS PROCESS STANDARDS

Problem Solving: (grid game) How many more buttons do you need to cover the rest of the bears?

Reasoning and Proof: (path games) Nathan says your mover should be here. Can you show him how you got to your spot on the path?

Communication: (path games) Lucas wants to catch up to you. How many spaces will he need to move?

Connections: (short path game) Are the two paths the same length? How can we tell? (Connects to Measurement)

Representation: (grid game) How many buttons would you need for each bear to have two buttons?

Winter Game Set

Many children experience the fun of snow in the winter. Even those who do not are fascinated by the thought of snow and snowmen. This set of three games, at three levels of difficulty, is based on winter. As with the previous game sets, each game has the potential to be more or less challenging, depending on the number of spaces, type of die, and counters used. While teachers may offer suggestions or model ways to play the game, they should be open to children's ideas. Kindergarten children may be more interested in making up rules for the games than preschool children.

Winter Grid Game

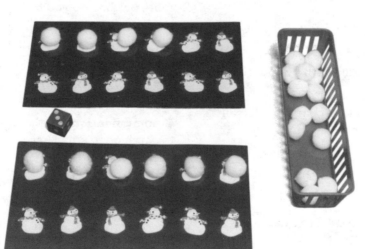

MATERIALS

☐ 2 posterboard grid boards, 12 × 6 inches, each with 12 snowman stickers

☐ 24 white pom-poms

☐ 1–3 teacher-made die

☐ small basket to hold the pom-poms

☐ lamination for protection and durability of the game

CHILD'S LEVEL

This grid game is most appropriate for younger preschool children.

WHAT TO LOOK FOR

• Children may roll the die, determine how many pom-poms to take, and place one pom-pom on each snowman.

MORE >

- Some children may place one pom-pom on each snowman without using the die to determine a quantity. They are creating a one-to-one relationship but do not yet understand the use of the die in quantification.

- Some children may compare quantities of pom-poms they each have.

- Children may count the snowmen on the grid board.

MODIFICATIONS FOR SPECIAL NEEDS OR SITUATIONS

Use counters that do not pose a choking hazard for children who still put things into their mouths. To increase the difficulty of the game, use three pom-poms for each snowman and a pair of dice.

Winter Short Path Game

MATERIALS

- ☐ posterboard, 12 × 18 inches
- ☐ 20 1-inch circles or snowflake stickers to form the straight path on each game board
- ☐ 2 small toy people, such as those from Duplo or Fisher-Price, for the movers
- ☐ silhouette sticker or clip art of a child for the starting point on each path
- ☐ snowman sticker or clip art for the end point on each path
- ☐ 1–3 die or spinner
- ☐ small items, such as sunglasses, top hats, carrots, and brooms, for collecting at the end of the path

- ☐ print, such as "Collect things for your snowman," on each board
- ☐ lamination for protection and durability of the game

CHILD'S LEVEL

The game is most appropriate for children who have played numerous short path games using a 1–3 die. Many children will repeat the cycle from start to finish several times in order to collect items for the snowman. This provides multiple opportunities to quantify from one to three.

MORE >

WHAT TO LOOK FOR

- Children may advance along the path according to the dots on the die.

- Some children will advance along the path several times to collect items for the snowman.

- A few children may play with the small items for collecting during the game but disregard the path. Teachers can take advantage of this incidental learning opportunity by asking questions focused on quantification, such as "How many things do you have for the snowman? Do you each have the same amount?"

MODIFICATIONS FOR SPECIAL NEEDS OR SITUATIONS

For children who have difficulty handling small pieces, put a larger snowman at the end of the path and use larger movers and collection pieces.

Winter Long Path Collection Game

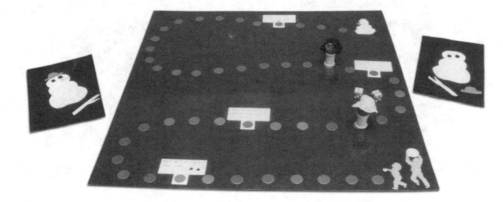

MATERIALS

- ☐ posterboard, 22 × 22 inches

- ☐ 50 1-inch circles to form the path

- ☐ 4 bonus spaces with 1 illustration per space of a carrot, scarf, hat, and coal eyes

- ☐ silhouette stickers of a child for the starting point of the path

- ☐ snowman sticker for the end point of the path

- ☐ 2 small people figures for movers

- ☐ 2 small felt boards, 6 × 8 inches

- ☐ 2 felt pieces each of a hat, carrot, and scarf, as well as 4 felt circles for the coal eyes

- ☐ a pair of 1–6 dice

- ☐ lamination for protection and durability of the game

CHILD'S LEVEL

This game is most appropriate for kindergarten children. It is a more complex path game with some specific guidelines for how to play. Kindergarten children like to play games with rules and are beginning to follow such guidelines. For this game, each player advances along the path and tries to finish building the felt snowman by collecting the hat, carrot nose, scarf, and coal eyes to place on the felt snowman. Directions can be written at each

MORE >

bonus space for collecting the items, such as roll seven to collect the hat, roll four to collect the scarf, roll two to collect the carrot nose, and roll twelve to collect the eyes. Children may want to discuss whether players must land *on* the bonus space or pass the bonus space to collect the items. Children will have to consider the probability of rolling the necessary quantities at the bonus spaces if one die or a pair of dice is used. They can decide among themselves when to use one die and when to use a pair of dice. This kind of mathematical problem solving encourages higher-level thinking and multiple perspectives.

WHAT TO LOOK FOR

- Children may move along the path according to the roll of a die or dice and stop at the bonus space to complete the task of collecting an item before advancing on the path.

- Some children will ignore the directions on the bonus spaces and place the hat, carrot nose, scarf, and coal eyes on the felt snowman at any point on the path.

- Children will discuss whether a player must land on the bonus space or pass the bonus space to collect the items for the snowman.

- Children will quantify the amount on a pair of dice by counting all the dots.

- Children may re-count the space their mover occupies when they take a new turn.

- Some children may "fix" the dice to a particular number of dots in order to land on a bonus space.

MODIFICATIONS FOR SPECIAL NEEDS OR SITUATIONS

Teachers can suggest that children play the Winter Grid or Short Path Game if the Winter Long Path Game is too difficult. For children with visual disabilities, use felt circles to mark the path.

MATHEMATICS CONTENT STANDARD CONNECTIONS

This game set aligns primarily with Number and Operations. The games encourage children to quantify, create and compare sets, and count. The path games are essentially number lines that give children experience moving a set distance. Because the games also allow children to model a mathematical problem, they incorporate aspects of the Algebra standard.

COMMENTS AND QUESTIONS RELATED TO MATHEMATICS PROCESS STANDARDS

Problem Solving: (long path game) How many more spaces will I move before I collect the scarf for my snowman?

Reasoning and Proof: (grid game) Ted, do you have enough pom-poms for all your snowmen?

Communication: (grid and path games) I rolled this on the dice. What should I do now?

Connections: (long path game) How far is it from the beginning of the path to the first bonus? (Connects to Measurement)

Representation: (grid and path games) Show me how many spaces the die indicates I should move.

Spider and Fly Game Set

Young children eagerly respond to stories that have a repeating text. This game set coordinates with the predictable book *The Very Busy Spider* by Eric Carle. In the story, a spider spins her web as different farm animals invite her to join them. After all the animals pass by and the web is finished, the spider catches a "pesky fly." This game set goes along with the theme of the book in grid, short path, and long path games.

Spider and Fly Grid Game

MATERIALS

- ☐ 2 grid boards, each with three rows of five boxes, with a spider illustration in the middle of each cell, mounted on 5 × 4 inch posterboard and laminated for durability
- ☐ 30 plastic flies
- ☐ 1–3 teacher-made die
- ☐ 2 small baskets for the counters
- ☐ a copy of the book *The Very Busy Spider* by Eric Carle (optional)

CHILD'S LEVEL

This grid game is most appropriate for children who are quantifying from one to three using a die.

WHAT TO LOOK FOR

- Many children will roll the die, take an equivalent set of plastic flies, and place one fly per spider on the grid.
- Children will quantify how many flies to take using a quantification strategy (global,

MORE >

one-to-one correspondence, or counting) based on their level of development.

- Some children may choose to place more than one fly on each space of the grid. They may quantify how many more spiders they would need to complete the grid in this manner.

MODIFICATIONS FOR SPECIAL NEEDS OR SITUATIONS

For children with visual disabilities or cognitive delays, use a plastic or wooden box divided into sections, each with a spider illustration in it. (The boxes can be found in fabric or craft stores.) Children with visual problems will be able to feel the grid spaces, and the boxes are a more concrete place to put counters than flat grid boards. The game with alterations will be interesting to all children. For older children, use a pair of dice and encourage them to try to catch two flies for each spider.

Spider and Fly Short Path Game

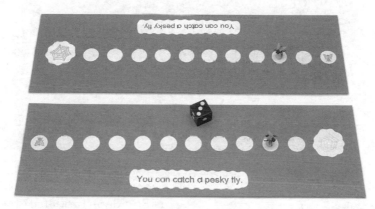

MATERIALS

- ☐ 2 pieces of posterboard, each 6 × 22 inches
- ☐ 20 white, 1-inch circles to form the straight path on each game board
- ☐ 2 small fly movers (glue a small plastic fly to a wooden spool or disk)
- ☐ illustration of a fly at the starting point
- ☐ illustration of a spiderweb at the end of each path
- ☐ print, such as "You can catch a pesky fly," on each board
- ☐ 1–3 die or spinner
- ☐ lamination for protection and durability of the game
- ☐ a copy of the book *The Very Busy Spider* by Eric Carle (optional)

CHILD'S LEVEL

Children who are just beginning to play path games, using a 1–3 die, will be able to play this game.

WHAT TO LOOK FOR

- Some children will roll the die and move an equivalent number of spaces along the path.
- Children often move the first two spaces when rolling two dots and then move just one space more when they roll three dots on the next turn. They do not yet perceive the sets as different but demonstrate an under-

MORE >

standing of the quantity of three. This error in thinking changes over time and with modeling by peers and teachers.

- Some children may hop to the end of the path without regard for the die. This also decreases with experience and modeling by peers and teachers when it's their turn to play.

MODIFICATIONS FOR SPECIAL NEEDS OR SITUATIONS

The path can be made more accessible to children who have a visual disability by gluing felt or foam circles on top of the laminated board. Children can then touch the circles to distinguish the spaces of the path.

Spider and Fly Long Path Game

MATERIALS

☐ posterboard, 16 × 22 inches

☐ 35 or more 1-inch circles to form the path

☐ illustrations of farm animals from the book mounted on black paper and placed in the center of the game board (as pictured)

☐ 5 fly stickers or illustrations for collection spaces

☐ 22 marble chips in a basket in the middle of the game board for collecting at each fly space

☐ 2 spider movers mounted on wooden spools (you can use spider rings with the ring removed and the legs cut short)

☐ 1–6 die or a pair of dice

☐ lamination for protection and durability of the game

☐ a copy of the book *The Very Busy Spider* by Eric Carle (optional)

CHILD'S LEVEL

This game is more complex than the short path game because it has more spaces, does not have a beginning and ending point, uses a more complex die, and has an added element of stopping each time the player lands on a fly sticker on the path. Children cover one of the farm animals each time they land on a fly space. Children may discuss whether players cover a farm animal each time they pass a fly space or only when they land on a fly space.

WHAT TO LOOK FOR

- Children may move along the path according to the roll of a die or dice and cover a

MORE >

farm animal picture each time they land on a fly space.

- Children may quantify how many animals they have each covered and how many more they need to cover.

- Some children may cover an animal each time they take a turn regardless of whether they land on or pass a fly space.

- Children may miscount the dots on the die or the path by double counting or skipping dots.

MODIFICATIONS FOR SPECIAL NEEDS OR SITUATIONS

No special adaptations are anticipated for this game. If it is too complex for some children, teachers can play the Spider and Fly Grid or Short Path Game with them. Kindergarten children might like to write the name of each farm animal as they cover it. They might make up other rules for the game, such as the farm animals must be covered in the order of their appearance in the book or you must land on the fly sticker to cover an animal.

MATHEMATICS CONTENT STANDARD CONNECTIONS

These games all align with the Number and Operations standard, albeit at different levels. The grid game focuses on one-to-one correspondence and counting, and the short path game moves the same concepts to a more abstract level. The long path game allows children to extend their quantification to larger sets and to begin adding sets together.

COMMENTS AND QUESTIONS RELATED TO MATHEMATICS PROCESS STANDARDS

Problem Solving: (grid game) How many flies do you have altogether?

Reasoning and Proof: (grid game) How do you know how many flies to take on this turn?

Communication: (path games) How did you decide how many spaces to move?

Connections: (short path game) Am I closer to the web, or are you closer to the web? How do you know? (Connects to Measurement)

Representation: (grid game) If two of my spiders eat their flies, what will my grid board look like?

Bear Hunt Game

DESCRIPTION

This game is suitable for a gross-motor area and correlates with the traditional "Going on a Bear Hunt" chant or book. Placing a math activity in a gross-motor area provides opportunities for children to demonstrate their knowledge in a nontraditional way. Some children who avoid path games in the classroom may look forward to playing this game in the gross-motor area because they learn and express themselves more easily in that realm. The game provides opportunities for assessment of children's mathematical understanding. Giant paw prints are taped to the floor to form a path. Children roll a giant die and hop along the path toward the bear's cave at the end. They may need some assis-

tance quantifying the dots on the die as it rolls out of reach. Teachers or other children can retrieve the die and bring it closer to the child who rolled it.

MATERIALS

- ☐ paw prints made from brown paper grocery bags and black, oval cutouts to form the path
- ☐ large box for the "cave" at the end of the path
- ☐ giant die made from a large stuffed fabric cube with 1–6 puff paint dots
- ☐ a copy of the book *We're Going on a Bear Hunt* by Michael Rosen and Helen Oxenbury (optional)

MORE >

CHILD'S LEVEL

This game is most appropriate for older preschool and kindergarten children. It is common for young children who are learning to play path games to re-count the space their mover occupies when they take their next turn; however, they often stop making this error after playing a game like this one in which they are the mover.

WHAT TO LOOK FOR

- Children may roll the die and attempt to move an equivalent number of spaces along the path.
- Some children may accurately count the dots on the die but not move an equivalent number of spaces on the path.
- Children may help others by quantifying the dots on the giant die.
- Some children will hop along the path without using the die.
- Some children who re-count the space they occupy on classroom path games will not do so when they are the mover for the game.

MODIFICATIONS FOR SPECIAL NEEDS OR SITUATIONS

The giant die is easier for some children to use for quantification, and the puffy paint circles are easy to feel on the die. The die can be made with one to three dots if one to six is too many for some children to quantify. For older or more experienced children, the path could be longer and include obstacles, such as those found in the chant. Perhaps children would need to roll seven dots to go through the forest or five dots to go through the grass.

MATHEMATICS CONTENT STANDARD CONNECTIONS

Because this game simulates a number line, it aligns strongly to Number and Operations. Children have many opportunities to use quantification strategies as they quantify. Movement along the path is also related to Measurement.

COMMENTS AND QUESTIONS RELATED TO MATHEMATICS PROCESS STANDARDS

Problem Solving: How many more paw prints are there until you reach the cave?

Reasoning and Proof: How can you tell what Julian would have to roll to land on the same paw print as Paul?

Communication: Dema, tell Skylar how many spaces she should move. The die is too far away for her to see.

Connections: If we made the path straight, would we need as many paw prints to reach the cave as we do on this curved path? (Connects to Measurement)

Representation: Show me with hops how many dots you rolled on the die.

Hop to the Mitten

DESCRIPTION

Many children are attracted to the tale "The Mitten," a Ukrainian story in which a number of different animals manage to fit inside a lost mitten. Several book versions of this traditional tale are available. In this gross-motor math game, children roll a large die and hop along a path made from carpet squares. They each carry a laminated drawing of one of the animals from the story to hang on a large paper mitten at the end of the path.

MATERIALS

☐ 10–12 carpet squares to form the straight path on the floor

☐ 1–3 die made from a large stuffed fabric cube with 1–3 dots on each side

☐ large mitten cut from paper and mounted on the wall

☐ drawings of the characters from the story (these may be available on the Internet)

☐ magnetic tape cut into small pieces and mounted on the mitten and on the back of the drawings

CHILD'S LEVEL

This activity is most appropriate for older preschool or kindergarten children.

WHAT TO LOOK FOR

• Many children will roll the die and hop an equivalent number of spaces along the path. They will carry one of the animals to attach to the mitten.

• Some children may hop to the end of the path without regard to the quantity on the die.

MORE >

- Some children will count the number of animals in the mitten.

- When playing board games, children may re-count the space their mover occupies each time they take a turn; however, when the child is the mover in a gross-motor game such as this one, he often does not make the same error.

MODIFICATIONS FOR SPECIAL NEEDS OR SITUATIONS

For younger children or children with cognitive delays, provide an optional die with one or two dots on each side. Teachers also can substitute a set of five-by-seven-inch index cards with one to three dots on each. Children may find it easier to quantify the dots on a card they can hold.

MATHEMATICS CONTENT STANDARD CONNECTIONS

The activity aligns with the Number and Operations standard as children quantify, compare quantities, count, and move along a simulated number line.

COMMENTS AND QUESTIONS RELATED TO MATHEMATICS PROCESS STANDARDS

Problem Solving: How many more spaces until you can put your animal on the mitten?

Reasoning and Proof: If Charles puts the badger on the mitten, how many animals will there be? How can you tell?

Communication: Andre, tell me how you decided how far to move on the path.

Connections: How far is it from the starting line to the mitten? (Connects to Measurement)

Representation: What will the mitten look like when two more animals crawl in?

Up the Downspout Race

DESCRIPTION

For this game, children use a die to decide how many spaces to move their spiders up a downspout. Magnets are attached to plastic spiders so they will stick to the metal downspout. Colored tape is used to divide the downspout into sections that form a path for the spiders. The downspout is then attached to a pegboard divider or the back of a shelf. Cover the top of each spout with tape to prevent children from putting spiders into the spouts where they tend to get stuck.

MATERIALS

☐ metal downspout with a 90-degree elbow joint

☐ several small spiders, each with magnetic tape attached to the underside

☐ 1–3 die

☐ basket for the spiders

CHILD'S LEVEL

This game is appropriate for preschool and kindergarten children.

WHAT TO LOOK FOR

• Children will use global, one-to-one correspondence, and counting strategies to decide how many spaces to move.

• Some children will compare how many spaces their spiders have moved.

MORE >

MODIFICATIONS FOR SPECIAL NEEDS OR SITUATIONS

For children with visual disabilities, use puffy paint to mark sections on the downspout. After the paint has dried, children can feel the marks. Increase the number of spiders used in the game for older children, who can quantify larger amounts. They can roll two dice and move a succession of spiders up the spout.

MATHEMATICS CONTENT STANDARD CONNECTIONS

This activity aligns with the Number and Operations standard because children count and compare the number of dots on the die with the number of spaces they move the spiders. Because they model a mathematical problem using concrete materials, the activity also aligns to the Algebra standard. Movement along a set of incremental spaces connects this activity to Measurement.

COMMENTS AND QUESTIONS RELATED TO MATHEMATICS PROCESS STANDARDS

Problem Solving: How many spaces does your spider get to move?

Reasoning and Proof: How can you prove that you moved the right number of spaces?

Communication: How many more spiders have to go up the spout to make six at the top?

Connections: How many sections tall is the downspout? (Connects to Measurement)

Representation: Show me where your spider will be if you roll a three on the die.

Butterfly Math Suitcase

These take-home versions of board games offer parents an opportunity to interact with their children by playing math games similar to those found in the classroom. The instructions for parents include information not only about how to play the games but also about what math concepts children learn while playing with their family members. Older siblings often enjoy playing with their younger brothers and sisters. This set of games focuses on children's common interest in butterflies. Teachers can use small backpacks or plastic boxes with a handle as a suitcase, within which the game pieces will be stored in containers. Suitcases can be sent home with children on a rotating basis. Teachers should include in the suitcase an inventory of materials and instructions to parents. A sample letter to parents is included in appendix B. Be sure to tell them the games contain small pieces and, so, should be kept out of reach of younger siblings who may still put things into their mouths.

MORE >

Butterfly Math Grid Game

MATERIALS

☐ 2 grid boards, 8 × 6 inches, made from blue posterboard, each with 12 butterfly stickers and laminated for protection and durability

☐ 24 large, clear marble chips for the counters

☐ 1–3 teacher-made die

Butterfly Math Long Path Game

MATERIALS

☐ 1 path game, 12 × 16 inches, made from blue posterboard, with 20–25 1-inch circles to form the path, an illustration of a child holding a butterfly net at the beginning, and a butterfly illustration at the end of the path, laminated and then cut in half or thirds, with the sections taped together so that the game folds to fit into a small case or backpack

☐ 2 people figure movers

☐ 1–6 die

☐ small case or backpack

CHILD'S LEVEL

This suitcase is appropriate for all preschool children. Because they are playing the games with their parents, children will receive more instruction for how to use the materials, as well as one-on-one attention. The adult acts as a model for how to play. In a classroom situation, children may play with each other in a variety of ways and with fewer instructions.

MODIFICATIONS FOR SPECIAL NEEDS OR SITUATIONS

Use milk or juice jug lids as the counters for children who may still put things into their mouths. For children with visual disabilities, use raised stickers to form the grid spaces and path spaces.

MATHEMATICS CONTENT STANDARD CONNECTIONS

The materials in the suitcase align closely with the Number and Operations standard. As children play the math games with their families, they may create and compare sets, count quantities of counters or of spaces on the path, and ponder questions such as, "Is five more than three?" "Do we each have the same number of butterflies on the grid?" "Does my sister have more than I do?"

SUGGESTED PROCESS STANDARDS COMMENTS AND QUESTIONS FOR PARENTS

Problem Solving: (grid game) How many butterflies do you get to cover on your board?

Reasoning and Proof: (grid game) Do we have enough marble chips to cover all the butterflies? How do you know?

Communication: (path game) What do I have to roll to catch up to your mover?

Connections: (path game) How much farther do I need to move to reach the butterfly at the end of the path? (Connects to Measurement)

Representation: (grid game) If I roll three on my die, will I cover the last butterflies? How would that look?

Grocery Shopping Math Suitcase

The games in this math suitcase relate to grocery shopping, which is a common experience for parents and children. The suitcase incorporates both math and literacy concepts for older children. This grid game is more complex than the Butterfly Math Grid Game (Activity 2.17) because children quantify using a pair of dice and place multiple items on each space of the grid. The directions for how to play the path game also include specific guidelines. Using the sample grocery list in the suitcase, children are encouraged to make a list of the items they collect. They may also be encouraged to graph results. Parents are asked to assist children and return copies of their written work back to school. It is important for parents to know this is not homework; children have a choice about whether they choose to play the games at all and whether they want to include the writing and graphing components. Parents should also be encouraged to take dictation from children if writing becomes too overwhelming. The suitcase is supposed to promote excitement about math and literacy for both the parents and children.

Grocery Shopping Grid Game

MATERIALS

□ 2 grid boards, each 8 × 8 inches, with illustrations of 16 grocery bags or cloth totes, glued to 9 × 9 inch posterboard and laminated for durability

□ 64 (or fewer) small toy grocery items, such as cans, bottles, and boxes (found in dollar stores or craft stores and catalogs)

□ a pair of dice

MORE >

Grocery Shopping Long Path Game

MATERIALS

- ☐ game board made from posterboard, approximately 16 × 12 inches or about twice the size of the suitcase (the board is cut into sections after lamination, taped together, and folded to fit into the suitcase)
- ☐ 40 or more 1-inch circles to form the path
- ☐ 2 people movers, such as those from Duplo or Fisher-Price
- ☐ 20 or more small toy grocery items (the same as used for the grid game)
- ☐ a pair of dice
- ☐ sample grocery list for children to copy as they collect items
- ☐ paper and pencil for recording grocery items
- ☐ 1-inch graph paper to graph the results of the collection of groceries (optional)

CHILD'S LEVEL

This suitcase is most appropriate for kindergarten children who will be excited to work with larger quantities of counters and a pair of dice. They typically enjoy directions for how to play as well. Both of the games are more complex than the suitcase games in Activity 2.17 because of the quantity of spaces on the grid and path game and the use of a pair of dice. Multiple counters require children to consider more than one-to-one correspondence as they place two or more items on each space of the grid. Younger children might be overwhelmed by the complexity of the games.

MODIFICATIONS FOR SPECIAL NEEDS OR SITUATIONS

For children with cognitive delays, use a cloth tote bag to hold the materials, and include a 1–3 die or spinner, empty sample sizes of boxed or canned foods, and empty pint-sized juice or milk jugs. Children can roll the die to decide how many food containers to take. The tote bag will be fun to take home, and the reduced number of foods in a larger size will be easier to handle than the small novelty foods.

MATHEMATICS CONTENT STANDARD CONNECTIONS

The suitcase games connect to Number and Operations. Children can create and compare sets using one-to-one correspondence and counting. Family members provide models for the sequence of counting words as well as more logical ways to solve problems. If children decide to graph the results of sorting the foods, they will use concepts that apply to the Data Analysis and Probability standard.

SUGGESTED PROCESS STANDARDS COMMENTS AND QUESTIONS FOR PARENTS

Problem Solving: (grid game) How many foods are on your grid?

Reasoning and Proof: (grid and path games) Have we each collected the same amount of food? How can we tell?

Communication: (grid and path games) How do I know how many pieces of food to take?

Connections: (grid and path games) Do we have just as many boxes of food as cans of food? (Connects to Data Analysis)

Representation: (path game) How can we show the foods we collected on this graph for your teacher?

CHAPTER 3

The Number and Operations Standard— Arithmetic Operations

Arionne and Sanjai quickly put away their coats and backpacks in order to be the first to play the new game at the math center. The Fish Bowl game (Activity 3.18) consisted of a drawing of a large fish bowl, from forty to fifty fish erasers, and a pair of dice. The children were familiar with this type of game and immediately began rolling the dice and taking turns placing an equivalent number of fish erasers in the fish bowl. The teacher joined them and observed for a while before making comments or asking questions. She had previous assessment information for the children, who often remembered the addition combinations without counting the dots on the dice. The teacher asked the children if they could remember how many of each type of fish they had in the fish bowl. They immediately began separating the fish by type and counting each group. Although they accurately quantified up to twenty and higher, neither child could remember the quantities of fish in each group. The teacher suggested they might like to use paper and pencils to help them. They agreed this would be a good idea.

Arionne counted two types of fish and wrote numerals to record the results— eight in one group and twelve in the other. Sanjai became very excited and said, "That's easy. Eight and two is ten, and you have ten more if you take away the two from the twelve—ten and ten is twenty!" Although Arionne accurately quantified and used numerals to represent the quantity, she wasn't convinced about the total until she lined up the fish in a row and counted them one by one from one to twenty.

. . .

Effective teachers assess math knowledge, plan interesting activities and experiences, and use both incidental and intentional teaching strategies to further children's understanding of Number and Operations. They understand the need for concrete materials and recognize that children solve complex mathematical problems involving addition, subtraction, multiplication, and division long before they solve simple problems using algorithms.

In the story above, both children demonstrate knowledge of addition, as they have played dice games so often they now remember many of the combinations. Sanjai is able to decompose the quantity twelve into ten and two because he understands relationships in reference to ten. He, like many five-year-olds, knows double combinations such as four plus four, five plus five, and ten plus ten. He uses this information to solve a problem by relying on his numerous experiences solving problems with concrete materials. Sanjai demonstrates a sophisticated understanding of Number and Operations. Would he have this understanding without the teacher-made math materials and appropriate teaching strategies? Arionne is not as sure of the mathematical relationships and continues to use concrete materials to validate the answer. Would she think about such problem solving solutions if the teacher had not accepted her previous attempts to come up with strategies for quantification? The answer is probably not.

Teachers' Questions

What does the operations component of the Number and Operations standard mean?

For young children, operations include combining sets (early addition), taking away from sets (early subtraction), distributing equal amounts through repeated addition (early multiplication), and dividing materials among friends (early division). Children must also use a variety of methods and tools to compute, including concrete objects, mental computation, estimation, and paper and pencil. According to NCTM Standards for Number and Operations (NCTM 2000, 78), by the end of second grade, children should be able to:

- understand and apply counting to find out how many are in a group;

- understand and represent base-ten place value using multiple models;

- understand magnitudes and relationships among whole numbers, including cardinal and ordinal representations;

- understand and work flexibly with whole numbers, including composing and decomposing them; and

- use physical models to represent number words and numerals.

The activities in this chapter provide opportunities for children to enhance the construction of those concepts in meaningful and authentic ways.

How does the operations component of the Number and Operations standard apply to young children?

Children develop an understanding of operations and higher-level thinking through both everyday play experiences and activities that are planned by the teacher. Children construct the meaning of operations through their play and daily interactions throughout the classroom. For example, a child thinks about addition when he has two crayons and a friend gives him another one. Subtraction occurs when three children are pretending to ride a bus and one gets off. Children may think about multiplication concepts when they give two mittens to each baby doll and begin to notice the pattern. Division happens routinely as children decide how to equitably share materials. Teachers not only design activities, such as math manipulative and board games, but also plan specific materials or experiences throughout the classroom and gross-motor areas.

Can young children really do addition, subtraction, multiplication, and division?

Yes! Young children do all of these operations in a manner that demonstrates their current level of thinking. They advance their thinking through experiences in the classroom and careful activity planning and scaffolding by the teacher. Children begin to solve mathematical problems by using what they already know. Their ideas change as new information is processed and adults or more knowledgeable peers offer just the right amount of information to move their thinking forward. They may pose questions that cause disequilibrium, or a conflict between what the child observes and what the child previously believed to be true. This helps children advance in thinking.

Young children use concrete materials or draw pictures when solving problems that require arithmetic operations rather than solving a written algorithm, such as five plus three or twenty-four divided by two. Children can solve more complex problems using their own method than they can solve in the written form. The use of their own strategies solidifies the underlying understanding of mathematical concepts better than memorization of "facts."

These are some examples of children using strategies commensurate with their level of thinking to solve mathematical problems.

- A child determines how many unit blocks (twelve) and double unit blocks (eight) she has altogether by counting all the blocks (addition).

- A child who has seven goldfish crackers but wants ten figures out how many more he needs by counting up the number line and making slash marks as he says, ". . . eight, nine, ten. I need three more" (subtraction).

- A teacher asks a child how many baby bears she has altogether. The child answers the question by drawing a picture of her mama and baby bears and then counting the baby bears in pairs: "One/two, three/four, five/six, seven/eight, nine/ten. I have ten" (multiplication). She has organized her counting into five groups with two number words needed per group. Later she will remember the even numbers she used and begin to skip odd numbers when counting.

- When asked to divide the frogs (twenty or more) so each person has the same amount, a child pushes the frogs into two piles or gives each person one at a time until all the frogs are distributed (division).

What are the early stages of addition?

Research has shown a hierarchy in children's responses to addition problems (Clements and Sarama 2007, 481–85). *Children initially rely on counting strategies that require the use of countable objects, such as fingers* (Baroody 1987).

Count All: When children begin adding, they start by counting the individual sets and then counting all the items together. For example, if a child rolled a four and a three, he would count, "One, two, three, four; one, two, three"; and then, "One, two, three, four, five, six, seven."

Shortcut-Sum: Preschool teachers who have implemented a mathematics game curriculum in which children quantify dots on dice before taking counters or moving along a path, have noted that many children quickly develop a true counting strategy consisting of counting both sets together to get the sum without having to first count them separately. This is often referred to as a *shortcut-sum strategy* (Clements and Sarama 2007).

Count On: Eventually children begin to *count on* from one of the addends. If they roll a five and a three, they start from one set and count forward, such as, "three"—then "four, five, six, seven, eight." With continued experiences playing quantification games, children eventually remember addition combinations (Kamii 2000).

Are there stages to subtraction, multiplication, and division?

Not in the same sense as addition. Children learn subtraction by realizing that it is the inverse of addition. They apply their knowledge of addition and subtraction to constructing concepts of multiplication and division. This happens during the elementary school grades and is beyond the purview of this book.

How can teachers support young children's construction of foundational concepts for the arithmetic operations?

Teachers use intentional planning strategies that encourage children to use their own thinking strategies to solve math problems. Telling children how to get the correct answer, such as moving the child's finger while counting, does not help children learn to think logically. Instead, it imposes the adult's thinking on the child and teaches children to look to adults to solve math problems. Children need many opportunities to think about mathematical relationships in order to develop their sense of number.

Teachers can invite children to discuss mathematical problems that emerge as they interact and play games together. Discussion and disagreement among peers do not inhibit children's autonomy and willingness to think about solutions to problems. Often, as children try to explain a viewpoint to another child, new ways of thinking emerge. Children learn from one another because they think and evaluate as they argue and discuss.

Teachers can use the intentional teaching strategy of modeling or demonstrating mathematical reasoning at a stage that is just above the thinking level of the child. For example, if a child is at the counting all stage of addition, the teacher might model counting on. Modeling and demonstrating are not the same as correcting errors. They simply offer alternative means to solve a problem.

Teachers should offer prompts to help children move forward in solving a problem. The teacher can give the child the name for twenty, thirty, forty, and so on as the child tries to count a larger quantity of objects. The teacher might ask leading questions, such as, "How many fewer cars do I have than you?" or "Do you have enough rattles to give each baby two?"

Teachers may sometimes directly teach or reteach some information. Although many children construct knowledge about the meaning of operations through incidental teaching, some children will not. It is important for teachers to thoughtfully assess children's understanding of operations, plan experiences or activities based on the assessments, and follow through with teaching opportunities. In most cases, the teacher may decide to directly model a strategy when it is her turn. Use of "self talk" can help. For example, when demonstrating *counting on* for sets of two and three, the teacher might say, "Hum, I already know that's two dinosaurs, so three, four, five."

What types of curriculum materials support arithmetic operations?

Teacher-made board games, math manipulative materials, graphing, dramatic play activities, gross-motor games, and solving everyday math problems all support the development of arithmetic operations. The following types of materials and experiences provide opportunities for children to engage in thinking about arithmetic operations.

Board Games: Children roll a pair of dice and add the quantities of dots together while playing a teacher-made board game.

Math Manipulative: As children play games with dice and counters, such as "Birds on a Wire" (Activity 3.10), they get into a discussion about who has the most birds. They conclude they should divide the set of birds so they each begin with the same amount; otherwise, it won't be fair.

Graphing: Children vote for their favorite book by Eric Carle, and the teacher graphs the results for use at group time. The children compare the votes and subtract quantities in one column from those in another to find out which book received the fewest votes.

Dramatic Play: The dramatic play area is set up for camping and includes a "Fish Fry" activity (Activity 3.16). Children compare the quantities of fish they each catch and decide to make a record by drawing a picture of each fish they catch.

Gross-Motor: Score sheets are available for the Ski Ball game (Activity 3.11) during gross-motor play. Children make marks, draw pictures, and use written numerals to represent their scores.

Incidental Math Problem: Several children want to make a book at the art table. The teacher gives them the job of determining how many pieces of paper they need in order for each child to have three pieces of white paper and two pieces of red.

How can teachers use play to support children's construction of arithmetic operations?

In addition to providing appropriate math materials and planning specific activities, teachers can use comments and questions to encourage mathematical processing skills as children engage in play. The Mathematical Processing Standards—Problem Solving, Reasoning and Proof, Communication, Connections, and Representation—are explained in chapter 1. They encompass the means that children use to learn mathematical concepts, as well as their methods for communicating results and describing their reasoning. Mathematical processes are critical because they reveal the thinking that underlies mathematical understanding. A focus on content that excludes an equal focus on process leads to students with a surface knowledge of mathematics. While they may have substantial memorized information, they may be unable to apply it to unique mathematical situations.

Marble Can Addends

DESCRIPTION

In this activity, children manipulate marbles in a divided can to form different combinations equaling quantities from one to ten. This can help children who are learning about number families.

MATERIALS

☐ 6 or more tuna fish cans spray painted and mounted on wood

☐ a sponge glued to the bottom of each can to partially divide it

☐ file folder stickers (dots) attached to the wood bases in consecutive quantities from 1 to 6 or 1 to 10

☐ container to hold the marbles

☐ 1–6 die, 1–10 die, or a pair of dice if 10 cans are used

CHILD'S LEVEL

This game is intended for kindergarten children who are beginning to focus on what combinations equal a particular sum.

WHAT TO LOOK FOR

• Children often use the dots on the wood to determine how many marbles to put into each can.

• Children may roll the dice to determine which can to add marbles to.

• Children may roll the marbles around the cans and observe the different configurations.

• Older children may focus on different groupings that add up to the same total.

• Some children may choose to write down the combinations if paper and pencils are provided.

MORE >

MODIFICATIONS FOR SPECIAL NEEDS OR SITUATIONS

For children who may have trouble handling the marbles, larger cans and larger marbles or wooden spheres can be used in place of the materials suggested.

MATHEMATICS CONTENT STANDARD CONNECTIONS

This activity aligns with Number and Operations. As children manipulate the quantity of marbles in each can, they focus on comparing quantities and forming relationships. The activity provides a concrete means for children to compose and decompose numbers.

COMMENTS AND QUESTIONS RELATED TO MATHEMATICS PROCESS STANDARDS

Problem Solving: How many ways can you arrange the marbles in the number 5 can?

Reasoning and Proof: What happens when the marbles roll around? Does the quantity of marbles stay the same?

Communication: Explain some of the ways you made a total of six with the marbles.

Connections: What do you have to do with the four marbles so that you have the same number on each side of the can? (Connects to Algebra)

Representation: Can you write down the combinations that made a total of five?

Subtraction

Ten in the Bed

DESCRIPTION

This activity is based on the traditional counting song "Ten in the Bed." Subtraction is a more challenging concept than addition. In this activity, children use concrete objects to represent subtraction. This is also an opportunity for children to read and possibly write the numerals in a meaningful activity.

MATERIALS

☐ wooden doll bed or teacher-made bed constructed from a cardboard box

☐ 10 small dolls, Duplo people, or stuffed bears, depending on the size of the bed

☐ numeral cards, 1–10

☐ paper and pencils

CHILD'S LEVEL

This activity is most appropriate for children who are counting or quantifying to ten and are beginning to recognize numerals 1 through 10. The paper and pencils are optional.

WHAT TO LOOK FOR

• Children often place the dolls on the bed and remove them as they sing the song.

• Some children will coordinate the quantity of dolls with the numeral cards and the words of the song.

• Children may debate how many dolls to put in the bed or whether the correct quantity of dolls is in the bed.

• Some children will accurately quantify one through five but make errors in thinking with quantities greater than that.

MORE >

MODIFICATIONS FOR SPECIAL NEEDS OR SITUATIONS

For younger children or children with cognitive delays, use a large doll bed and fewer but larger dolls or stuffed animals.

MATHEMATICS CONTENT STANDARD CONNECTIONS

This activity connects to Number and Operations, as children determine the quantity of dolls in the bed with each verse of the song after removing one more doll. Children are interested in solving problems such as those found in this activity, which aligns it to the Algebra standard as well. The use of concrete materials provides opportunities for young children to quantify amounts and solve problems they could not solve using pencil and paper.

COMMENTS AND QUESTIONS RELATED TO MATHEMATICS PROCESS STANDARDS

Problem Solving: We need ten bears to begin the song. Are they all here?

Reasoning and Proof: If five bears have fallen out of the bed, how many are left in the bed?

Communication: Which numeral card did you use first? What comes next?

Connections: Let's line up the bears. Are there more bears in the bed or out of the bed? (Connects to Measurement)

Representation: How many bears will be in the bed if one climbs back in? What would that look like?

Multiplication

Chicken Grid Game

DESCRIPTION

Many children enjoy the book *Rosie's Walk* by Pat Hutchins. Rosie the hen walks across the farmyard to get back to the henhouse in time for dinner. This grid game, which includes multiple pictures of the hen, is designed for children to "feed" Rosie quantities of corn. Children may determine how many pieces of corn to feed each Rosie before the game begins. Older children may want to write the numeral for how much they will feed Rosie, while younger children may need assistance from the teacher or a peer. Children continue to play the game until each space on the grid has the same quantity of corn. This leads to repeated addition, or multiplication, as children quantify the corn.

MATERIALS

☐ 2 grids, 8 × 5 inches, each with 12 rubber stamp pictures of Rosie the hen

☐ 48 or more kernels of feed corn

☐ 1–3 or 1–6 spinner made with corn kernels

☐ basket to hold the corn

☐ lamination for protection and durability of the game

☐ a copy of the book *Rosie's Walk* by Pat Hutchins (optional)

CHILD'S LEVEL

This game is most appropriate for children who can quantify to at least six and can play

MORE >

more challenging grid games using multiple cover-ups or counters. Younger children may be overwhelmed by the large quantity of counters. Kindergarten children may choose a large quantity of corn to feed Rosie and make up other rules for the game.

WHAT TO LOOK FOR

- Children will use the spinner and take that quantity of corn kernels to place on the grid.

- Some children will give each hen an equal set of corn kernels without using the spinner. They are thinking about multiplication through repeated addition.

- Some children will begin by giving each hen one corn kernel and repeat the process to give each hen multiple corn kernels until they each have the same amount. They are also thinking about multiplication through repeated addition.

- Children who predetermine the quantity of corn to collect for each hen may want to keep track of how many kernels of corn they have collected for each hen.

MODIFICATIONS FOR SPECIAL NEEDS OR SITUATIONS

Teachers may want to make larger "kernels of corn" using craft clay, which can be baked in the oven. This would allow some children to more easily pick up the pieces of corn. This game is challenging because of the large quantities of counters for the grid. Some children might like to use paper and pencil to record information about quantities of corn they collect.

MATHEMATICS CONTENT STANDARD CONNECTIONS

This activity aligns primarily with Number and Operations. It incorporates concepts of one-to-one correspondence, counting, set comparisons, addition, and multiplication through repeated addition. Because the activity allows children to model a mathematical problem, it also incorporates aspects of the Algebra standard.

COMMENTS AND QUESTIONS RELATED TO MATHEMATICS PROCESS STANDARDS

Problem Solving: If each hen eats one kernel of corn, how much corn will you need? If each hen eats two pieces, how much corn will you need?

Reasoning and Proof: Ellie says some of your hens have more pieces of corn than others. Can you show her what you did to give each hen the same amount of corn?

Communication: How should we decide how much corn to give each hen?

Connections: Do you have enough corn for each hen to have two pieces? How can you find out? (Connects to Algebra)

Representation: Let's write the number for how many pieces of corn to give each hen. That way we won't forget in the middle of the game.

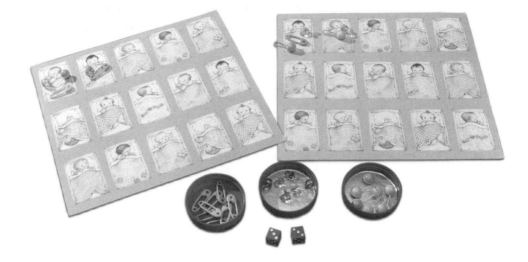

Multiplication

Baby Grid Game

DESCRIPTION

Children collect a variety of baby items to complete this grid. The illustrations of babies and the novelty baby items used as counters attract children to the game. Children use their knowledge of number sense to collect equivalent sets of objects for each baby on their game board. In the process, they explore multiplication at the conceptual level.

MATERIALS

☐ 2 grids, 12 × 12 inches, each with 15 illustrations of babies

☐ 30 counters each of novelty plastic rattles, pacifiers, and diaper pins found in the baby shower departments of craft and party stores

☐ a pair of dice, or 10-sided die

☐ small containers to store the counters

☐ lamination for protection and durability of the game

CHILD'S LEVEL

This grid game is most appropriate for children who are quantifying to at least six and beginning to add a pair of dice together.

WHAT TO LOOK FOR

• Children often roll a die or dice and take a corresponding amount of one type of counter to place one per grid space.

• Some children will notice that five babies with two objects each makes ten objects. This supports a conceptual understanding of multiplication.

MORE >

- Some children will try to collect one of each type of counter for each baby. This will give them an equivalent quantity of objects on each space.
- Some children will add the dice together by counting all the dots.
- Some children will remember combinations of dots without counting.

MODIFICATIONS FOR SPECIAL NEEDS OR SITUATIONS

Stickers of bottles and other baby toys can be mounted on milk or juice jug lids to use as the counters or cover-up pieces. These will be easier to handle and also be attractive. Reduce the quantity of baby items to fifteen per grid and use a 1–3 die to make the game less challenging. Older children might like to record how many bottles, rattles, and diaper pins they collect, using paper and pencil for computation.

MATHEMATICS CONTENT STANDARD CONNECTIONS

This grid game incorporates concepts of Number and Operations, as children think about the relationship between how many of each baby item they have collected. They will be motivated to count to determine the amount. Children will think about repeatedly counting sets of baby items, for example, "One, two, three; four, five, six; seven, eight, nine," when three babies have three items each. This focuses on the repetitive nature of multiplication through repeated addition.

COMMENTS AND QUESTIONS RELATED TO MATHEMATICS PROCESS STANDARDS

Problem Solving: If you give each baby one more rattle, how many rattles will you need?

Reasoning and Proof: Yumi, the list tells us to collect five baby bottles. How do you know you have collected enough?

Communication: Tell me how many more bottles I need for the last babies on my grid.

Connections: Do you have just as many rattles as you do bottles? (Connects to Algebra)

Representation: How will you record how many of each item you have, Stephen?

Egg Cartons and Eggs

DESCRIPTION

Plastic eggs and egg cartons are easy to add to the dramatic play area. They have great math potential because children attempt to divide the eggs equitably, find out how many eggs they each have, or place one egg in each space in the egg carton. The teacher's role in modeling, commenting, or asking leading questions increases the mathematical value of the experience. Sometimes children divide by saying, "One for you and one for me." At other times, they make two piles of eggs that look like about the same amount. The use of concrete materials lays the foundation for later division using algorithms.

MATERIALS

☐ plastic or foam egg cartons

☐ plastic or wooden eggs

CHILD'S LEVEL

This activity is popular with a wide range of children, from young preschoolers who like to put one egg into each space in the egg carton to older preschool or kindergarten children who will enjoy solving math problems such as dividing the eggs.

WHAT TO LOOK FOR

- Children will use a variety of strategies to try to divide the eggs equitably (division).

- Many children will fill each space in the egg carton with an egg (one-to-one correspondence).

- Some children will count to see how many eggs they have (quantification).

- Children will compare how many eggs each person has (comparison of sets).

MORE >

- Some children will give the same number of eggs to each person and then quantify the eggs (multiplication).
- Children may give away some of their eggs and then determine how many eggs are left (subtraction).

MODIFICATIONS FOR SPECIAL NEEDS OR SITUATIONS

The materials for this activity are sturdy and large enough to be used by all children. Teachers may want to purchase inexpensive plastic egg containers used for camping.

MATHEMATICS CONTENT STANDARD CONNECTIONS

This activity includes aspects of the Number and Operations standard as well as concepts about Algebra. Children create, model, and solve problems using concrete materials. As they solve problems, they create and compare sets, quantify objects by counting, and think about relationships of equality.

COMMENTS AND QUESTIONS RELATED TO MATHEMATICS PROCESS STANDARDS

Problem Solving: How can you divide the eggs so that each person has the same amount?

Reasoning and Proof: Do you each have the same amount of eggs? Are there any left over?

Communication: Tell me how many eggs you need so we each have two.

Connections: We have five eggs and two people. If we use all the eggs, will each person have the same amount? (Connects to Algebra)

Representation: What will my egg carton look like if you give me two more eggs?

Addition/Subtraction

Hide the Ducks

DESCRIPTION

This activity introduces five toy ducks into the block area. Children take turns hiding several ducks in a small duck house. The other children look at the remaining ducks and try to determine how many are hidden (subtraction). Children may also think about addition as they remove ducks from the duck house to bring them back to the group and re-quantify how many ducks they have. This is similar to the algorithms children encounter later in school (3 + 2 = ☐ or 5 - ☐ = 3). Children form a deeper understanding of the under-lying concepts of addition and subtraction when they solve interesting problems using the materials in this activity. This game could also be incorporated into the manipulative area or sensory table. It is an extension of the familiar children's song "Five Little Ducks."

MATERIALS

☐ 5 small toy ducks

☐ duck house made from unit blocks or a small box

CHILD'S LEVEL

This activity is most appropriate for older preschool or kindergarten children. Younger children may use the ducks in other ways that are appropriate for their level of thinking, such as reenacting the song with the ducks.

WHAT TO LOOK FOR

• Children will use a variety of strategies to determine how many ducks are hidden.

• Some children will count on to find out how many ducks are left. They will start with the

MORE >

number of ducks they can see and count the missing ducks on their fingers until they reach five.

- Some children will quantify the ducks they can see but be unable to figure out how many ducks are hidden.

- Children will watch one another and discuss ways to solve the missing ducks problem.

MODIFICATIONS FOR SPECIAL NEEDS OR SITUATIONS

This activity is accessible to all children, but teachers must be aware of the level of mathematical thinking for individual children and adjust their questions and comments appropriately. Reduce the amount of ducks to three until children have more experience if needed.

MATHEMATICS CONTENT STANDARD CONNECTIONS

This activity directly aligns to Number and Operations as well as Algebra. Children model the problem of how many ducks, employing concepts of Algebra, and also quantify by counting and comparing quantities of ducks, which are components of Number and Operations. As children compare sets of ducks, they must also think about addition and subtraction mathematical operations.

COMMENTS AND QUESTIONS RELATED TO MATHEMATICS PROCESS STANDARDS

Problem Solving: How did you decide how many ducks are hidden?

Reasoning and Proof: I see one, two, three, four ducks outside the duck house. I wonder how many ducks are inside.

Communication: I can't see the ducks inside the duck house. Can you tell me how many are inside?

Connections: Are there more ducks outside or more ducks inside the duck house? (Connects to Algebra)

Representation: If one more duck goes into the duck house, how many ducks will be left outside?

Addition/Multiplication

One or More for Each

DESCRIPTION

As children interact with one another in the dramatic play area, many opportunities arise for them to create and compare sets, quantify small amounts, and think more deeply about the operations of addition and multiplication. The teacher's selection of materials, the organization of materials, and well-timed, intentional teaching strategies facilitate children's construction of the concepts of addition and multiplication.

MATERIALS

☐ basic household furniture

☐ plates, cups, dolls and doll clothes, bottles, etc., arranged in multiples of 4 or a quantity equal to the number of children allowed in the area at a time

☐ food items, jewelry, dress-up clothes, etc., assembled in quantities that allow each child to have more than 1 of each item (to encourage addition and multiplication)

CHILD'S LEVEL

This is an appropriate activity for preschool and kindergarten children. Younger children will focus on quantities of less than three, and older preschool and kindergarten children may focus on quantities of five or more. They may also use addition and multiplication during play.

WHAT TO LOOK FOR

• Children will take a set of items, such as bracelets, and then add more to their set.

MORE >

- Some children will give two items to each child and then decide to add them all up, which presents a multiplication problem.

- Children may explore concepts of pairing, or multiplying by two, when they give each doll two mittens or each person two shoes.

- Some children will be able to create one-to-one correspondence with materials but will not be able to think about the operations of addition or multiplication.

MODIFICATIONS FOR SPECIAL NEEDS OR SITUATIONS

No modifications are anticipated for this activity. As always, teachers should adjust their questions to meet the needs of individuals.

MATHEMATICS CONTENT STANDARD CONNECTIONS

This activity aligns with Number and Operations.

COMMENTS AND QUESTIONS RELATED TO MATHEMATICS PROCESS STANDARDS

Problem Solving: Do you have enough baby bottles to give one to each baby? How many bottles do you need for each baby to have two?

Reasoning and Proof: You have four plates. Is that enough to give each person a plate? How many more do you need? How many do you have left over?

Communication: I need to know if the babies have two diapers each. How will you find out for me?

Connections: Can you find something round to give each baby? Something rectangular? (Connects to Geometry)

Representation: If each person wants two slices of pizza, what will you do to remember the order?

Addition/Multiplication

How Many Treats

DESCRIPTION

Teachers can plan for children to assist with the distribution of snack. They make decisions about which foods to include based on their knowledge of children's allergies and school policy about food. Children might each be responsible for distributing snack to a table of six children. Later, after some experience, children might distribute snack to all tables. Teachers plan intentional strategies for distribution of such items for snack. For example, one day the teacher may tell children to give everyone two pretzels, one cookie, and three crackers for snack. On a different day children might be asked to get three pretzels, three cookies, and three crackers for each of the children at the table. Additional snack items may be distributed during snack.

MATERIALS

☐ varieties of food, such as teddy bear cookies, square crackers, and circle pretzels

☐ small plates for serving snack

☐ paper and pencils for recording the quantities of each food to be distributed

CHILD'S LEVEL

Older preschool and kindergarten children will be able to accomplish this activity. Initially they may be part of a small group working with the teacher to set up snack, but eventually they will be able to distribute snack independently with supervision and attention to health and sanitation concerns.

MORE >

WHAT TO LOOK FOR

- Some children will distribute one type of snack item to each plate before going on to the next item. For example, they will give every plate two pretzels before distributing one cookie or two crackers. They repeat the process until each plate has the appropriate amount of each food.

- Children may distribute every snack item and quantity to one plate before going on to the next, until each plate has the appropriate amount of each food. For example, plate number one gets two pretzels, one cookie, and three crackers. The process is repeated for each plate until all snacks have been distributed.

- Some children may need further assistance to distribute the snacks appropriately.

- Some children will quantify how many plates they have and determine the number of each of the snack items needed for all the plates. They will collect the appropriate quantity of each snack item before beginning the distribution.

MODIFICATIONS FOR SPECIAL NEEDS OR SITUATIONS

No specific modifications are needed for this activity. The teacher is making decisions about the orders in many instances.

MATHEMATICS CONTENT STANDARD CONNECTIONS

This activity aligns with the Number and Operations and Algebra standards. Children analyze, represent, and model mathematical problems using concrete materials. They create and compare sets of objects, strengthening an understanding of patterns and relationships in the number system.

COMMENTS AND QUESTIONS RELATED TO MATHEMATICS PROCESS STANDARDS

Problem Solving: Each child can have two pretzels, two teddy bear cookies, and two crackers for snack today. How many snacks will each person have altogether?

Reasoning and Proof: How will you be able to prove that every child got the same amount of each snack?

Communication: Will is going to help us today. Tell him what each child should get for snack.

Connections: How many squares will we eat today? Circles? (Connects to Geometry)

Representation: Can you draw a picture of what each child should get for snack?

Counting by 5s

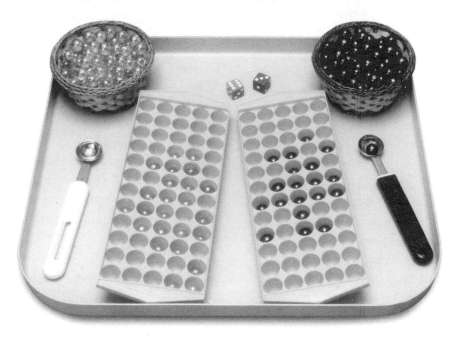

DESCRIPTION

Ice cube trays used for making small balls of ice along with dice and marbles create an unusual and intriguing game that encourages children to count rows of marbles organized in a 5 × 12 pattern of spaces. Arrays such as this are presented later in elementary school when multiplication is formally taught. A melon scoop is used to pick up the marbles and place them into the spaces of the ice cube tray. The activity should be displayed on a suitable tray, because the marbles must be dumped out of the ice cube tray at the end of the game. This keeps them contained and prevents them from rolling around the floor.

MATERIALS

☐ 2 ice cube trays with round holes

☐ 120 marbles

☐ 2 melon scoops

☐ a pair of dice or 10-sided die (1–10 dots per side)

CHILD'S LEVEL

Because this game has so many marbles, it is appropriate for older preschool or kindergarten children who are beginning to combine the quantity of dots on a pair of dice or are interested in a ten-sided die. Kindergarten children may use the game to help them count by fives.

WHAT TO LOOK FOR

• Some children will add dots on the pair of dice by counting all the dots.

• Some children will count to create rules, such as having to fill up a row of five before going on to fill the next row.

MORE >

- Some children will quantify how many marbles they have by counting each row of five holes and emphasizing the last number word in the sequence, such as one, two, three, four, five; six, seven, eight, nine, ten; eleven, twelve, thirteen, fourteen, fifteen; and so on, emphasizing the multiples of five as they count.

MODIFICATIONS FOR SPECIAL NEEDS OR SITUATIONS

This activity may be overwhelming for some children. Teachers can substitute twelve-space ice cube trays and larger, refreezable ice shapes for the sixty-space ice trays and marbles. Add a 1–3 die when children are ready to determine quantity by rolling a die or using a spinner. Tongs can be used for children who are working on hand strength.

MATHEMATICS CONTENT STANDARD CONNECTIONS

This complex activity encourages children to think more deeply about Number and Opera-tions. Children think about counting as a method of quantification. The specific materials ensure that the pattern of 5s emerges in a natural way as children think about more, less, and equal amounts.

COMMENTS AND QUESTIONS RELATED TO MATHEMATICS PROCESS STANDARDS

Problem Solving: How many dots do I need to roll to fill up this row?

Reasoning and Proof: How will I know if I have just as many marbles as you do?

Communication: You've filled up three rows with marbles. How many marbles is that?

Connections: Does it take more marbles to fill a row across or up and down? (Connects to Measurement)

Representation: Can you write down how many marbles you have each time you fill a row?

Addition/Subtraction

Birds on a Wire

DESCRIPTION

Children often observe birds sitting on telephone wires. For this game, each child has a telephone pole and wire frame made from wooden dowels and plastic-coated wire. They also have small birds to clip onto the wires. A spinner or die determines how many birds children add to the wire with each turn, or how many birds fly away with each turn. The quantity of birds and the type of die or spinner varies with the mathematical levels of children in the group.

MATERIALS

☐ telephone pole frame made by gluing 2 8-inch lengths of ¾-inch dowel rods into ¾-inch holes at either end of a 4 × 15 inch wooden base, inserting and gluing 5-inch lengths of ¼-inch dowels into holes drilled

at the tops of the larger dowels, and stretching plastic-coated wire between these crossbars

☐ 20–30 small wooden or flocked birds secured to pinch clothespins using a hot glue gun

☐ bird spinner with 1–4 bird stickers in each section, or 1–6 die or a pair of dice, depending on the quantity of birds used for the game

☐ 2 bird's nests or baskets for holding the birds

☐ paper and pencils for recording quantities of birds on the wire (optional)

CHILD'S LEVEL

This game is most appropriate for older preschool or kindergarten children who can

MORE >

more easily manipulate the clothespins for clipping and removing the birds on the wire and are interested in beginning addition and subtraction.

WHAT TO LOOK FOR

- Children will use a spinner or dice to determine how many birds to put on their wire and will quantify how many are on the wire by counting the birds at the end of each turn.

- At first, some children may clip birds to the wire without regard to the spinner or dice. Teachers can use these teachable moments to ask mathematical questions focusing on addition or subtraction.

- Some children will compare how many birds they each have on their wire by using one-to-one correspondence. Other children will quantify by counting the birds on each wire and making comparisons.

- Some children will quantify how many birds are on the wires at the end of the game or at the beginning of the game.

- At the start of the game, some children may determine how many birds to place on the wire and use the spinner or dice to decide how many birds fly away.

- Children will notice that as more birds are added to the wire, there are fewer birds in the nests. As more birds are subtracted from the wire, there are more birds in the nests.

MODIFICATIONS FOR SPECIAL NEEDS OR SITUATIONS

The small clip clothespins may be too challenging for children with physical or visual disabilities. The birds can be glued onto push clothespins, and the lip of a cardboard box could represent the wire. Children could choose a number card made with 1–6 bird stickers on index cards in place of the small spinner.

MATHEMATICS CONTENT STANDARD CONNECTIONS

This activity aligns primarily with Number and Operations. It incorporates concepts of one-to-one correspondence, counting, set comparisons, addition, and subtraction. It also incorporates aspects of the Algebra standard as children model mathematical problems of more, less, and equal amounts.

COMMENTS AND QUESTIONS RELATED TO MATHEMATICS PROCESS STANDARDS

Problem Solving: Do we have enough birds for ten birds to sit on each wire? How many birds will be left after these two fly away?

Reasoning and Proof: Do the wires each have the same number of birds? How do you know?

Communication: Tell me how many birds are left on your wire. Is that more than I have or fewer than I have left?

Connections: Let's see. We each had five birds. Then one of your birds flew away, and two of my birds flew away. Who do you think has more birds left? (Connects to Algebra)

Representation: How many birds should we begin with on each wire? What will that look like if we want to write it down?

Ski Ball

DESCRIPTION

This teacher-made game is similar to games found in an arcade. Create a ramp that slopes upward to about twelve to eighteen inches and is about twenty-four inches wide. Hollow blocks, wooden planks, or heavy cardboard are possibilities for creating the ramp. Place three empty, three-pound cans at the high end of the ramp. Children roll a small ball up the ramp in an attempt to land the ball in one of the cans. At any point during the game, children can check the number of balls in the cans. The cans could have a point value of one, two, and three or more if children choose to make the game harder. Score sheets are available for children to document how many balls go into the cans.

MATERIALS

☐ wide ramp

☐ 3–6 tennis balls

☐ 3 empty 3-pound cans each painted a different color or covered in a different color of paper

☐ score sheets and pencils can be introduced after children practice rolling the balls up the ramp and aiming for a particular can

CHILD'S LEVEL

Older preschool and kindergarten children will be most interested in this game, which involves both eye-hand coordination and the end result of keeping score. Younger children may have difficulty rolling the ball up the ramp and will most likely be interested in rolling balls down the ramp.

WHAT TO LOOK FOR

• Children will experiment with how to roll the ball up the ramp and make it land in one of the cans. Once they master the skill, they

MORE >

will be more interested in keeping score and may aim for a particular color of can or the can with the highest assigned point value.

- Some children will keep score by making hash marks, drawing pictures, or using numerals.

- Older children will increase the point value or make other rules to increase the challenge and complexity of the game.

- Some children may try to get all the balls in one can or two balls in each can.

MODIFICATIONS FOR SPECIAL NEEDS OR SITUATIONS

Side rails can be made to keep the balls from rolling off the ramp. This is similar to bumper bowling. For children with visual disabilities, place a bell on each can so that when the ball hits it, a sound will be made.

MATHEMATICS CONTENT STANDARD CONNECTIONS

Keeping score is an interesting component of this activity. As children take turns, they are motivated to keep track of how many balls are in the can or how many points they have compared to their last score or compared to another child. This requires addition. All of these components align with Number and Operations.

COMMENTS AND QUESTIONS RELATED TO MATHEMATICS PROCESS STANDARDS

Problem Solving: How many balls will you need to land in the two-point can to get a score of four?

Reasoning and Proof: How many more points will Christian need to have the same score as you?

Communication: I want to record my score. What should I write?

Connections: Which color can has the most balls? (Connects to Data Analysis)

Representation: What does the score sheet tell you about how many balls have landed in the cans?

ACTIVITY 3.12

Subtraction

Pendulum Target Game

DESCRIPTION

A pendulum is a weight suspended from a fixed point. The weight swings freely when released and moves back and forth. The pendulum for this gross-motor math game could be made from a small peanut butter jar partially filled with sand and suspended from a tire swing frame. Then make a target consisting of empty water bottles, small cardboard blocks, toy bowling pins, or other containers about eight to ten inches tall. The targets should be easy for children to line up on the floor in the area of the pendulum. The weight should be heavy enough to knock over the targets but not so heavy that it can injure someone. Children focus on subtraction as they quantify how many bottles are left standing at the end of each turn.

MATERIALS

☐ large teacher-made pendulum

☐ 6 or more empty plastic bottles or other containers for the targets

☐ paper and pencil

CHILD'S LEVEL

The pendulum can be used by children at all levels of mathematical thinking. This activity incorporates elements of both science and mathematics. Young children may explore the physical knowledge aspects of the pendulum and gain mathematical knowledge by watching older children knock over the bottles while quantifying, comparing, communicating, and keeping score verbally and in a written form. Teachers use intentional

MORE >

teaching strategies to encourage all children to focus on counting, comparing sets, and using mathematical operations, especially subtraction.

WHAT TO LOOK FOR

- Children will initially concentrate on the properties of the pendulum and may not be able to answer mathematical questions. Learning about how their actions affect the reaction of the pendulum may require a long period of exploration.

- Some children will count to quantify how many bottles they knocked down and compare this to the number of bottles they started with.

- Some children will use the paper and pencil to record how many bottles they knocked down by making hash marks, drawings, or written numerals on the paper.

MODIFICATIONS FOR SPECIAL NEEDS OR SITUATIONS

Children may need assistance placing the bottles in a stable position, but they should decide where to place the bottles rather than the teacher making the decision. For children with visual disabilities, use an object that makes a sound when the pendulum strikes it, such as a metal can.

MATHEMATICS CONTENT STANDARD CONNECTIONS

This activity focuses on Number and Operations, with special attention to subtraction to determine how many bottles are left standing.

COMMENTS AND QUESTIONS RELATED TO MATHEMATICS PROCESS STANDARDS

Problem Solving: How many bottles are left after you knocked over these three?

Reasoning and Proof: It looks like you have knocked over three bottles. Is that more or fewer bottles than you have left standing? How will you find out?

Communication: Where should I stand to knock over all the bottles?

Connections: Do you think you will knock over more bottles if you place them in a line or in a triangular shape? (Connects to Geometry)

Representation: How will you show your parents your score today?

Addition

Walking Upside Down Long Path Game

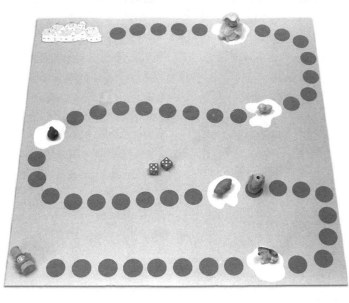

DESCRIPTION

Many children love to imagine acting silly like the characters in the book *Silly Sally* by Audrey Wood. Silly Sally walks to town backwards and upside down. Along the way she meets a dog, loon, pig, and sheep. In this path game, children advance the upside-down movers along a path that includes bonus spaces. At each bonus space, children collect toy animal figures for the dog, loon, pig, and sheep. They will quantify how many animals they each have at the end of every turn. They may add together the quantities of animals they each have collected, or they may use one-to-one correspondence to quantify by lining up the animals in rows across from each other. Each time they add one animal, they use concrete materials to represent the pattern of the number system; each number is one more than the previous number.

MATERIALS

- [ ] posterboard, 22 × 22 inches
- [ ] 45 1-inch circles to form the path
- [ ] 5 irregular shapes to form the bonus spaces for the animal figures
- [ ] 2 silhouette stickers placed upside down for the starting point
- [ ] illustration of a town at the ending point
- [ ] 2 or more people figures mounted upside down on wooden disks
- [ ] small rubber or plastic figures of dogs, loons, pigs, and sheep
- [ ] a pair of dice or 10-sided die
- [ ] 2 small baskets for collecting the animals along the path

MORE >

☐ lamination for protection and durability of the game

☐ a copy of the book *Silly Sally* by Audrey Wood (optional)

CHILD'S LEVEL

The complexity of the path makes this game most appropriate for older preschool and kindergarten children. The path is fairly long, has an irregular shape, and includes bonus spaces. Children who are ready to add together the quantities of dots on a pair of dice or quantify up to ten will find this game both interesting and challenging. Younger children may be overwhelmed by the design and choose to play with the animal figures instead of advancing along the path. Some children may want to keep track of which animals they have collected by recording the information on paper. Other children might want to write the name of each animal as they collect it.

WHAT TO LOOK FOR

- Some children will roll two dice and add them together by counting all the dots before moving along the path.

- Some children will add the quantities of dots on the pair of dice by counting on. Children who roll five dots and three dots may recognize the quantity on one die as five and add the other die by continuing to count, "six, seven, eight."

- Some children will remember the addition combinations without counting the dots on the dice. Teachers could add a third 1–6 die to the game.

MODIFICATIONS FOR SPECIAL NEEDS OR SITUATIONS

Use a single 1–6 die for children not yet ready to quantify by combining sets of dots on a pair of dice. For children with visual disabilities, use raised circles for the path and dice.

MATHEMATICS CONTENT STANDARD CONNECTIONS

This path game directly aligns to Number and Operations. Children count dots on the die or add together the quantities on a pair of dice. They are motivated to use quantification strategies on each turn to advance their mover to the end of the game. Many children will also "check" the accuracy of addition by other players, increasing reasoning and proof as well as communication about mathematics.

COMMENTS AND QUESTIONS RELATED TO MATHEMATICS PROCESS STANDARDS

Problem Solving: If I roll seven dots on the dice, will I move past the loon or stop before the loon?

Reasoning and Proof: How will you find out how many animals have been collected altogether?

Communication: How shall we play this game? Do I have to land on the bonus space to collect the animal, or do I collect the animal if I pass the bonus space? How will we remember what to do?

Connections: I am only two spaces from the pig. Do I have a good chance of rolling just two dots? (Connects to Probability)

Representation: You can use the paper to keep track of which animals or how many animals you have collected.

Addition

Pirate Treasure Long Path Game

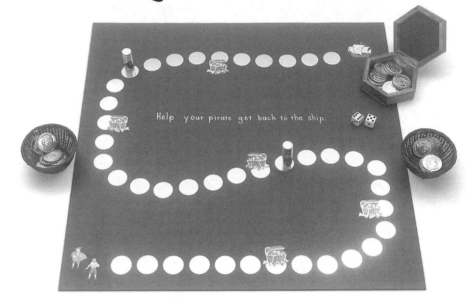

DESCRIPTION

Children are often fascinated with pirates and the prospect of finding treasure. This long path game coordinates well with pirate books, such as *Tough Boris* by Mem Fox. Children advance a mover along a path that sometimes crosses a treasure chest bonus space. Children collect gold coins or other treasure at each of the treasure chests along the path. As they advance along the path, they quantify and compare the amount of treasure they have collected. At the end of the game, they may choose to record the amount on paper. Children may also be interested in sorting a collection of different types of coins or pretend jewels. The teacher may provide one-inch graph paper for children to represent the quantities of each type of treasure they collect.

MATERIALS

☐ posterboard, 22 × 22 inches

☐ 40 or more gold squares or circles to form the path

☐ 2 pirate stickers or illustrations for the starting point

☐ 1 pirate ship sticker or illustration for the end point

☐ 5 treasure chest stickers or illustrations for the bonus spaces

☐ 20 or more gold coins or other treasure to collect at bonus spaces

☐ 2 different pirate movers or other small toy people

☐ a pair of dice or 10-sided die

☐ basket or fancy box to hold the treasure

MORE >

☐ paper and pencils (optional)

☐ lamination for protection and durability of the game

☐ a copy of the book *Tough Boris* by Mem Fox (optional)

CHILD'S LEVEL

Older preschool and kindergarten children are very interested in collecting things, especially treasure of any kind. They are more able to understand the idea of using the bonus spaces on the path as part of the game. Teachers may want to suggest collecting treasure on the bonus spaces as they introduce the game formally or informally. Teachers or more competent peers will also model this on their turn to play.

WHAT TO LOOK FOR

- Children will add the dice together by counting all the dots and advance an equivalent number of spaces along the path.

- A few children may count the dots on one die and advance on the path before counting the dots on the second die and advancing further along the path. This is an opportunity for the teacher to model combining the two dice by counting all the dots when it is her turn to play.

- Some children will *count on*—recognize the quantity on one die and count forward from that amount for the dots on the second die; for example, "I have five and six, seven, eight. I have eight."

- Some children will remember the addition combinations after repeated experience adding two dice.

MODIFICATIONS FOR SPECIAL NEEDS OR SITUATIONS

Larger-sized dice can be found in many novelty stores. They often have indentations for the dots. These would be easier for a child with a visual disability to count, because they can feel the indentations. Also, raised spaces can be used for the path so that children can feel it. Some children may enjoy starting the game with a quantity of coins and losing some each time they land on a treasure chest. In this case, they will be thinking about subtraction.

MATHEMATICS CONTENT STANDARD CONNECTIONS

This activity aligns with Number and Operations. Children typically count to determine how many spaces to move on the path, which helps them develop a deeper understanding of the number system. Children compare quantities of dots on the die to the number of spaces they move on the path. They add the quantities of dots on the pair of dice together, which is the operation of addition.

COMMENTS AND QUESTIONS RELATED TO MATHEMATICS PROCESS STANDARDS

Problem Solving: What should happen if I land on a treasure chest bonus space? (Many children will suggest collecting treasure or perhaps going back a space or ahead a space as well as collecting treasure. These rules should be negotiated among the players until an agreement is reached. Some children may want the teacher to write down the rules they generate.)

Reasoning and Proof: How many coins will you have at the end of the game if you collect two coins at each treasure chest bonus space?

Communication: Should players collect one coin at each treasure chest bonus space, or should players begin with ten coins and take one away if they land on a treasure chest?

Connections: How will you sort your treasure into groups? How many groups will you have? (Connects to Algebra)

Representation: Is there a way for you to keep track of how much treasure you collect along the path?

Grandma's Cookies

DESCRIPTION

Kindergarten children often explore the concept of division during the daily activities of school. They might divide the markers used for an art activity or the packages of pretzels for snack. In this path game, children advance along the path and collect cookies at the bonus spaces. At the end of the game, children can compare the number of cookies they each have and discuss what they would have to do to divide the cookies equally among themselves. The game coordinates with the book *The Doorbell Rang* by Pat Hutchins, in which children must solve the problem of how to divide the cookies each time more children join the group.

MATERIALS

☐ posterboard, 22 × 22 inches

☐ 50 white, 1-inch circles

☐ illustration of a chocolate chip cookie for each bonus space

☐ plastic cookies to collect

☐ 2 or more people movers, such as those by Duplo or Fisher-Price

☐ a pair of dice

☐ a small basket or cookie jar for the end point to hold the cookies

☐ 1 small basket or tray per child for collecting cookies along the path

☐ paper and pencil for recording and computation (optional)

☐ lamination for protection and durability of the game

☐ a copy of the book *The Doorbell Rang* by Pat Hutchins (optional)

MORE >

CHILD'S LEVEL

This game is most appropriate for kindergarten children who can quantify using a pair of dice and have played games with guidelines. The bonus spaces and the inclusion of two 1–6 dice make this game too complex for younger or less experienced children. The teacher may need to discuss the game with children before it is available for use. Children may generate additional or different rules for how to play the game. The paper and pencils may be included for those interested in recording how many cookies they have collected.

WHAT TO LOOK FOR

- Some children will add the dice together by counting all the dots, move an equivalent number of spaces along the path, collect cookies at the bonus spaces, and compare how many cookies each player has collected at the end of the game.

- Children may discuss whether the division of cookies is equal or not equal.

- Children can decide how to distribute the cookies so that each player has the same amount.

MODIFICATIONS FOR SPECIAL NEEDS OR SITUATIONS

Children with cognitive delays can play an easier version of the game with a single 1–6 die and by focusing on the addition of cookies as they pass bonus spaces.

MATHEMATICS CONTENT STANDARD CONNECTIONS

The operations of addition and division are a major part of this activity; therefore, it aligns directly to Number and Operations. Children must employ their understanding of the number system in order to engage in the activity.

COMMENTS AND QUESTIONS RELATED TO MATHEMATICS PROCESS STANDARDS

Problem Solving: How many cookies will we need if everyone wants to collect five by the end of the game?

Reasoning and Proof: Does each player have the same amount of cookies so far? How will you find out?

Communication: Tell me how many more cookies you have than I do.

Connections: Is it the same distance between each bonus space? (Connects to Measurement)

Representation: How will you keep track of how many cookies you have collected each time you land on a bonus space?

Addition/Division

Fish Fry in Dramatic Play

DESCRIPTION

Teachers should include math activities in many areas of the classroom to provide multiple ways for children to demonstrate their understanding of mathematical concepts and for teachers to use authentic experiences for assessment. Children like to pretend to cook and serve food to other children and to the teacher. In this activity, small blocks of wood in various shapes represent fish sticks in the dramatic play area, which is set up as a restaurant. A menu posted on the wall and printed on cards for the customers encourages children to consider how many fish sticks in each shape they wish to order. Each order requires the cook to add together the quantities of fish to fry or to determine if the fish can be divided among the patrons. If the menu includes prices for different shapes, the cook or cashier will collect pennies from customers when they pay for their order.

MATERIALS

☐ 20 or more small blocks of wood (bags of wooden shapes are available in craft catalogs)

☐ divided trays for displaying the fish sticks in an organized manner

☐ small frying pans or trays for cooking the fish in the dramatic play area

☐ menus posted on the wall and printed on cards (prices for each shape can be included)

MORE >

☐ pennies for customers to purchase fish sticks (optional)

☐ paper and pencils for recording the orders

CHILD'S LEVEL

This activity is most appropriate for older preschool and kindergarten children, but younger children enjoy participating in the play.

WHAT TO LOOK FOR

- Children will quantify as they fill orders for the fish fry, such as two star-shaped fish and one triangle-shaped. They will add together the quantities of each fish shape.

- Some children will place one fish shape on each plate at the table in a one-to-one correspondence manner.

- Children may place one of each fish shape on each plate at the table and quantify how many they need altogether.

- Some children will order from the menu and pay for their purchase using pennies.

- Some children will take the orders and add the totals.

MODIFICATIONS FOR SPECIAL NEEDS OR SITUATIONS

No modifications are anticipated for this activity because it is self-leveling.

MATHEMATICS CONTENT STANDARD CONNECTIONS

This activity directly aligns with Number and Operations. Children think about one-to-one correspondence and counting, as well as the operations of addition and division.

COMMENTS AND QUESTIONS RELATED TO MATHEMATICS PROCESS STANDARDS

Problem Solving: I want one of each fish shape. How many fish will I get in my order?

Reasoning and Proof: Do you have enough pennies to pay for your order?

Communication: Here is my order. How many fish will you tell the cook to prepare?

Connections: Is there a way to divide the triangle-shaped fish so we each have the same amount? (Connects to Geometry)

Representation: What will my order look like if I want two more star-shaped fish?

Addition/Subtraction

Getting to School Graph

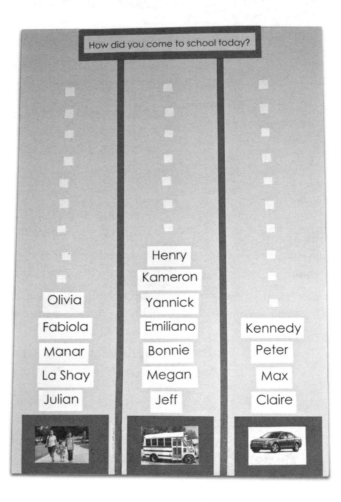

DESCRIPTION

How do you get to school? In this activity, the answer to this question is represented by a class graph. Children get to school each day by car, bus, or walking. Graphing the results is interesting, relevant, and helps children visualize the quantities involved. It also facilitates making comparisons. Children both create and compare sets of names on the graph. The graph of results can change on a daily basis, providing new opportunities to quantify and compare sets.

MATERIALS

☐ posterboard or paper divided into 3 columns and a number of rows equal to the number of children in the class

☐ illustrations for a car, bus, and children walking to place at the bottom of each column

☐ a printed message at the top of the graph, such as "How did you come to school today?"

MORE >

☐ name tag for each child, sized appropriately to fit the graph

☐ magnetic tape or Velcro to secure the name tags in the columns on the graph

CHILD'S LEVEL

This graph is appropriate for both preschool and kindergarten children. Younger children will use the illustrations on the graph to help them understand the concept of a graph. This type of graph has a more authentic purpose than voting, for example, for a favorite color or flavor of ice cream. Children will begin to understand the need for accuracy in their responses because the bus total may have to be delivered to the office. Also, for this graph, children are unlikely to respond in a way that agrees with a friend or votes for the "winning" column, as they may be inclined to do on other graphs. Younger children can identify their name tag with their response, while children who can write their own name can do so on the slips of paper. There is a concrete, one-to-one correspondence relationship between each child and each name on the graph.

WHAT TO LOOK FOR

- Children may count to quantify how many people get to school in each manner.

- Children may compare column heights to determine whether there are more, fewer, or the same number of children who come to school by car, bus, or walking.

- Some children may subtract to determine how many more name tags one column has than another.

- Some children may count all the responses to verify that the number equals the number of children present on that day.

- A few children may want to record the responses each day and compare the results with other days of the week.

MODIFICATIONS FOR SPECIAL NEEDS OR SITUATIONS

Teachers may need to assist some children in placing their name tag on the graph. Braille or raised print can be used on the graph if there are children with visual disabilities in the class.

MATHEMATICS CONTENT STANDARD CONNECTIONS

This graphing activity directly connects to Number and Operations, as children add together the quantities of votes in each category. Some children may use subtraction to determine how many more votes one category received than another. The activity incorporates concepts of the Data Analysis and Probability standard as well, because children collect the data, record it, and interpret it.

COMMENTS AND QUESTIONS RELATED TO MATHEMATICS PROCESS STANDARDS

Problem Solving: How many children have responded today?

Reasoning and Proof: Fifteen children are at school today. Can you tell from the graph if everyone has responded?

Communication: Sara wants to know how many children came to school on the bus. How can she find that out?

Connections: If three more children come on the bus to school today, will that be more or fewer than the children who come by car? (Connects to Data Analysis)

Representation: What will the graph look like if one more person walks to school today?

Fish Bowl

DESCRIPTION

The illustration of a large fish bowl and colorful fish erasers make this activity interesting to all children. They can create and compare sets and may use written numerals to record the quantity of fish they catch. Children work together to catch fish for the fish bowl. This reduces competition and provides opportunities for peer modeling to occur. During the game, children count fish as well as sort them into groups and compare quantities. Teacher questions and intentional teaching strategies encourage children to think more deeply about quantifying large amounts of fish, addition and subtraction, and also representing quantities by using written numerals.

MATERIALS

☐ large fish bowl drawn on blue posterboard, 20 × 15 inches

☐ 30 or more fish erasers or other small plastic fish

☐ a pair of dice or 10-sided die

☐ slips of paper with the words, "There are _____ fish in the fish bowl," written on each

☐ pencils

CHILD'S LEVEL

This activity is most appropriate for older preschool and kindergarten children. The quantities of fish and type of dice available may be overwhelming for younger children.

WHAT TO LOOK FOR

• Children may begin by placing fish in the fishbowl without regard for the die. Teachers can use these opportunities to ask mathematical questions that focus children's attention on quantity.

MORE >

- Some children will create a set of fish equal to the quantity of dots on the die and place them in the fish bowl.
- Children may add the quantities of dots on the dice together and take an equivalent amount of fish to place in the fish bowl.
- Children may sort the fish by type and quantify how many of each type they have.
- Some children will count the fish in the bowl each time they take a turn. They may use the paper and pencils to record the amount, using hash marks or other representations.
- Some children will use written numerals to fill in the blank on the slips of paper available with the game.

MODIFICATIONS FOR SPECIAL NEEDS OR SITUATIONS

The game can be designed using a large plastic fish bowl or other plastic bowl and plastic fish. This design would be interesting to all children, but it would be especially accessible to children with a physical disability or with IEP goals related to eye-hand coordination. The type of die and quantity of fish are determined by the developmental level of children who are playing the game.

MATHEMATICS CONTENT STANDARD CONNECTIONS

This activity aligns with Number and Operations, as children determine quantity by counting fish they have collected and compare amounts by adding or subtracting. The use of concrete materials makes this easier for children. If children sort the fish into categories, the activity also connects to Algebra and Data Analysis.

COMMENTS AND QUESTIONS RELATED TO MATHEMATICS PROCESS STANDARDS

Problem Solving: Are there more fish with stripes or more fish with dots?

Reasoning and Proof: Your paper says there are twenty-four fish in the bowl. How did you decide that?

Communication: How many fish will I have if I collect all the striped fish and all the blue fish?

Connections: After you sort the fish, do you think you will have more fish with dots or more fish with stripes? (Connects to Data Analysis)

Representation: If you catch five more fish, will you have more than twenty fish or fewer than twenty fish in the bowl?

CHAPTER 4

The Algebra Standard

Jeffrey sorted tiny dinosaurs from a basket into groups of three. The teacher could observe no common attributes among the dinosaurs of each group. He asked Jeffrey how he decided which dinosaurs to put together. Jeffrey answered, "Well, I wanted three in each group, but I wanted each of the three to be totally different." If the teacher had not asked a probing question, he would not have had accurate assessment data for Jeffrey. The erroneous assumption might have been that Jeffrey lacked an understanding of sorting and classifying.

Annabelle sorted a button collection several times over a period of two weeks. She first grouped the buttons by color, but later she focused on size. Eventually Annabelle noticed some buttons were both the same color and the same size. She placed the buttons into new groups to reflect her expanded and flexible observations of attributes. Buttons can be grouped in a variety of ways.

• • •

Did you ever spend a quiet morning playing with your grandmother's jewelry box? Perhaps you put all the bracelets together in one pile, all the rings in another, and the earrings in a third pile. Later maybe you put the jewelry you liked best in one pile, the jewelry you "sort of" liked in another, and the jewelry you didn't like much at all in a third pile. As the time slipped away, you were sorting and re-sorting the collection, thinking intently about how to group that jewelry.

Children are intrigued with the classification of materials. If you didn't find a jewelry box to rummage through, perhaps you found a button box or a drawer full of toy cars and other vehicles. As you played with the materials, you were learning how to think about things in more than one way. Collections are introduced to the classroom to provide children with the opportunity to experiment with sorting and classifying and to help them develop flexible thinking—a necessary disposition for mathematics learning.

Teachers' Questions

How does the Algebra standard apply to young children?

Algebra involves understanding patterns and relationships. It also includes analyzing, representing, and modeling mathematical situations (NCTM 2000, 90). *Children construct mathematical relationships by sorting and classifying materials and eventually forming them into patterns.* Many teachers wince at the idea that algebra is a mathematics standard for young children, but actually, many of the experiences that children have in the home and school settings relate to this category. The language of mathematics that permeates math-rich classrooms helps children analyze problem situations, such as whether three friends can go to the gross-motor room together when only two spaces are open on the waiting list.

What concepts related to algebra should teachers look for in young children?

Children begin to sort, classify, and order objects into a variety of categories long before they enter a formal school setting. They also recognize, describe, and extend patterns and begin to analyze how both repeating and growing patterns are generated. Infants construct the knowledge that some people are familiar and some are not—we call this stranger anxiety. It is also classification. A toddler lines up her stuffed animals from smallest to largest. This act of play is a sequencing pattern. As children develop and explore the world, they continue to sort and classify and make patterns. Young children might group a collection of rocks into categories or sort the laundry. Many children seem to perceive patterns naturally. Often they become interested in patterns in clothing, nature, or other everyday experiences. Many children walk across a tile floor in a store, stepping only on the blue ones. Playing around with patterns is intriguing.

Children also solve everyday math problems of equality, such as whether each sibling has the same amount of ice cream or whose turn it is to sit in the best seat in the car. This problem solving helps them construct the concept of equality. According to NCTM, "Equality is an important algebraic concept that students must encounter and begin to understand in the lower grades" (NCTM 2000, 94). Children must experience and begin to understand equality in the early grades so they can readily solve for unknown variables in later schooling.

What concepts related to sorting and classifying do young children develop?

Children carefully observe similarities and differences in the attributes of objects, make comparisons, and construct relationships among objects. This helps them develop more flexible thinking and begin to take another person's perspective. As children play with the objects in collections, they make note of distinguishing features, such as color, size, shape, texture, ornamentation, and detail. They then begin to compare objects within the collection, look for similarities or differences, and group them accordingly. This construction of relationships, such as *same*, *different*, *more*, and *less*, provides a framework for all later mathematical understanding.

Collections encourage children to become more flexible in their thinking. There is no predetermined, correct way to sort the objects. The goal is for children to find a variety of ways to group materials. For example, a child playing with a key collection might initially separate all the brass keys from the silver keys. On another day, she might focus on the number or type of holes in the keys. While, at a later time, she might sort them by size.

Collections can help children take another person's perspective. Young children are egocentric. They assume everyone thinks the same way they do. As children discuss or argue about how to group the items in a collection, they become aware that different people view the same objects in different ways. This helps them move away from such an egocentric viewpoint.

Why is patterning an important mathematical concept?

Perceiving patterns helps children understand mathematical structures. Mathematical thinking involves constructing relationships among ideas and concepts. Although not all mathematical relationships involve patterns, exploring patterns helps children learn to view items in relationship to one another rather than individually. Formation of these logical-mathematical relationships is the basis of future mathematical problem solving.

How are sorting and classifying related to patterning and algebra?

Sorting and classifying are integral parts of patterning and later algebraic reasoning. In order to sort materials into categories, children must learn to focus on a particular attribute and identify it in a variety of materials or situations. Later, children will use this knowledge of attributes to recognize, create, and extend patterns.

On a practical level, children who want to create a pattern with particular materials, such as colored beads, can do this more easily if the beads are presorted into different colors. It is easier for them to remember the pattern if they don't need to search through a container of eight different colors of beads.

Teachers may notice children creating symmetrical patterns with art or manipulative materials. For example, the child may start with a central bead or block and then extend outward with identical objects on each side. This experimentation with symmetry forms a backdrop for later algebraic equations in which both sides must be equal.

How can teachers support children's construction of concepts related to sorting and classifying?

Teachers must observe carefully, model appropriately, and direct questioning to encourage a variety of sorting possibilities. Teachers should allow ample time for the class to explore materials in a collection and observe how children begin to group the items. They may discover a variety of sorting possibilities. As interest wanes or the children appear to have exhausted all the possibilities, the teacher can model sorting by a new attribute or ask questions to possibly lead their thinking in another direction.

- Is there another way to put these together?

- Do you have any that will fit in my group?

- Where can I put these?

- What would you do if you could only have four groups?

- How will (or did) you decide which ones go together?

What are the attributes of a good collection?

A good collection is highly interesting to young children and can be sorted in several ways. Look for

- objects that are intriguing to young children;

- objects that share at least three attributes, such as color, shape, size, or detail, so they can be sorted in several different ways;

- objects that coordinate with the overall curriculum, such as a collection of shells when children are interested in or learning about the ocean; and

- an appropriate number of objects, so that children have enough to make many cross comparisons yet are not overwhelmed.

Commercial collections often have only one or two attributes. For example, a child might be able to sort a set of teddy bears only by color. This does not encourage flexible thinking that develops when children can group and regroup objects by several different attributes. Many commercial collections are the standard didactic shapes or cubes. Children have often seen this type of material and do not find such collections nearly as interesting as Grandma's buttons.

How can teachers support children's construction of patterning concepts?

Teachers can provide opportunities for children to learn to recognize, extend, and create patterns. This happens after they understand the underlying relationship among the items forming the patterns. While patterning relationships cannot be directly taught to children, teachers can facilitate the construction of patterning concepts by planning activities that expose children to patterns and providing them with materials for creating their own. For example, children may learn to recognize patterns in teacher-designed pattern strips, particularly if the patterns are introduced at group time and chanted rhythmically. Children can place manipulative pieces in empty boxes on pattern strips to extend patterns, such as in Cookie and Pretzel Pattern Strips (Activity 4.15) and Shell Patterns (Activity 4.16). Children begin to create patterns once they become aware of the patterns around them. They often create patterns in their artwork, such as stringing beads or painting stripes in a repeating color order.

Children may also construct some mathematical relationships built on patterns. The realization that, when counting, each number is one more than the previous number or the discovery that even and odd numbers alternate are examples of mathematical relationships that involve patterns.

Teachers can help children discover patterns that exist naturally throughout their environment, both indoors and outdoors. Children are surrounded by patterns, from alternating colors of floor tiles to the stripes on their own clothes. It is the teacher's role to draw attention to patterns and initiate discussions about them so that children begin to discover patterns themselves.

Teachers can also design specific materials and activities that encourage children to create and extend patterns. Their ability to use the same objects to create many different relationships increases as children interact with the materials and with one another. This helps young children develop more flexible thinking and problem-solving capabilities.

Teachers may model creating patterns to help get children started. They may ask leading questions to draw children's attention toward patterns. When teachers choose to model, it should be with the intent of showing another way to use the materials, not the "correct" way. If children show an interest in patterns, they can continue on their own. If children are not interested in creating patterns, teachers can wait for another opportunity. Although the teacher may have designed a particular material to stimulate patterning, the children may use it to construct other concepts.

How does assessment guide planning?

Think of assessment like a tourist guide. Tourists use the guide to help them plan their vacation. Teachers use assessments to plan activities for individual children and for groups of children. There are discrete points of interest throughout the year, just as there are points of interest at a vacation destination. There are some sites you must see and some that are optional. Sometimes you make decisions based on time, and other times based on interest. The tourist guide may suggest that you visit one site before the other. In the same way, teachers sometimes introduce a developmentally appropriate and important concept to all children at group time or another class meeting. At other times, they use their observations and ongoing assessments of individual children to pose questions or introduce curriculum that is geared toward an individual child or small group of children.

Can teachers directly teach algebra concepts?

No, algebraic concepts involve logical-mathematical thinking that each individual must construct. However, the concrete materials that are a mainstay in quality programs enable children to represent mathematical problems in ways they can understand. Are there enough drivers to put one in each car? How can we find out? Are there more cows or horses? If there are more cows, which kind of animal will need a bigger pen? These are the types of experiences encountered by children through their play that help them form the basis for later algebra. Over time, a play situation involving one child with three cars and another child with two cars will help the children perceive that $5c = 3c + 2c$.

How can teachers modify algebra activities for children with disabilities?

Teachers can simplify the language used with children and use smaller quantities of objects for some activities. For example, rather than asking children to create a pattern with three colors of beads, the teacher might reduce the color choices to two.

Children may understand patterns more easily if they are approached within a play context. For example, the teacher might ask a child to find a baby sheep for each mama sheep. This may make more sense to the child than asking him to show a big-little alternating pattern.

Patterning should be introduced to all children through a variety of modalities, including movement and music. Many teachers have discovered that children recognize patterns more easily when they are chanted rhythmically and particularly if accompanied by body movements. For example, one group of young kindergarten children who were having difficulty identifying and extending an alternating pattern of pumpkins and cats amazed their teacher by catching on immediately when they chanted "pumpkin, cat, pumpkin, cat" during music time.

Bears and Balloons

DESCRIPTION

Algebra for preschool children involves analyzing, representing, and modeling mathematical situations. The colorful bears and balloons provide numerous opportunities for children to construct those concepts while engaging in an interesting activity. The bear and balloon cutouts can be made from different materials and used in a variety of ways. They can be cut from construction paper and laminated, with magnetic tape on the back. These will stick to some whiteboards or most metal surfaces, such as the cover to the classroom heating and cooling unit. Stiff, craft felt is another material to use. The cutouts adhere to a flannel board fairly easily. Bears and balloons can also be cut from thin craft foam and used in the sensory table with a Plexiglas easel or plastic tray, as in Geometry Comes to the Water Table (Activity 5.2). A small amount of water is needed to make the foam stick to the surface.

MATERIALS

☐ 5 or more bear cutouts

☐ 10 or more balloon cutouts in 2 or more shapes and 2 or more colors

CHILD'S LEVEL

Children at all developmental levels benefit from the mathematical potential embedded in this activity. Teachers of very young children may begin with two or three bears and fewer than five balloons in one color. The focus of the activity will be one-to-one correspondence for younger children, as in "Do you have enough balloons to give each bear one

MORE >

balloon?" Older or more experienced children benefit from representing more complex concepts and problems, such as "Do you have enough balloons to give each bear a red balloon and a yellow balloon?"

WHAT TO LOOK FOR

- Children may initially be interested in playing with the bears in a storylike manner.

- Some children will give each bear one or more balloons.

- Children may respond to teacher questions by representing the solution using the bears and balloons.

- Children will approximate answers to teacher questions.

- Children may try to equally divide the balloons by color or shape so each bear has the same amount of each.

MODIFICATIONS FOR SPECIAL NEEDS OR SITUATIONS

No special modifications are needed. Teachers will select the most appropriate material to use to meet the needs of children in the group.

MATHEMATICS CONTENT STANDARD CONNECTIONS

This activity aligns with the Algebra and Number and Operations standards. Children can use the bears and balloons to model problems and also to quantify using one-to-one correspondence or counting to determine amounts of bears and balloons.

COMMENTS AND QUESTIONS RELATED TO MATHEMATICS PROCESS STANDARDS

Problem Solving: I need three balloons for my bears. Can you get enough for me?

Reasoning and Proof: How do you know you have enough red balloons for all the bears to have one red balloon?

Communication: Tell me how many yellow balloons to give to each bear.

Connections: How many balloons do you have altogether?

Representation: My bears each want two balloons. What will that look like?

Stinky Socks

DESCRIPTION

All children seem to like their socks. Toddlers take them off, preschoolers show them off, and even kindergartners compare the designs and talk about differences between regular socks and soccer socks. This activity encourages children to match pairs of baby socks while saying this poem:

> Socks in the basket for me and you.
> Let's make a pair; here's a clue (hold up a sock or give verbal hints).
> Some of you have (_____) socks too.
> Hang them on the line if you do.
> Stinky, stinky socks—P-U!

The socks can be clipped to a small shelf extender that looks like a clothesline.

MATERIALS

☐ 5 or more pairs of colorful baby socks (dollar stores have a large selection)

☐ basket for the socks

☐ shelf extender for hanging up the pairs of socks

☐ clothespins

CHILD'S LEVEL

Many children are interested in their own shoes and socks, and they also delight in silly poems with a surprise ending. This activity provides opportunities to match pairs of interesting socks and laugh at the silly poem.

WHAT TO LOOK FOR

• Some children will clip the socks individually on the rack.

• Children will match pairs of socks and clip them on the rack or set them aside.

• Some children will group the socks by categories and clip a group of socks together on the rack.

MORE >

- Children will count all the socks. Some will count the pairs they make.

- Some children will group the socks by a particular attribute.

MODIFICATIONS FOR SPECIAL NEEDS OR SITUATIONS

For children with motor problems, use larger socks, larger clothespins, and a larger drying rack or clothesline strung up in the classroom. Pinch type or push type clothespins can be used, depending on the needs of the children.

MATHEMATICS CONTENT STANDARD CONNECTIONS

This activity deals with solving problems, creating pairs, and sorting by attributes. It aligns directly to the Algebra standard. Because many children will quantify how many socks they have, it also coordinates with the Number and Operations standard.

COMMENTS AND QUESTIONS RELATED TO MATHEMATICS PROCESS STANDARDS

Problem Solving: Do you have two socks that are the same?

Reasoning and Proof: Hung-Jun says she has four pairs of socks, but one sock is leftover. Hung-Jun, how do you know you have four pairs of socks?

Communication: How did you decide these socks go together?

Connections: I see that you put the socks into three piles. How did you decide which socks go together? (Connects to Data Analysis)

Representation: What will my drying rack look like if I have three pairs of socks?

Cars and People

DESCRIPTION

Duplo or Lego blocks and accessories are a staple component of most preschool and kindergarten programs. Children build houses, make cars and trains, and engage in pretend play. They usually decide to put people in the cars and trains. Teachers can take advantage of both incidental and intentional teaching opportunities to encourage children to analyze and represent mathematical situations. Children who might otherwise lack confidence in their math ability, may eagerly respond to questioning strategies during play with the blocks and accessories. Teachers who have observed children and assessed their mathematical knowledge can plan specific questions or pose problems for them to solve during play with the blocks and accessories. This leads not only to further math knowledge but also further assessment opportunities.

MATERIALS

☐ 5 or more Duplo or Lego cars

☐ 10 or more Duplo or Lego people

☐ set of Duplo or Lego blocks

CHILD'S LEVEL

All children can play with the materials. The teacher's decisions about how many cars and people to make available for children help determine the level of difficulty for problem solving and representing mathematical situations.

WHAT TO LOOK FOR

- Initially, children will play with the blocks and accessories in a pretend play manner.

- Some children may discuss how many people they need.

MORE >

- Some children will place one person in each car. They will think about other possibilities when teachers pose questions or in discussions with their peers.

MODIFICATIONS FOR SPECIAL NEEDS OR SITUATIONS

For children with fine motor problems, use the larger Duplo blocks and people. For younger children or children with cognitive delays, reduce the number of cars and people to three of each.

MATHEMATICS CONTENT STANDARD CONNECTIONS

This activity focuses on using concrete materials to solve mathematical problems of equality, a vital component of the Algebra standard.

COMMENTS AND QUESTIONS RELATED TO MATHEMATICS PROCESS STANDARDS

Problem Solving: If I want two people to sit in each of the cars, how many people will I need?

Reasoning and Proof: Hemi, Paul doesn't think the people are divided equally. He thinks you have more. Can you show him what you think?

Communication: Do you have enough people to put two in each car?

Connections: How many people do you have altogether? (Connects to Number and Operations)

Representation: If I have five cars and three people want to ride in each car, how many people will I need?

Caterpillar Manipulative Game

DESCRIPTION

The book *The Very Hungry Caterpillar* by Eric Carle is a popular story with children of all ages. This activity encourages children, individually or with the teacher, to reenact the fanciful story of a pretend caterpillar who eats food very unlike a real caterpillar. During this activity, children think about relationships and patterns, important concepts of Algebra. How many more oranges than plums did the caterpillar eat? Which fruit did he eat first and last? How many more foods does he eat on each page? The representation of problems using concrete materials helps children construct mathematical knowledge needed to solve problems using algorithms later in school. Teachers may initially display the activity with exactly enough fruits to retell the story, but at a later date, or for more experienced children, teachers may want to include more of each fruit than needed. The added fruit assures that children figure out how many they need to reenact the story.

MATERIALS

- ☐ plastic fruits that correspond to those in the book

- ☐ small toy caterpillar, commercially available or teacher-made

- ☐ a board book copy of *The Very Hungry Caterpillar* by Eric Carle (optional)

MORE >

CHILD'S LEVEL

This activity is appropriate for preschool and kindergarten children who are quantifying to at least five.

WHAT TO LOOK FOR

- Children often reenact the story by taking the quantity of fruits available for each day of the week as they look at the book or as the teacher reads the story.

- Children may discuss how many of each fruit they need.

- Older children will take the appropriate quantity of fruit for each day of the week by counting or comparing sets, even when more than enough fruits are available.

- Some children may notice that the caterpillar takes one more of each successive fruit than the day before—a growing pattern.

- Younger children may continue to use all the available fruits without creating a set equal to the set of fruits in the story.

- Some children may count all the fruit.

- Children will sequence the fruits as in the story.

MODIFICATIONS FOR SPECIAL NEEDS OR SITUATIONS

Larger plastic fruit is available and might be easier for some children to pick up.

MATHEMATICS CONTENT STANDARD CONNECTIONS

This activity aligns to the Algebra standard due to the repeated modeling of a mathematical problem. Because many children will quantify how many fruits, it also aligns to the Number and Operations standard.

COMMENTS AND QUESTIONS RELATED TO MATHEMATICS PROCESS STANDARDS

Problem Solving: Which fruit did the caterpillar eat the most of? Which did he eat the least of?

Reasoning and Proof: Hirvin, you said you have more oranges than other fruit. Show me how you figured this out.

Communication: What did the caterpillar eat first, second, third, etc.?

Connections: What numeral would I use to show how many strawberries the caterpillar ate? (Connects to Number and Operations)

Representation: If the caterpillar ate one more of each fruit each day, what would that look like?

One in the Bed

DESCRIPTION

Counting songs often begin with five or ten and take away one with each verse. Children quickly learn the words to songs, such as "Five Little Ducks" or "Five Little Speckled Frogs," but may not fully understand the mathematical concepts involved due to the backward counting. Many teachers sing the popular song "Ten in the Bed" at group time. This variation begins with one in the bed and continues to ten or more. Children model and represent the pattern of the number system using concrete materials. Every number is one more than the number before. Children can add one more doll to the bed with each verse of the song. The exploration of this pattern is part of Algebra for young children.

The song begins:

There was one in the bed and the little one said, "I'm lonely."

So she rolled over and another climbed in. There were two in the bed and the little one said, "I'm lonely."

So she rolled over . . .

The song ends:

There were ten in the bed and the little one said, "Too crowded!"

MATERIALS

☐ small doll bed or a box decorated to look like a bed

☐ 10 or more small dolls or stuffed animals

MORE >

CHILD'S LEVEL

This version of the traditional song is appropriate for both preschool and kindergarten children.

WHAT TO LOOK FOR

- Some children will attempt to hold up their fingers to coordinate with the number of dolls in the bed.
- Children will sing the song and say the number words with the teacher.
- Children will probably want to use the materials independently and add one doll to the bed for each verse of the song.
- Some children will compare the number of dolls in the bed with the number of dolls out of the bed for each verse.

MODIFICATIONS FOR SPECIAL NEEDS OR SITUATIONS

No modifications are anticipated for this activity because the materials are large and easy to handle. If ten dolls is too large a quantity, teachers may choose to use five or fewer dolls at a time. Older preschool and kindergarten children may like to use numeral cards with every verse.

MATHEMATICS CONTENT STANDARD CONNECTIONS

One of the key components of the Algebra standard is modeling situations that involve the addition and subtraction of whole numbers using objects. This activity directly aligns to the Algebra standard, as children use the manipulative pieces to demonstrate their understanding of a problem. The growing pattern of one more person each time is a concrete representation of the counting pattern that underlies our number system. Because many children will also count and re-count the dolls, the activity also aligns to Number and Operations.

COMMENTS AND QUESTIONS RELATED TO MATHEMATICS PROCESS STANDARDS

Problem Solving: How many dolls are in the bed now?

Reasoning and Proof: When one more doll climbs in the bed, how many will you have?

Communication: How many dolls will you put in the bed altogether?

Connections: Are there more dolls in the bed or not in the bed? (Connects to Number and Operations)

Representation: What numeral should I write for the dolls in the bed now?

Five Little Ducks

DESCRIPTION

Most children are familiar with the song "Five Little Ducks" or with book versions of the song. Teachers can use small figures to represent the problem of how many ducks to start with, how many ducks came back, and how many ducks are still playing. These are Algebra problems solved using concrete materials.

MATERIALS

☐ 5 small rubber or plastic ducks and 1 mother duck

☐ blue felt or thin foam cut to represent a pond

☐ tray or basket for storing the ducks

☐ a board book of the song "Five Little Ducks" (optional)

CHILD'S LEVEL

This activity is best suited for children who count or quantify to at least five. Children will count and re-count the ducks as they sing each verse.

WHAT TO LOOK FOR

• Children will play with the ducks in a pretend play manner. Teachers can focus questions on mathematical thinking to take advantage of this incidental learning opportunity.

• Children may attempt to quantify how many ducks they have altogether by including the mother duck in the group.

• Some children will separate the ducklings from the group when they count.

MORE >

- Some children will subtract one duck with each verse, but most will need to re-count the remaining ducks to determine how many are left.

- Some children will mentally subtract one duck with each verse and quantify how many are left.

- Some children will be able to quantify how many ducks go out to play but be unable to answer the question of how many are left.

MODIFICATIONS FOR SPECIAL NEEDS OR SITUATIONS

This activity does not require specific modifications because the concrete materials are easily handled by most children. You can reduce the quantity of ducks to three if five is overwhelming.

MATHEMATICS CONTENT STANDARD CONNECTIONS

Since this activity uses concrete materials to model situations that involve addition and subtraction, it aligns to the Algebra standard. The particular focus of this activity is subtraction, a difficult concept for children to construct. Most children count the ducks for each verse; therefore, this activity also aligns to Number and Operations.

COMMENTS AND QUESTIONS RELATED TO MATHEMATICS PROCESS STANDARDS

Problem Solving: How many ducklings do you have?

Reasoning and Proof: How many ducklings will be left if three go out to play?

Communication: Tell Alexi how many ducklings came back.

Connections: How many ducklings has mother duck lost so far? (Connects to Number and Operations)

Representation: What will the pond look like if all the ducklings are swimming in it?

Cookie Sharing

DESCRIPTION

Children negotiate the sharing of materials in many situations at school and at home. This activity coordinates with the predictable book *The Doorbell Rang* by Pat Hutchins, in which children share chocolate chip cookies. The story begins with two children who have twelve cookies to share; then the doorbell rings and more children arrive to share the cookies. Eventually there are twelve cookies and twelve children with one cookie each. The book does not need to be part of the activity. Teachers may want to present the problem of dividing cookies equally with different numbers of people.

MATERIALS

☐ 12 Duplo children figures or other small figures to represent the children

☐ 12 small cookies made from modeling dough or 12 black marble chips to represent cookies

☐ a copy of the book *The Doorbell Rang* by Pat Hutchins (optional)

CHILD'S LEVEL

This is a challenging book extension and is most appropriate for kindergarten children or older preschool children in a small group situation. The process of dividing and redividing the cookies requires children to solve the problem multiple times.

WHAT TO LOOK FOR

• Children often begin by giving one cookie to each of the twelve figures.

MORE >

- Some children will read the book and try to follow the story line as they divide the cookies.
- Some children will initially be able to divide the cookies equally but then become overwhelmed by the problem.
- Some children will accurately quantify and requantify by dividing the cookies equally among a successive number of people.

MODIFICATIONS FOR SPECIAL NEEDS OR SITUATIONS

If the problem is too challenging, begin with two or three figures and four or six cookies to divide. Place pretend cookies in the dramatic play area and pose the question of how to equally divide the cookies among the children in that area. This will make the problem more concrete for some children.

MATHEMATICS CONTENT STANDARD CONNECTIONS

Like many activities in this chapter that use concrete materials to model problems, this activity aligns with the Algebra and Number and Operations standards.

COMMENTS AND QUESTIONS RELATED TO MATHEMATICS PROCESS STANDARDS

Problem Solving: How many children are there altogether?

Reasoning and Proof: Marina, you say that every child should get two cookies. How did you decide that?

Communication: Do you have just as many cookies as children?

Connections: How many more children just came? Six! Will there be enough cookies for each child to have one? (Connects to Data Analysis and Probability)

Representation: What will it look like if two more children come to share the cookies?

Stack and Fall—
Keeping Score

DESCRIPTION

Educators agree that children learn in different ways. Some children learn best when they use their whole body in a gross-motor manner. This simple target game is made with empty salt boxes and beanbags. A whiteboard and magnets provide a method for keeping score. Children can write their names on the board and use magnets to represent how many boxes they knock over. This game encourages quantification (how many boxes fell down), subtraction (how many boxes are left standing), and other opportunities for mathematical thinking and problem solving as children compare scores, keep track of how many boxes they knock over, and calculate whether they have more or fewer than another child.

MATERIALS

☐ 10 empty salt boxes attractively covered or painted

☐ 3 beanbags

☐ magnetic board and magnets

CHILD'S LEVEL

This self-leveling activity is appropriate for all children. Young children are usually interested in stacking and knocking down the boxes, while older children are interested in quantification and keeping score. Teachers can direct children's attention to keeping score by encouraging them to use the whiteboards and magnets or through verbal discussions about how many boxes they knocked down and how many are left.

MORE >

WHAT TO LOOK FOR

• Children will explore a variety of methods for knocking down the most boxes and observe the results.

• Some children will quantify how many boxes they knocked down and how many are left.

• Some children will count how many beanbags they need to throw to knock over all the boxes.

• Some children will use the magnets for keeping score of how many boxes they knocked down.

MODIFICATIONS FOR SPECIAL NEEDS OR SITUATIONS

If the physical challenge of throwing the beanbag is too difficult, children can roll a ball at the stack of boxes or kick them over after an adult arranges them. For older or more advanced children, teachers can cover the boxes in different colors of contact paper and allow children to assign a point value to each color for score keeping.

MATHEMATICS CONTENT STANDARD CONNECTIONS

This activity includes components of both the Algebra and Number and Operations standards. Children think about the addition and subtraction of whole numbers as they engage in this gross-motor activity. They may represent numbers using the magnetic board and magnetic pieces.

COMMENTS AND QUESTIONS RELATED TO MATHEMATICS PROCESS STANDARDS

Problem Solving: How many more will you have to knock over to have a score of ten?

Reasoning and Proof: Teresa says her score is higher than yours. Do you agree or disagree?

Communication: Kevin, tell me how you know you have knocked over the most boxes.

Connections: If you knock down the last three boxes, will your score be higher or lower than Evan's score? (Connects to Number and Operations)

Representation: Show me what you will do with the magnets to remember how many you knocked over on your first turn.

Button Collection

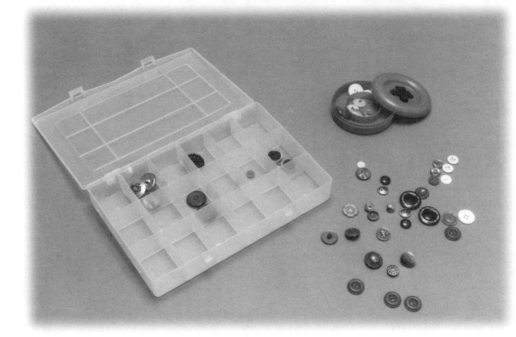

DESCRIPTION

This collection of interesting buttons encourages children to carefully observe similarities and differences and to construct relationships among the buttons. Sorting and classifying the buttons into categories such as same, different, more, and less provides a framework for later mathematical understanding. This framework is important for children as they learn about Algebra later in school.

MATERIALS

Example for preschool or introductory collection

☐ 25–30 buttons in red, white, and black

☐ large and small buttons of each color

☐ buttons with 2 holes, 4 holes, and a shank in each color

Example for kindergarten or more complex collection

☐ 40 or more buttons in red, white, black, and gold

☐ large and small buttons of each color

☐ buttons with 2 holes, 4 holes, and a shank in each color

☐ buttons in some of the colors with additional attributes, such as fabric, a stamped design, metal, or other shapes

☐ divided container for sorting the buttons

☐ basket or other container for storing the buttons

CHILD'S LEVEL

Both preschool and kindergarten children benefit from explorations of a button

MORE >

collection. Tailor the quantity of buttons and the number of different attributes to the age and experience of the children in the group. Younger children may be overwhelmed by large quantities of buttons and dump them on the floor rather than sorting them. Older children will become bored if the collection is too small or does not contain enough different attributes for sorting.

WHAT TO LOOK FOR

- Children often focus on color when they initially sort buttons. Color is a very obvious attribute.

- Children may sort by other attributes, such as size, number of holes, or design, as they have repeated opportunities to observe similarities and differences in the buttons.

- Some children may spend a long time grouping and regrouping the buttons as they closely observe the similarities and differences.

- Some children may group the buttons together in different ways each time they play with the collection.

MODIFICATIONS FOR SPECIAL NEEDS OR SITUATIONS

For young children or children with cognitive delays, reduce the quantity of buttons available at first to a selection of extra large buttons that vary only by size and color. For children with visual challenges, choose buttons with extreme contrasts, such as extra large and small or smooth and textured.

MATHEMATICS CONTENT STANDARD CONNECTIONS

This activity aligns with both the Algebra and Data Analysis and Probability standards, as children sort, classify, and order buttons by size, number, and other properties.

COMMENTS AND QUESTIONS RELATED TO MATHEMATICS PROCESS STANDARDS

Problem Solving: How should we sort these buttons today?

Reasoning and Proof: How did you decide which buttons go together?

Communication: Which of these buttons go in this group?

Connections: Do you have more red buttons or more white buttons? (Connects to Data Analysis and Number and Operations)

Representation: Here are some new buttons. Where can they fit?

Hat Collection

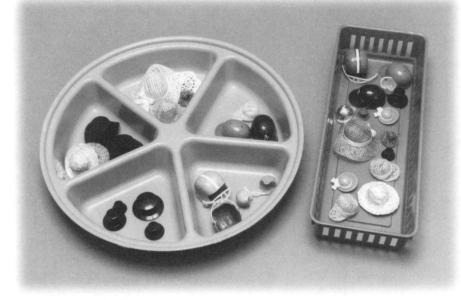

DESCRIPTION

Commercial collections rarely interest children in the same way as a teacher-designed collection, such as this hat collection, which attracts children and sustains their interest. Small novelty hats are available in craft stores and catalogs. Some are made of plastic and others are made of fabric. They come in a variety of colors, types, and sizes. A collection of such hats is intriguing to children and provides many opportunities for sorting and classifying. Children learn to think in a more flexible manner as they discuss and consider possible attributes for sorting. Do the sunbonnets go with the fabric hats or with the large hats? Can the blue hat be part of the blue group one day and part of the small hat group the next? These types of problems facilitate an understanding of the underlying concepts of sorting and classifying, which is a key precursor to patterning.

MATERIALS

☐ 30 or more hats in 2 or 3 colors, 3 or 4 different styles, and 2 different materials (e.g., blue, brown, and white hats; sunbonnets, top hats, cowboy hats, and helmets; plastic and fabric)

☐ additional hats to add to the collections at a later time (e.g., felt hats, big and small sunbonnets, and top hats)

CHILD'S LEVEL

Both preschool and kindergarten children benefit from explorations of the hat collection. Tailor the quantity of hats and the number of different attributes to the age and experience of the children in the group. Younger children may be overwhelmed by large quantities of hats and dump them on the floor rather than sorting them. Older children will become bored if the collection is too

MORE >

small or does not contain enough different attributes for sorting.

WHAT TO LOOK FOR

- Some children will initially sort hats by color; others will focus on the type of hat.
- Children may sort by attributes of their own invention.
- Some children will compare the quantity of each type of hat.

MODIFICATIONS FOR SPECIAL NEEDS OR SITUATIONS

For young children or children with cognitive delays, begin with a small number of hats with very obvious differences in size, color, and texture. Increase the variety of attributes for more experienced children.

MATHEMATICS CONTENT STANDARD CONNECTIONS

This collection, like the other collections in this chapter, aligns to both the Algebra and Data Analysis standards, as children sort and classify the miniature hats according to their attributes and organize the data into categories by placing them into the divided container.

COMMENTS AND QUESTIONS RELATED TO MATHEMATICS PROCESS STANDARDS

Problem Solving: Which hats should go together?

Reasoning and Proof: Is there a different group these can go with?

Communication: Tell me where to put this hat.

Connections: Do you have more big hats or more baseball caps? (Connects to Number and Operations and Data Analysis)

Representation: How would you group these into just three groups?

Clothespin and Clip Collection

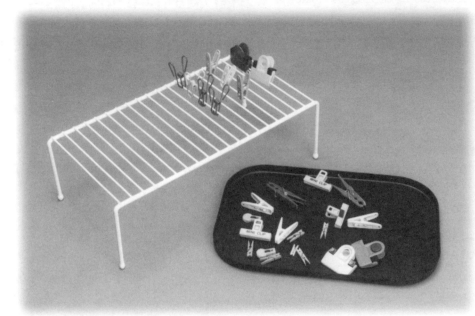

DESCRIPTION

Clothespins and office-type clips are abundantly available in dollar stores. This collection combines math and fine-motor skills as children sort the clothespins and clips onto a small shelf extender that represents a clothesline. The clothespins and clips have numerous cross attributes, such as size, type, color, decoration, print, shape, and type of material.

MATERIALS

☐ 30–35 clothespins and clips, with the following crossover attributes:

- 2 or 3 colors
- 2 or 3 styles (e.g., slot-peg clothespins, spring clothespins, binder clips)
- large and small sizes
- 2 or 3 materials (wood, plastic, and metal)

☐ shelf extender to hold the sorted clips

☐ basket to hold the unsorted clips

☐ add 10–15 clothespins and clips at a later time in the activity to increase the complexity of the collection

CHILD'S LEVEL

The smaller collection of clothespins and clips is appropriate for older preschool and kindergarten children. Younger children might have difficulty clipping the items to the rack. The larger collection might be appropriate for most kindergarten children who have had experiences sorting and classifying.

WHAT TO LOOK FOR

- Children usually concentrate on clipping the clothespins onto the rack when they first use the collection.

MORE >

- Some children initially sort clothespins and clips by one attribute, such as color or type.
- Children will sort by color, size, type, material, print, or attributes of their own invention, such as "These are the ones my mommy has, and these are the ones my grandma has."

MODIFICATIONS FOR SPECIAL NEEDS OR SITUATIONS

Use larger clothespins for children who have a physical disability. To draw a more reluctant child into the activity, make a clothesline in the dramatic play area and set up the area as a laundromat. Children can sort and classify clothespins as part of their pretend play.

MATHEMATICS CONTENT STANDARD CONNECTIONS

This activity directly aligns to the Algebra standard as children pose questions about the materials and represent the answer using concrete materials. Because children also sort the clothespins and clips according to attributes, the activity aligns to Data Analysis and Probability as well.

COMMENTS AND QUESTIONS RELATED TO MATHEMATICS PROCESS STANDARDS

Problem Solving: Where should I put this big clip with the magnet?

Reasoning and Proof: Why are these clothespins together?

Communication: Jenni, tell me how to sort these clips.

Connections: Are there more small clothespins or more big clothespins? (Connects to Data Analysis and Measurement)

Representation: Show me how to sort my clips into just three groups.

Key Collection

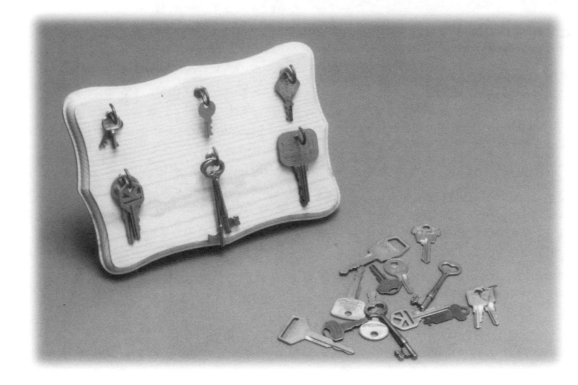

DESCRIPTION

Children's interest in keys begins in infancy. Many parents find that car keys entertain a bored infant or toddler when the family goes on errands. Keys are readily available and free! Teachers can begin the collection by asking parents and friends for old keys found around the house. Hardware stores are willing to donate those keys made by mistake when cutting duplicates for customers. The attributes are plentiful and interesting to children. Keys are made of different types of metal and come in different colors, sizes, and shapes. Some keys have plastic tops, and the number or type of holes in keys varies widely. Sorting and classifying is an intriguing activity with a collection of keys.

MATERIALS

☐ an assortment of approximately 40 keys with the following crossover attributes:

- 2 colors (brass and silver)
- big and small
- 2–3 different types, such as keys that vary by shape or the number of holes

☐ a frame made with cup hooks for sorting the keys, or a divided container (hooks can be added to a peg-board room divider)

☐ add more keys to increase the complexity or vary the way the keys can be sorted (e.g., add big and small keys in different colors, keys with plastic tops, and keys with different shapes)

MORE >

CHILD'S LEVEL

All children will be interested in the key collection. Younger children may be more interested in using them to "unlock" something but will also focus on sorting possibilities if teachers ask well-timed questions or make comments to direct their attention to the various attributes of the keys. Older preschool and kindergarten children will be very interested in the details of the keys.

WHAT TO LOOK FOR

- Children often initially sort the keys by the colors "silver" and "gold."
- Some children will make groups that do not seem to have common attributes until the teachers ask what makes them go together.

MODIFICATIONS FOR SPECIAL NEEDS OR SITUATIONS

No modifications are anticipated, but teachers may want to eliminate the smallest keys if they are too challenging to pick up.

MATHEMATICS CONTENT STANDARD CONNECTIONS

This activity aligns to the Algebra and Data Analysis standards, as children sort and classify the collection of keys by various attributes.

COMMENTS AND QUESTIONS RELATED TO MATHEMATICS PROCESS STANDARDS

Problem Solving: Where should I put this key?

Reasoning and Proof: Why did you decide this key goes with this group?

Communication: Tell Andrew how you grouped your keys.

Connections: Which of your groups has the most keys? (Connects to Number and Operations)

Representation: Look! This key has lines. I wonder if it goes with any others. Can you help me decide?

Ice Cream Cone Patterns

DESCRIPTION

Mathematics is based on relationships. Patterning activities provide many opportunities for children to consider relationships and discuss them with teachers and peers. For this activity, children create ice cream cone patterns by placing large beads on a dowel frame. The beads are painted to represent ice cream flavors, such as chocolate, vanilla, strawberry, and mint. Children can select a pattern card and re-create the pattern or create their own patterns. They may need to describe the pattern to others or answer questions about what comes next in the pattern. This communication helps children think more deeply about the relationships in a pattern—an important component of Algebra.

MATERIALS

☐ wooden frame made with 4 9-inch lengths of dowel glued into a wooden base, 12 × 12 inches

☐ 4 small, wooden flowerpots with holes drilled in the bottom so they fit over the dowels

☐ an assortment of large-hole beads painted with acrylic paint in ice cream flavor colors with a hole large enough to slide onto the dowel

☐ pattern cards made on index cards by using 1-inch circles for the scoops of ice cream on top of an illustration of a cone (vary the pattern—a/b, a/b, a/b; a/bb, a/bb, a/bb; etc.)

CHILD'S LEVEL

This activity is appropriate for preschool and kindergarten children. Teachers should make decisions about the complexity of the pattern cards based on the ages and experiences of children in the group.

MORE >

WHAT TO LOOK FOR

- Children will recreate and extend the patterns on the cards.
- Children will create new patterns using the beads.
- Some children will sort the beads by color.
- Some children will quantify the number of scoops of ice cream they have on each dowel.

MODIFICATIONS FOR SPECIAL NEEDS OR SITUATIONS

Begin with a simple a/b pattern for children with cognitive delays. Larger beads and frames can be used for children who still put objects into their mouths. For older children, add more beads to represent more flavors of ice cream. Kindergarten children may enjoy using press-on dots to create their own patterns of ice cream scoops.

MATHEMATICS CONTENT STANDARD CONNECTIONS

This activity encourages children to recognize, describe, and extend patterns and translate them from one representation to another. These are key components of Algebra.

COMMENTS AND QUESTIONS RELATED TO MATHEMATICS PROCESS STANDARDS

Problem Solving: How will you decide which flavors to put on this cone?

Reasoning and Proof: What flavor should I add next to make this pattern?

Communication: Can you tell Jessie what the pattern is on your ice cream cone?

Connections: Do you have more chocolate or more vanilla in your pattern? (Connects to Number and Operations)

Representation: What pattern would you like to make?

Barrettes on Braids

DESCRIPTION

A small doll with long braids and a basket of selected barrettes inspires patterning in this manipulative activity. Children can place the barrettes in patterns on the braids to show their friends.

MATERIALS

☐ 1 or more small dolls with long braids

☐ barrettes in 3 or 4 colors

☐ divided container or tray for display of the barrettes

☐ pattern cards with illustrations of barrettes in a variety of patterns to copy and extend (optional)

CHILD'S LEVEL

This activity is most appropriate for older preschool and kindergarten children who can more easily manipulate the barrettes.

WHAT TO LOOK FOR

- Children will form patterns with the barrettes, especially if this is suggested as a possibility.

- Children will create a/b patterns, such as red/blue, red/blue.

- Some children will create more complex patterns by considering multiple attributes of the barrettes, such as red bow/blue bow, red bow/blue bow.

MORE >

- Some children will randomly clip the barrettes to the braids. They may begin to form patterns after observing other children.

MODIFICATIONS FOR SPECIAL NEEDS OR SITUATIONS

Encourage children with communication disorders to point to which barrette to place on the braids. Teachers may assist children with physical challenges by clipping the barrettes onto the braids. For children with motor delays, use large, butterfly style clips instead of barrettes. They are much easier to manipulate. Include more barrettes with different attributes for children with experience making patterns.

MATHEMATICS CONTENT STANDARD CONNECTIONS

Creating patterns with concrete materials, such as the barrettes, incorporates components of the Algebra standard.

COMMENTS AND QUESTIONS RELATED TO MATHEMATICS PROCESS STANDARDS

Problem Solving: Can you make a pattern with three colors?

Reasoning and Proof: What color should I add next to continue Max's pattern?

Communication: Can you explain your pattern to Loren?

Connections: How many barrettes are on each braid? (Connects to Number and Operations)

Representation: Is there a way to write down this pattern so we can remember it?

Cookie and Pretzel Pattern Strips

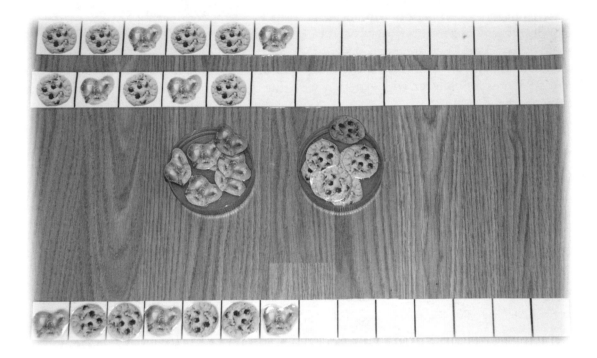

DESCRIPTION

Children are interested in both cookies and pretzels. The pattern strips, which are made with clip art pictures, provide opportunities for children to recognize, copy, extend, and create patterns. Teachers can plan the complexity of the pattern on each strip based on their assessment of the children. Examples of appropriate patterns include the a/b pattern (cookie/pretzel, cookie/pretzel) and the a/a/b pattern (cookie/cookie/pretzel, cookie/cookie/pretzel). Be sure to include at least one blank pattern strip to keep the activity open-ended and multilevel.

MATERIALS

- [ ] pattern strips made from white poster-board, 2½ × 22 inches, marked into sections large enough to hold the illustrations

- [ ] posterboard cut into 2-inch squares to hold the illustrations

- [ ] illustrations of cookies and pretzels for designing the pattern strips and for making the cards to place on the strips (be sure to have enough for children to copy or extend)

- [ ] a divided container to display the cookie and pretzel cards (this organization helps children consider the possibilities)

MORE >

CHILD'S LEVEL

Preschool and kindergarten children will be able to use this activity.

WHAT TO LOOK FOR

- Children will use cookie and pretzel cards to extend patterns on the pattern strips.

- Some children will create patterns using the pattern cards and blank pattern strip.

- Children will chant the pattern as they extend it.

- Some children will match the pattern but be unable to extend it.

MODIFICATIONS FOR SPECIAL NEEDS OR SITUATIONS

For younger children or children with cognitive delays, limit the selection of patterning possibilities to alternating patterns. Encourage children to chant the pattern and move their bodies left to right as they chant.

MATHEMATICS CONTENT STANDARD CONNECTIONS

This activity aligns primarily with the Algebra standard due to its focus on patterning. It also connects to the Number and Operations standard because children may compare quantities of cookie and pretzel cards.

COMMENTS AND QUESTIONS RELATED TO MATHEMATICS PROCESS STANDARDS

Problem Solving: What should come next on this pattern strip, the cookie or the pretzel?

Reasoning and Proof: How can I tell which card goes next on my pattern strip?

Communication: What pattern can you create with the cookie and pretzel cards? How do you decide which card to use next?

Connections: Do you have just as many cookie cards as pretzel cards on your pattern strip? (Connects to Number and Operations)

Representation: What will the pattern look like if you use two cookie cards and one pretzel card?

Shell Patterns

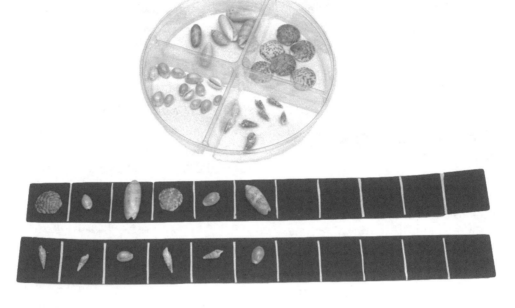

DESCRIPTION

For this activity, children create patterns by placing different types of shells onto gridded strips. Children can work individually or create patterns for a peer to copy or extend. Teachers should use an appropriate and accurate label for each type of shell whenever possible. This is an opportunity for vocabulary development as well.

MATERIALS

☐ 3 types of small shells (dollar stores sell baskets of shells)

☐ black posterboard strips, 2½ × 22 inches, divided into sections every 1½ inches

☐ divided container for display of the shells

CHILD'S LEVEL

This activity is appropriate for older preschool and kindergarten children. Younger children may be most interested in merely manipulating the shells but not as interested in making patterns.

WHAT TO LOOK FOR

• Children will use two or more types of shells to create patterns.

• Some children may begin by placing one shell in each box in a one-to-one correspondence manner, without regard for patterning. They may change their focus if teachers ask leading questions and model possibilities.

MODIFICATIONS FOR SPECIAL NEEDS OR SITUATIONS

The shells are three-dimensional and easy to handle, so no modifications are needed. Teachers may want to begin with two very different types of shells, for example, fan-shaped

MORE >

and spiral. Increase the size of the shells and the corresponding size of the pattern strips for children who still put objects in their mouths.

MATHEMATICS CONTENT STANDARD CONNECTIONS

This activity aligns primarily with the Algebra standard due to its focus on patterning. It also connects to the Number and Operations standard because children may compare quantities of each type of shell in the patterns they create.

COMMENTS AND QUESTIONS RELATED TO MATHEMATICS PROCESS STANDARDS

Problem Solving: What pattern can you create with the shells?

Reasoning and Proof: Ian made a pattern with the shells. Can you tell what comes next in his pattern?

Communication: Tell Elena what pattern you created.

Connections: Can you find some shells that are symmetrical? Symmetrical means one side looks the same as the other side in reverse. (Connects to Geometry)

Representation: If you make a pattern with two kinds of shells, what will it look like?

Bingo Marker Patterns

DESCRIPTION

Graph paper and bingo markers often suggest the idea of patterning to children. This activity can be added to the art area or used as a special activity.

MATERIALS

☐ bingo markers in 2 or 3 colors to begin with

☐ 1-inch graph paper

CHILD'S LEVEL

Preschool and kindergarten children benefit from the use of the materials for this activity. Typically older, more-experienced children create more complex patterns, but this is not always the case.

WHAT TO LOOK FOR

• Some children will use the bingo markers to create alternating patterns, especially if only two colors of bingo markers are available for the activity.

• Some children will make an entire row of each color and repeat the pattern.

• Some children will think about one-to-one correspondence and randomly place one mark in each box without creating a pattern.

MODIFICATIONS FOR SPECIAL NEEDS OR SITUATIONS

If the bingo markers are too difficult for some children to manipulate, substitute detergent bottle lids dipped in paint. Larger grid spaces can be created by drawing large boxes on easel paper. Measure the size of the lid and draw boxes slightly larger. For more experienced children, offer more colors of bingo markers for creating more complex patterns.

MATHEMATICS CONTENT STANDARD CONNECTIONS

This activity directly aligns with the Algebra standard due to the focus on patterning.

MORE >

COMMENTS AND QUESTIONS RELATED TO MATHEMATICS PROCESS STANDARDS

Problem Solving: How did you decide what colors to use for your pattern?

Reasoning and Proof: How do you know you have a pattern?

Communication: What pattern do you think George tried to make in this row?

Connections: How many dots are in your pattern? (Connects to Number and Operations)

Representation: What comes next in your pattern—red/red/blue, red/red/blue, red/red/____?

Cookie Cutter Patterns

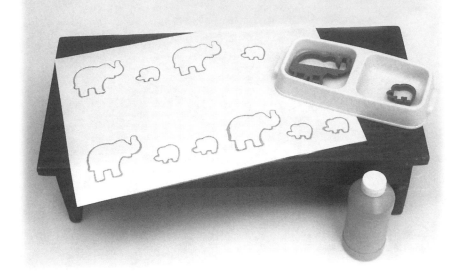

DESCRIPTION

The art area is another part of the classroom ideal for encouraging pattern making. Teachers often plan painting activities using cookie cutters as printing tools. Big and small cookie cutters of the same shape naturally inspire children to create patterns. They begin to perceive the relationship between the two sizes and a repeating pattern, such as big/small, big/small or mama/baby/baby, mama/baby/baby. Displaying the materials in an organized manner enhances the perception of patterning possibilities.

MATERIALS

☐ 2 sizes of the same shape cookie cutter

☐ 1 color of tempera paint

☐ paper, 12 × 18 inches

☐ pet food dish with 2 sections

CHILD'S LEVEL

This activity is appropriate for preschool and kindergarten children. Older children may create more complex patterns. Teachers may alter the activity by including cookie cutters in more shapes so that more complicated patterns can be created.

WHAT TO LOOK FOR

• Children will create alternating patterns.

• Some children may create more complex patterns.

• Children may describe the pattern they created.

MODIFICATIONS FOR SPECIAL NEEDS OR SITUATIONS

No modifications are anticipated for this activity.

MORE >

MATHEMATICS CONTENT STANDARD CONNECTIONS

This activity like the other patterning activities in this chapter aligns with the Algebra standard. Some children may also quantify how many of each type of cookie cutter print they have, which connects the activity to Number and Operations.

COMMENTS AND QUESTIONS RELATED TO MATHEMATICS PROCESS STANDARDS

Problem Solving: Let's see. Big/big/little; big/big/little. What comes next?

Reasoning and Proof: If you put one little elephant after each big elephant, will it make a pattern?

Communication: Audrey made one little elephant inside each big elephant. Did she make a pattern too?

Connections: Are there more elephants in the row of little ones or the row of big ones? (Connects to Measurement)

Representation: What kind of pattern can you make if you use only the big elephant?

Stringing Straws and Pasta Wheels

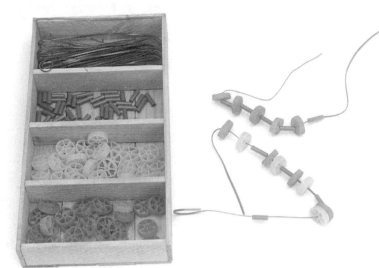

DESCRIPTION

Teachers often observe children creating patterns during stringing activities, especially when there are two or three shapes or types of objects to string. This activity combines straws cut into pieces and pasta wheels as an art activity. Children more easily perceive patterning possibilities when the materials are displayed in an organized manner. If they must sort through a basket full of cut straws and pasta wheels, they will be less likely to create a pattern. Teachers can dye the pasta using food coloring, and straws are available in a variety of colors.

MATERIALS

☐ 1 or 2 colors of straws cut into pieces ½-inch long

☐ pasta wheels in 1 or 2 sizes or colors

☐ plastic cord for stringing

CHILD'S LEVEL

This activity is appropriate for preschool and kindergarten children. Younger children may need fewer options, such as one color of straw pieces and one size of pasta wheel. Older children will be able to make choices from a wider variety of options, such as those described above.

WHAT TO LOOK FOR

• Children may alternate the straws and pasta wheels to create a pattern.

• Children may use the materials to make a variety of types of patterns.

• Some children may start a pattern but lose track of the pattern as they continue their project.

MORE >

- Some children will use the materials for stringing but may not create a pattern. They may begin creating patterns at a later time after watching other children and listening to their discussions.

MODIFICATIONS FOR SPECIAL NEEDS OR SITUATIONS

Straws intended for use with smoothies or bubble tea have a much larger opening and will be easier for some children to manipulate. Tape the end of the string to the table to help prevent the straw pieces from dropping off the string. Use pipe cleaners as a substitute for string.

MATHEMATICS CONTENT STANDARD CONNECTIONS

Patterning is an important component of the Algebra standard. The organization of this activity aligns it directly with that standard.

COMMENTS AND QUESTIONS RELATED TO MATHEMATICS PROCESS STANDARDS

Problem Solving: How can you use these materials to make a pattern necklace?

Reasoning and Proof: Ellie, your necklace ends with the pattern, red/ yellow/ blue straws. Where does the pattern begin on your necklace?

Communication: Describe your pattern to us.

Connections: Did you use more pasta wheels or more straws in your pattern? (Connects to Number and Operations)

Representation: If you want to make another necklace for your sister, is there a way to draw a picture of the pattern so you will remember it?

Can Band Patterns

DESCRIPTION

Music is filled with patterns, so the music area is a logical part of the classroom for children to explore patterns. This activity includes a variety of sizes of empty cans and a wooden mallet for striking them. Each size can has a different pitch. The can band seems to naturally foster patterning as children compare the sound of the cans. Teachers can also create patterns for children to try to recognize or reproduce on the various sizes of cans.

MATERIALS

☐ several sizes of empty aluminum cans without sharp edges

☐ wooden mallet or 8-inch length of wooden dowel (do not use a metal striker)

CHILD'S LEVEL

All children can use this activity, including toddlers, preschool, and kindergarten children.

WHAT TO LOOK FOR

• Children will experiment with striking the cans to hear how they sound.

• As children go back and forth between cans to compare sounds, patterns will emerge. The teacher can point out the patterns.

• Some children will create complex patterns with the cans.

MORE >

MODIFICATIONS FOR SPECIAL NEEDS OR SITUATIONS

This activity is accessible to all children. Teachers may want to limit the selection of cans to three if they believe children will be overwhelmed by more than that. Children with limited or delayed language development may communicate their mathematical knowledge using an activity such as this one. This activity provides opportunities for turn taking as teachers play a simple, alternating pattern and suggest children do the same or ask children to make a pattern for teachers to repeat.

MATHEMATICS CONTENT STANDARD CONNECTIONS

This activity aligns with Algebra because it provides opportunities for children to recognize, describe, and extend patterns using sequences of sounds.

COMMENTS AND QUESTIONS RELATED TO MATHEMATICS PROCESS STANDARDS

Problem Solving: What comes next in your pattern?

Reasoning and Proof: Will I make a pattern if I play each can twice?

Communication: Make a pattern for me to repeat.

Connections: How many times should I hit the big can for the pattern? (Connects to Number and Operations and Measurement)

Representation: What will the pattern sound like if you use only the biggest can and the smallest can?

Rhythm Patterns for Group Time

DESCRIPTION

Rhythm pertains to patterns of sound perceived in relationship to a recurring beat or pulse (Moomaw 1997, 53). The first rhythmic pattern of life is the heartbeat of the mother. Because patterns and relationships are essential components of mathematics, it is important for children to develop an understanding of them. This activity allows children to use their hands and feet to create rhythmic patterns, which may help them perceive patterns in mathematics and other curricular areas. No materials are needed for this activity. Teachers can plan rhythm pattern activities for large or small group experiences and take advantage of other times throughout the day to create rhythm patterns with children.

Suggested Patterns

Include simple songs, poems, and chants at group time. Look for those that have a strong, steady beat with rhyme and repetition. Lead children in repeating the beat first by clapping. Then incorporate the suggested patterns. For example, clap hands/slap knees, clap hands/slap knees during a song or chant. Later make the pattern more challenging, such as clap hands/clap hands/slap knees/slap knees. Here is how it would look for "Twinkle, Twinkle, Little Star."

MORE >

Clap Hands/Slap Knees/Clap Hands/Slap Knees
(* represents a clap; # represents a knee slap.)

Twin-	kle,	twin-	kle,	lit-	tle	star,	—
*	#	*	#	*	#	*	#

How	I	won-	der	what	you	are.	—
*	#	*	#	*	#	*	#

Up	a-	bove	the	world	so	high,	—
*	#	*	#	*	#	*	#

Like	a	dia-	mond	in	the	sky.	—
*	#	*	#	*	#	*	#

Clap Hands/Clap Hands/Slap Knees/Slap Knees

Twin-	kle,	twin-	kle,	lit-	tle	star,	—
*	*	#	#	*	*	#	#

How	I	won-	der	what	you	are.	—
*	*	#	#	*	*	#	#

Up	a-	bove	the	world	so	high,	—
*	*	#	#	*	*	#	#

Like	a	dia-	mond	in	the	sky.	—
*	*	#	#	*	*	#	#

Reverse the pattern on a different day—slap knees/clap hands, slap knees/clap hands. Include other body parts—stamp feet, snap fingers, wiggle, pat head, etc.

CHILD'S LEVEL

Children at all levels, from infancy and beyond, engage in rhythm activities. Careful planning by teachers ensures that both incidental and intentional strategies enhance children's understanding of patterning.

WHAT TO LOOK FOR

- Children will be able to repeat the simplest pattern but get confused with more complex patterns of rhythmic movements.
- Some children will identify the pattern by saying clap/slap, clap/slap, for example.

MODIFICATIONS FOR SPECIAL NEEDS OR SITUATIONS

Begin with clapping the steady beat. This helps build an understanding of the beat. Later add one other movement, such as slap knees or pat head.

MATHEMATICS CONTENT STANDARD CONNECTIONS

This activity directly aligns to Algebra because it incorporates patterning. The pattern may be more easily perceived and internalized when children use their bodies to produce it.

COMMENTS AND QUESTIONS RELATED TO MATHEMATICS PROCESS STANDARDS

Problem Solving: We're going to use this pattern for our song—clap/slap, clap/slap. What should come next?

Reasoning and Proof: If we alternate our feet while we stamp (like this), will that make a pattern? Why?

Communication: Show us a pattern we can use for this song.

Connections: Let's do a new pattern while we sing—arms high/arms low. (Connects to Measurement)

Representation: How will the pattern sound if we clap three times before we slap our knees?

Dance Patterns

DESCRIPTION

Most children can participate in some form of movement, either independently or with assistance from an adult. Teachers plan the movements for this dance patterning activity according to the needs of the children in the group. This activity is similar to Rhythm Patterns for Group Time (Activity 4.21) except children use their whole body for Dance Patterns. Begin with simple body movements and increase the level of difficulty as children become familiar with using their body to create a pattern. You might need to place small mats or tape an X on the floor to mark the place for each child to stand. This gives you control over how close children stand to one another. Remember that chanting a pattern helps children develop a deeper understanding of the concept. Encourage them to say the words with you.

Suggested Pattern

Step/step/bend your knees (pause for one or two seconds), step/step/bend your knees is a simple pattern. Teachers should begin by having children repeat the movements very slowly. It takes time for young children to process the directions and follow through with the movement of their bodies. You don't want children to move so fast they bump into one another. You can decrease the pause between repetitions as children have experience with the dance patterns.

MORE >

Other Patterns

- Sway/sway/turn around, sway/sway/turn around
- Step/step/point, step/step/point
- Plié/relevé, plié/relevé (Note: A plié is a knee bend, and relevé means to stand on tiptoe.)

CHILD'S LEVEL

Patterning activities are appropriate for all age groups. Teachers can determine the level of difficulty of the pattern based on age, experience, temperament of the group, and gross-motor development.

WHAT TO LOOK FOR

- Children will be able to repeat the simplest pattern but get confused with more complex patterns of dance movements.
- Children will want to create their own dance patterns.

MODIFICATIONS FOR SPECIAL NEEDS OR SITUATIONS

For children who have motor disabilities, such as those who use a wheelchair, think of movements that they will be able to do along with the rest of the class, such as "forward, back, bow your head," or "arms high, arms low, arms in a hug."

MATHEMATICS CONTENT STANDARD CONNECTIONS

This activity directly aligns to Algebra because it incorporates patterning. The pattern may be more easily perceived and internalized when children use their whole body to produce the pattern.

COMMENTS AND QUESTIONS RELATED TO MATHEMATICS PROCESS STANDARDS

Problem Solving: What pattern can we make using just our arms? Who wants to give us one?

Reasoning and Proof: Watch while I copy your pattern. Did I do it right? What mistake did I make?

Communication: Tell us a new pattern we can use for our dance.

Connections: Let's make shape patterns with our arms—triangle/circle, triangle/circle. (Connects to Geometry)

Representation: How does our dance look if we go forward, back, turn right, turn left?

Guess the Pattern at Group Time

DESCRIPTION

In this game, the teacher creates patterns with the children's shoes during group time. The children try to figure out the teacher's pattern. There are endless variations of the game. Some possibilities are:

- brown/white, brown/white
- sneaker/sandal/sandal, sneaker/sandal/sandal
- shoe pointing up/shoe pointing down, shoe pointing up/shoe pointing down

MATERIALS

☐ children's shoes

CHILD'S LEVEL

This activity is most appropriate for kindergarten children.

WHAT TO LOOK FOR

- Children will eagerly attempt to deduce the patterns created in this game.
- Children will become more skilled at recognizing patterns with experience and will also think of more pattern possibilities.
- Some children will begin to create their own shoe patterns after playing this game. For many children, patterns that alternate two items will be the easiest to recognize.

MORE >

MODIFICATIONS FOR SPECIAL NEEDS OR SITUATIONS

Demonstrate patterns for several days before expecting children to perceive the pattern made by the teacher.

MATHEMATICS CONTENT STANDARD CONNECTIONS

This activity aligns to the Algebra standard because of the focus on analyzing how repeating patterns are generated.

COMMENTS AND QUESTIONS RELATED TO MATHEMATICS PROCESS STANDARDS

Problem Solving: What pattern did I make? (This is harder for children than creating a pattern, because it requires them to take another person's perspective.)

Reasoning and Proof: What kind of shoe should come next in my pattern?

Communication: Does anyone have an idea for another pattern using the shoes? I will try to create it, and you can tell me if I get it right.

Connections: Does this pattern use just as many shoes as the first pattern? (Connects to Number and Operations)

Representation: Do we have enough shoes for me to create a pattern of Velcro/Velcro/tie, Velcro/Velcro/tie?

CHAPTER 5

The Geometry Standard

Peter and David were busy building cubes at the math activity table in their kindergarten classroom. "When we get enough, we can make a circus," Peter said. "These can be the crates for the animals."

The boys started each cube by laying a square tile on the table. Next they slid another square into each side of their central square until the tiles clicked together. David then raised the sides to form a box and clicked them together. When he tried to add a tile for the top to the cube, however, it kept falling into the box.

"You don't have to do it that way," said Peter. "Look." Pulling apart the sides of the box, he quickly spread them flat on the table so that a central square once again showed squares attached to each side. Peter quickly added another square tile to one of the side squares. As he raised the four sides and clicked them together, the top tile also closed into place.

The teacher had been watching the boys as she helped some other children measure and record the height of various plants in the class garden. "Are there any other ways you can position the square tiles on the table so they fold into a square?" she asked the boys.

"Yes," said Peter. "You can put three in an up and down row and then add three sideways from the middle square. I did that before." He quickly demonstrated.

"Great," said the teacher. "These flat formations are called nets in geometry. You can fold them to create geometric solids. Why don't you and David

figure out how many different nets you can create that will make a cube? We're going to start talking about nets next week, and you can help us."

"Can we trace around the nets so we can remember them?" asked David.

"Good idea," said the teacher. "Then you can show us what the nets look like."

• • •

From their earliest years, young children are busy constructing concepts related to geometry. As they maneuver through space, carefully sidestepping around tables and chairs, they begin to form concepts of lines, angles, and perimeter. Their position in space, as compared to the other objects in their environment, is of paramount importance, as numerous bumps and bruises from miscalculations can attest. In addition, young children explore shapes, such as carefully tracing the yolk in a poached egg, lining up peas along the perimeter of their plate, and attempting to stack and build with all sorts of found objects.

Unfortunately, young children may be more comfortable with geometry than their teachers. Number has long been the centerpiece of preschool and kindergarten mathematics curriculum, and geometry has often been relegated to shape sorters and the rote naming of shapes, which children eventually find boring. Clements comments that because most teachers have had little experience with geometry in their own professional development, they do little to extend geometric understanding in their students (Clements and Sarama 2007, 510). The current focus on geometry as one of the key areas of early mathematics has changed our understanding of its importance in the early childhood curriculum (NCTM 2006).

Teachers' Questions

Why is geometry an important area of mathematics for young children?

Young children's environment is filled with shapes and forms, including flat shapes, such as the designs on fabric, and three-dimensional objects, such as toys and furniture. Constructing relationships among familiar shapes and forms helps young children connect logical reasoning to other areas of mathematics. Geometry was selected as a focal area for preschool and kindergarten mathematics curriculum because it meets the three criteria set forth by NCTM (NCTM 2006). First, it is mathematically important.

Virtually all students will eventually study geometry in school, and all will use geometry in some form in their adult lives. Second, young children are already engaged in learning geometric concepts during their daily lives. Third, studying geometry in preschool and kindergarten forms a logical connection between what children already know and what they will later learn.

How does the Geometry standard apply to young children?

The understanding of foundational concepts in three areas of geometry—two- and three-dimensional shapes, spatial relationships, and symmetry and transformations—should be a focus of curriculum experiences for young children (NCTM 2000, 96). Children need many opportunities to explore and discuss all three of these areas of geometry throughout the curriculum. In this chapter, we suggest activities in art, music, science, cooking, blocks, and gross-motor areas as well as outside to help children develop important concepts in geometry.

What geometry concepts should teachers look for in young children?

Research indicates that concepts about shape begin forming in preschool and often stabilize during kindergarten (Clements and Sarama 2007). While young children quickly learn to name common shapes, such as circle, triangle, and square, they often recognize these shapes only when they are in their most commonly presented forms. In other words, if a triangle does not have two sides that are equal in length, it may not be regarded as a triangle. Or a square that is rotated forty-five degrees may be labeled a diamond and no longer be considered a square. Once these misconceptions are solidified, they are difficult to change. For this reason, preschool and kindergarten teachers should be especially careful to present shapes in many different configurations and rotations. Examples will be presented throughout this chapter.

What are the stages of development in geometry?

Dutch educator Pierre van Hiele has developed a series of stages that delineate children's levels of thinking as they progress in their understanding of geometry (van Hiele 1999). First is the *visual level*, which begins with nonverbal thinking. Children label familiar objects based on their appearance, so may call a circle a "ball" or a square a "box" before settling on the common geometric labels. Most preschool children and many kindergarten children are at the visual level. The second stage is called the *descriptive level*, during which children begin to describe the attributes of geometric shapes. They begin to understand that all closed figures with three straight sides are triangles, regardless of their differences in appearance. Therefore, a goal of preschool and kindergarten teachers should be to move children's thinking toward the descriptive level. For this to occur, children need many opportunities to play with materials that allow them to create, compose (put together), and decompose (take apart) shapes. In later elementary school, children begin to use their knowledge of the properties of geometric objects to form logical deductions. It is at this stage that children begin to understand why a square is always a rectangle but a rectangle may not be a square. Van Hiele calls this stage the *informal deduction level*.

How can teachers help children develop an understanding of two- and three-dimensional forms?

Teachers can introduce activities that allow children to explore two- and three-dimensional forms throughout the curriculum. The block area is especially rich in geometric potential. Children can combine shapes to create new shapes, such as putting two triangular blocks together to make a square. Children can explore blocks with straight and curved edges to form various shapes or enclosures. Or children can compare the construction potential of geometric solids, such as cylinders and rectangular solids. In the art area, children can compose shapes by drawing, painting, gluing, or modeling with clay. They can also decompose shapes by cutting them up. At the sensory table, children can compare the amount of sand or water that various three-dimensional forms will hold. Finally, there are a wealth of materials that children can explore in the manipulative area, including tangrams, pattern blocks, shape sorters, and table blocks.

While materials with geometric potential are important components of the curriculum, the conversations that teachers have with children as they interact with these materials are equally important. For this reason, questions and comments related to the mathematical process standards are included with each activity in this chapter.

How can teachers help children understand and express spatial relationships?

Children's spatial awareness develops as they explore their environment. In addition to constructing physical knowledge related to distance, position, and direction, children must learn the language to describe those concepts. Teachers should plan activities that help children develop both the physical knowledge and the language related to spatial awareness.

The conversations teachers have with children throughout the day provide an important means to reinforcing the connection between spatial awareness and descriptive language. As children engage in activities, teachers can make comments that relate the children's actions to distance, position, and direction. For example, the teacher might say, "Susie, you've climbed halfway up the climber." Teachers should be careful to include spatial terms in the directions they give to children. Rather than saying, "Go put the book away," the teacher could be more specific. "Please put the book on the bottom shelf, next to the other farm books." Teachers can also introduce books and songs that reinforce positional language, such as the traditional "Going on a Bear Hunt," and plan activities such as obstacle courses that encourage children to explore various positions with their bodies.

What are geometric transformations?

A transformation means that a shape has changed position while retaining the same size, angles, area, and line lengths. The three main transformations are the *turn, flip,* and *slide.* A turn means that the shape has been rotated a certain number of degrees, such as when a child rotates a shape to try to fit it into a puzzle. A flip indicates a shape is in a position that is a reflection, or mirror image, of its original position. A child who holds a shape up to a mirror sees the same image as when he flips the shape over an imaginary line, called the mirror line. A flipping action is similar to turning the page of a book. Finally, a slide means that a shape has been moved without rotating, resizing, or flipping it. In other words, every point in the shape has moved the same distance and direction. Moving a shape a particular distance across the floor would be a slide. This is also referred to as a translation.

What is symmetry?

Symmetry refers to a similarity of form, arrangement, or design on either side of a dividing line or around a point. There are several types of symmetry, of which reflective symmetry and rotational symmetry are two of the more common types. They are included in this book because they can be explored with young children.

Reflective symmetry refers to images in which half of the image is exactly like the other half, but in reverse order. An imaginary line, or axis, divides the two mirror images. The human body is an example of reflective symmetry. The left side of the body is essentially a mirror image of the right side.

Rotational symmetry means that when an object is rotated a specified number of degrees, it looks exactly the same as before it was turned. If a square is rotated 90 degrees, it looks the same as when it was in its original position; however, a rectangle that is not also a square must be rotated 180 degrees before it looks the same. A circle can be turned any number of degrees and still look the same. All are rotationally symmetrical. Starfish, daisies, and sand dollars are objects in nature that are rotationally symmetrical.

Why is it important to explore transformations and symmetry with children?

Exploring transformations and symmetry helps children develop a deeper understanding of mathematical relationships. As with patterns in algebra, in order to perceive transformations and symmetry, children must view the individual components of an object or a pairing of objects in relationship to one another. Only then does the symmetry or the transformation become apparent. Young children have difficulty thinking about parts in relationship to the whole. Activities that help them focus on transformations and symmetry also advance their ability to deal with part-whole relationships.

How can teachers help children understand and represent symmetry and transformations?

Teachers can provide materials that are symmetrical or that lend themselves to transformations and talk with children as they explore them. Teachers can also encourage children to create symmetry and transformations with art and building materials. Many natural materials, such as leaves, are symmetrical, so they make excellent mathematics or science displays. Manipulative materials, such as shape sorters, kaleidoscopes, and gears, help children understand rotational symmetry. In the art area, fold-over paintings allow children to explore reflective symmetry. By building with blocks in front of mirrors, children can view symmetrical images of their block structures.

Both natural play opportunities and planned activities provide opportunities for teachers to support children's understanding of transformations. For example, when children place moistened foam shapes on a Plexiglas easel in the activity Geometry Comes to the Water Table (Activity 5.2), they can see both the original shape and the flipped image, which appears on the opposite side of the easel. Teachers can design games in which transformations of various shapes form the game boards, such as in the Shape Match Game (Activity 5.1). As children attempt to match the corresponding shapes, they can discuss turning, flipping, and sliding.

How can teachers modify geometry activities for children with disabilities?

Most children with disabilities can participate in and enjoy the same geometry activities as the rest of the class. Teachers can make modifications to activities when necessary and before *they are introduced to make them fully accessible to individual children.* Children with cognitive delays may need more experiences with geometry materials and more scaffolding by the teacher to achieve success. For example, a child who is having difficulty fitting shapes into a shape puzzle may need specific directions from the teacher, such as, "See the point on the triangle? Turn it until the point fits in here." Children with language delays may benefit from simple songs that focus on shape recognition and positional awareness. Finally, teachers may need to make adaptations to some materials for children with physical disabilities. For example, a child who cannot see clearly would need raised shapes that she could feel on her shape game board.

How does assessment guide planning?

Ongoing assessment allows teachers to monitor the learning trajectories of both individual children and the group. Careful observations of mathematical content and processes guide the teacher in appropriate questions to ask, comments to make, and potential modeling of new problem situations to extend children's learning. In addition, careful focus related to ongoing learning in geometry helps teachers plan new curriculum or projects and ensure that all areas of geometry are addressed in the curriculum.

Shape Match Game

DESCRIPTION

In this activity, children match two- or-three-dimensional shape blocks to teacher-made game boards. The boards are made by tracing the shapes onto colored construction paper, cutting them out, and mounting them onto white posterboard. Children take turns passing around a grab bag that contains geometric shapes and trying to feel a shape that matches an empty space on the board. To avoid confusion, the shapes on the game board should all be the same color. The objects in the grab bag can be flat, such as pattern blocks or puzzle pieces, or three-dimensional, such as table blocks or geometric solids.

MATERIALS

☐ wooden or plastic manipulative pieces in geometric shapes (shape sorters, table blocks, geometric solids, pattern blocks, and attribute blocks are common preschool manipulative materials that can be used for this activity)

☐ several pieces of white posterboard, approximately 8 × 8 inches, with construction paper cutouts of the shapes glued to them

☐ grab bag to hold the game pieces

CHILD'S LEVEL

This game is appropriate for both preschool and kindergarten children. The flat shapes are easiest for younger children to match. Older preschool and kindergarten children will find more of a challenge in matching three-dimensional forms to the flat outline of shapes that appear on the game board.

MORE >

WHAT TO LOOK FOR

- Children will help one another match the manipulative shape pieces to their game boards.

- Some children will search for the shapes they need by feeling the pieces in the grab bag.

- Children using the three-dimensional forms may be surprised by the shapes some of the forms match; for example, although a pyramid has triangular sides, it may have a square base. Children may expect it to match a triangle but find that it matches a square.

- Children will use transformations, including flips, turns, and slides, to position the shapes on their boards.

MODIFICATIONS FOR SPECIAL NEEDS OR SITUATIONS

For younger children or children with cognitive delays, begin with just a few flat shapes to match. For children with visual disabilities, use black construction paper on the white posterboard for high contrast or shapes cut from felt that children can feel.

MATHEMATICS CONTENT STANDARD CONNECTIONS

This activity connects directly to the Geometry standard.

COMMENTS AND QUESTIONS RELATED TO MATHEMATICS PROCESS STANDARDS

Problem Solving: Can you feel a shape that matches this square on your board?

Reasoning and Proof: Is there more than one shape on your board that this block will match? How can you tell?

Communication: Tell me what to feel for so that I can match this triangle.

Connections: How many sides does that block have? (Connects to Number and Operations)

Representation: Later we'll press the sides of these shapes into playdough so we can see them better.

Geometry Comes to the Water Table

DESCRIPTION

Many young children spend time daily playing in the water table. Introducing foam shape blocks into this area of the classroom provides another milieu in which children can explore geometric relationships. Moist foam blocks adhere readily to a Plexiglas easel or a plastic tray. Children at the visual level of geometric reasoning may sort and name the different shapes. Children moving into the descriptive stage may use them to compose (put together) and decompose (take apart) larger geometric forms.

MATERIALS

☐ 2 Plexiglas easels made by mounting a piece of Plexiglas in an inexpensive picture frame that has wooden strips attached to the bottom for support

☐ 4 plastic trays (to use as a substitute for the easels)

☐ foam blocks, commercially available or made by tracing shapes onto craft foam and cutting them out

☐ water table or plastic wash tubs with water

CHILD'S LEVEL

This activity is self-leveling and is therefore appropriate for all preschool and kindergarten children. Older children can compose and decompose shapes with the foam blocks.

MORE >

WHAT TO LOOK FOR

• Young children will explore sticking the wet shapes onto their easel or tray and looking at their creations.

• Some children will sort the blocks by shape.

• Some children will combine shapes to create new shapes.

MODIFICATIONS FOR SPECIAL NEEDS OR SITUATIONS

Younger children who may want to put the shapes into their mouths need close supervision. Some children who are tactilely defensive may prefer to place dry foam blocks on a dry surface.

MATHEMATICS CONTENT STANDARD CONNECTIONS

This activity connects to the Geometry standard. If children sort the shapes or create patterns, this activity would also connect to the Algebra standard.

COMMENTS AND QUESTIONS RELATED TO MATHEMATICS PROCESS STANDARDS

Problem Solving: What shape can you make by putting two squares together?

Reasoning and Proof: Will you always get the same shape when you put these two squares together no matter which two sides are touching?

Communication: Tell me how to make a house like yours. How many sides does it have? What shapes did you use?

Connections: Do you have more shapes with flat sides or curved sides? (Connects to Number and Operations and Data Analysis)

Representation: Show me what shapes you can create with these two triangles.

Geometry Nets

DESCRIPTION

Young children are builders and creators. While they often use geometric forms in their block structures and puzzles, they may not have opportunities or incentives to analyze the features of these forms. Geometric building materials, such as Polydrons, enable children to create geometric solids and then combine them to create new structures. For example, they may create a cube and a pyramid and put them together to build a house.

Simply speaking, geometry nets are three-dimensional forms spread open on a flat surface to reveal the two-dimensional shapes that comprise them. Children can create geometry nets with manipulative materials or shapes cut from craft foam or tagboard. The nets can be the first step toward building three-dimensional forms, or they may appear as children decompose structures they have already built. Children may need scaffolding by the teacher to guide them in experiment-

MORE >

ing and reasoning about the various shapes needed and the ways they can be positioned to create specific three-dimensional forms.

MATERIALS

☐ Polydrons or other commercial, snap-together geometric building materials, or shapes that comprise the faces of geometric solids, precut from craft foam or tagboard with tape to hold them together

CHILD'S LEVEL

This activity is most appropriate for older preschool and kindergarten children.

WHAT TO LOOK FOR

• Many children will be eager to experiment with creating three-dimensional forms.

• With teacher guidance, children can decompose their three-dimensional forms and discuss or trace their component parts.

• Some children will begin to remember the geometry nets (configurations) used to create specific three-dimensional forms and may teach others how to make them.

MODIFICATIONS FOR SPECIAL NEEDS OR SITUATIONS

Some children with fine-motor challenges may need help snapping the blocks together or may need teachers to support their struc-tures while they tape them. Younger children or children with cognitive delays may prefer to create two-dimensional (flat) forms with the materials.

MATHEMATICS CONTENT STANDARD CONNECTIONS

Geometry nets connect directly to the Geometry standard. Because particular shapes must be organized in specific configurations or patterns to create a given geometric solid, this activity also aligns to the Algebra standard.

COMMENTS AND QUESTIONS RELATED TO MATHEMATICS PROCESS STANDARDS

Problem Solving: What shapes and how many of each do we need to make this tent? In geometry this shape is called a triangular prism.

Reasoning and Proof: Are two rectangles enough to make a prism? How can you prove that?

Communication: Joy wants to make a tent shape like yours. Can you tell her how you made your triangular prism?

Connections: Is there another net that will also make your triangular prism? How many ways can you do it? (Connects to Algebra)

Representation: Can you draw the net you used to make this pyramid?

Geometric Solids on a Roll

DESCRIPTION

Children are much more interested in geometric solids when they can experiment with them. In this activity, children place geometric solids on a simple incline, or ramp, and watch how they respond. The results encourage children to examine the geometric properties of the objects more closely to determine why they react the way they do. For example, the cylinder rolls when placed on its curved side but not when set on one of its flat ends. The cone follows a similar pattern, but when it rolls, its path curves and it often falls off the side of the ramp. Children quickly discover that objects with all flat sides don't roll well. Of course, the best roller on the ramp is the sphere, or ball.

MATERIALS

☐ ramp made by elevating one end of a flat piece of wood or sturdy cardboard with a block underneath

☐ several wooden or plastic geometric solids, commercially available or familiar objects that have the same forms as geometric solids, such as a ball (sphere), plastic or wooden egg (elliptical solid), bottle cork (cylinder), die (cube), or rectangular-shaped eraser (rectangular solid)

CHILD'S LEVEL

This activity is appropriate for all preschool and kindergarten children. Even toddlers like to place toys on their toddler slides and watch what happens.

MORE >

WHAT TO LOOK FOR

- Children will experiment with the materials and observe the results.

- Some children will examine the objects more closely to determine why they move the way they do.

- Some children may want to adjust the height of the ramp to see what happens.

- Children will notice that the curved shapes roll the best.

MODIFICATIONS FOR SPECIAL NEEDS OR SITUATIONS

For younger children or children with cognitive delays, the number of objects can be reduced to encourage comparisons.

MATHEMATICS CONTENT STANDARD CONNECTIONS

This activity aligns directly with the Geometry standard. Because some children may want to compare how far or how fast various objects move, it may also coordinate with the Measurement standard.

COMMENTS AND QUESTIONS RELATED TO MATHEMATICS PROCESS STANDARDS

Problem Solving: Here are some new materials to use with the ramp. Can you predict which objects will roll the best?

Reasoning and Proof: How can you prove that the cylinder rolls better than the cone?

Communication: Why does the cylinder roll and the block (rectangular solid) get stuck? They're both long and skinny.

Connections: How can we tell exactly how far each object rolled? (Connects to Measurement and Physics)

Representation: Can you set up the same experiment in the block area? That way more people can play.

Find My Object in Your Bag

DESCRIPTION

This game is designed to help children move toward the descriptive level of geometric thinking. Unlike more traditional "feely bag" activities, which are designed for one child to use at a time, this activity requires children to work in pairs. Each child has a grab bag with a selection of identical objects. First, children reach into their bags and feel the objects without looking. Then one child describes one of the objects he can feel. Based on the description, the other child tries to find the matching object in his or her bag. Then both children pull the object from their bags and see if they have selected the same thing. If they have picked different objects, the teacher can help them revise their descriptions. Children take turns describing objects and finding the match. Initially, small toys or familiar objects can be used. Later, geometric forms can be substituted.

MATERIALS

☐ 2 drawstring bags, each with identical objects like those listed below

☐ 4–6 small, familiar objects, such as a comb, toy car, plastic animal, box, artificial flower, spool, etc.

☐ several commercially available geometric shapes or solids, or familiar objects that have geometric shapes, such as a ball (sphere), plastic or wooden egg (elliptical solid), bottle cork (cylinder), die (cube), or rectangular-shaped eraser (rectangular solid)

CHILD'S LEVEL

This activity is most appropriate for older preschool or kindergarten children who are nearing the descriptive level of geometric reasoning. Because the activity is rich in language and sensory input, younger children may also benefit, particularly if fewer objects are used.

MORE >

WHAT TO LOOK FOR

- Some children will accurately describe the objects in their bags.
- At first, children may not give enough information for their partner to find the object.
- Children will compare the objects they select.
- With teacher input, children will discuss why they selected the same or different objects.

MODIFICATIONS FOR SPECIAL NEEDS OR SITUATIONS

Younger children or children with cognitive delays may need fewer objects (two or three at first) to differentiate among. Children who are tactilely defensive can listen to their peer describe an object and then visually select a matching item from a tray.

MATHEMATICS CONTENT STANDARD CONNECTIONS

This activity aligns with the Geometry standard.

COMMENTS AND QUESTIONS RELATED TO MATHEMATICS PROCESS STANDARDS

Problem Solving: What would Milan need to know to tell whether you're feeling a triangle or a square?

Reasoning and Proof: How can you tell that you both picked the same shape even though the colors are different?

Communication: Describe what object you're feeling so Claire can try to find it in her bag.

Connections: How many different objects do you feel? (Connects to Number and Operations)

Representation: Can you draw the object in the air? That might help Ken find it.

Pretzel Geometry

DESCRIPTION

Creating a geometric shape and then eating it is a yummy way to represent and experiment with geometric shapes. Children first work in small groups to create pretzel dough. Then they select a geometric shape and copy it with their pretzel dough. Teacher comments and questions are important when children are comparing their pretzel shapes to the geometric models. As a mathematical extension of the activity, teachers can record the shape of each child's pretzel and later graph the results. See chapter 7 for graph-related questions. Once the pretzels are formed, they can be baked and, of course, eaten.

MATERIALS

☐ Pretzel Recipe

- 2 teaspoons dry yeast
- 2 teaspoons sugar
- ¾ cup hot water (at least 105°F)
- 2 cups flour
- Dissolve the yeast in water. Stir in the sugar. Add the flour.
- Divide the dough into equal parts.
- Knead, and form shapes.
- Bake at 325°F for 15 minutes. Cool.

MORE >

□ bowl, measuring cups and spoons, stirring utensil, and baking sheets

□ geometric models showing the perimeter of various shapes, premade from self-hardening clay, playdough, or pipe cleaners

CHILD'S LEVEL

All children like to bake and eat their creations. The geometric modeling aspect of this activity is particularly suited to older preschool and kindergarten children.

WHAT TO LOOK FOR

- Some children will successfully copy the shapes with pretzel dough.

- Some children may need to use the models directly, perhaps by laying strips of dough over them.

- Some children will want to create their own shapes and should be allowed to do so.

MODIFICATIONS FOR SPECIAL NEEDS OR SITUATIONS

Children with visual disabilities may need to feel the geometric models. Children with physical or motor disabilities may need help forming the dough but should be allowed as much freedom as practical.

MATHEMATICS CONTENT STANDARD CONNECTIONS

This activity connects directly to the Geometry standard. If children are encouraged to count sides, the activity also connects to Number and Operations.

COMMENTS AND QUESTIONS RELATED TO MATHEMATICS PROCESS STANDARDS

Problem Solving: Choose a shape and see if you can make it with pretzel dough.

Reasoning and Proof: How can you tell that you made a triangle and not a square?

Communication: I want to turn my circle shape into an egg shape (ellipse). What should I do?

Connections: How many people made round pretzels? We'll put your names in this column of our graph. (Connects to Data Analysis and Number and Operations)

Representation: Look at all the shapes we made with pretzel dough!

Food Geometry—Cutting Up and Eating Geometric Solids

DESCRIPTION

When geometric solids (foods) are sliced in various ways, the cut side (*face* in geometric terms) forms a geometric shape. By pressing the face onto a lightly buttered surface, children can see and describe the shape that was created. Teachers can extend and preserve the results of these mathematical experiments by recording what the children do and say, photographing the results, or helping children draw the shapes that appear in the butter. Because children can eat the food when they are finished, this should allay concerns some families may have about wasting food. This activity can be implemented over a series of days, perhaps during lunch or snack, with one or two food items introduced each time. Make sure to maintain proper hygiene with food preparation and handling.

MATERIALS

☐ several small cutting boards or trays

☐ plastic knives

☐ small plastic plates, lightly coated with butter

☐ an assortment of foods in geometric shapes, such as the following:

  • large marshmallows (cylinders)

MORE >

- grapes (elliptical solids)
- cheese sticks (rectangular solids)
- melon balls (spheres)
- cheese cubes (cubes)

CHILD'S LEVEL

This activity is most appropriate for older preschool and kindergarten children who can safely manipulate the plastic knives.

WHAT TO LOOK FOR

- Children will be eager to cut the food.
- Children will be surprised at the shapes that some of the cut faces produce.
- Some children will have difficulty describing the cut shapes and need teacher support. Directed questions can help.
- Some children will want to trace the shapes created in the butter.

MODIFICATIONS FOR SPECIAL NEEDS OR SITUATIONS

This activity has several steps. Children with cognitive, language, or attention concerns may need the activity to be broken down into clear, discrete steps.

MATHEMATICS CONTENT STANDARD CONNECTIONS

This activity strongly supports the Geometry standard. If children are encouraged to count and compare sides, the activity also connects to Number and Operations.

COMMENTS AND QUESTIONS RELATED TO MATHEMATICS PROCESS STANDARDS

Problem Solving: If you cut the cheese stick in a slant rather than straight down, will the cut side look the same?

Reasoning and Proof: How can you tell that the two cut faces are different?

Communication: Tell Taizo what you did to create this shape in your butter.

Connections: How many cubes can you make from your cheese stick? (Connects to Number and Operations)

Representation: Let's save your butter plates. After lunch we can trace the same shapes in fingerpaint.

Shape Prints

DESCRIPTION

Teachers often introduce materials to create imprints as an art activity. Children may press objects into clay or dip them into paint before pressing them onto paper. This activity is similar and focuses on geometric forms and the shapes that can be created by combining them.

A variety of materials can be used for this activity. Geometric shape templates with handles are commercially available, as are geometric solids made from a sponge material. Some of the shape templates create an outline of the shape, which focuses on perimeter; others create a filled-in shape, which lets children visualize the area of a flat shape or the face (side) of a geometric solid.

This is another activity that is best repeated over a succession of days. At first, children are intrigued with the forms the various shapes make in the art medium. For example, they may be surprised to find that the base of a pyramid is square rather than triangular like the sides. Eventually teachers can encourage children to explore what composite shapes can be created by positioning the various shapes so that the edges touch.

MATERIALS

☐ shape templates, commercially available or made by cutting the shapes from craft foam and gluing them to wooden blocks

☐ geometric solids, preferably foam or plastic if paint is used

☐ clay or playdough, or tempera paint in a shallow dish, and paper

MORE >

CHILD'S LEVEL

This activity is appropriate for all preschool and kindergarten children.

WHAT TO LOOK FOR

- Younger children may focus on producing and naming the shapes.
- Older or more advanced children may be interested in the relationship between the shape template or geometric solid and the shape it produces in the art medium.
- Older children may combine shapes to create composite shapes, designs, or pictures.

MODIFICATIONS FOR SPECIAL NEEDS OR SITUATIONS

For younger children or children with cognitive delays, start with just two shapes. This focuses children's attention on comparing the two shapes. Children with fine-motor challenges often need templates with handles. Children with visual disabilities may benefit from using dark-colored paint that contrasts sharply with white paper or a modeling medium, such as clay, which is especially appropriate for feeling the imprint.

MATHEMATICS CONTENT STANDARD CONNECTIONS

This activity aligns with the Geometry standard. If children notice or are encouraged to create patterns with shapes, the activity also connects to Algebra.

COMMENTS AND QUESTIONS RELATED TO MATHEMATICS PROCESS STANDARDS

Problem Solving: Which of these geometric solids will make a triangle in the clay?

Reasoning and Proof: James, why do you think this shape is a triangle? Robin, why do you think it isn't a triangle?

Communication: Can you explain how you ended up with a square when the only template you used was a triangle?

Connections: Do you have more circles or triangles on your paper? (Connects to Number and Operations)

Representation: How many different shapes can you make by putting triangles together?

Creating Quilts with Iron-On Shapes

DESCRIPTION

Most children are familiar with quilts and may have a special one of their own. Many quilts are composed of geometric shapes placed in positions that create symmetrical forms. In this activity, children can combine geometric shapes cut from iron-on fabric to create their own quilt squares. Children do the creating and adults do the ironing. Once the squares are completed, they can be sewn together to create a class quilt.

MATERIALS

☐ iron-on fabric precut into geometric shapes

☐ denim, or other fabric with a solid color, cut into squares 12 × 12 inches to use as the background for the quilt squares

☐ iron for an adult to use to adhere the iron-on fabric to the background squares

☐ tape to temporarily hold the shapes in place until they can be ironed

☐ puffy paint or fabric marker to label each square with the name of the child who created it

CHILD'S LEVEL

This activity is most appropriate for older preschool or kindergarten children.

WHAT TO LOOK FOR

• Some children will combine shapes to form composite shapes or designs.

• Some children will create patterns.

MORE >

- Some children will use the shapes to create pictures.
- Some children will place the shapes randomly on the background to create a collage.

MODIFICATIONS FOR SPECIAL NEEDS OR SITUATIONS

No modifications are anticipated for this activity.

MATHEMATICS CONTENT STANDARD CONNECTIONS

This activity aligns with the Geometry standard. If children form symmetrical designs or create patterns, it would also connect to the Algebra standard.

COMMENTS AND QUESTIONS RELATED TO MATHEMATICS PROCESS STANDARDS

Problem Solving: What designs can you create with these shapes?

Reasoning and Proof: What pattern did you create in your pinwheel design? If you add another triangle, will you still have the same pattern?

Communication: What shapes did you put together to create your boat?

Connections: How many triangles of each color did you use to make your pinwheel pattern? (Connects to Algebra and Number and Operations)

Representation: You can create as many designs as you want with the shapes. When you decide on the one you like best, I'll iron it onto your square.

How Artists Use Shapes

DESCRIPTION

Many artists and illustrators are known for the geometric elements in their artwork. In this activity, children examine selected artwork and discuss how the artists use lines, shapes, and symmetry. Children then choose a style they like and create their own artist- and geometry-inspired artwork. Teachers may wish to record the children's descriptions of the artist samples and their own creations, including how they are similar or different.

MATERIALS

☐ an assortment of artwork with a strong geometric perspective, available from art books, calendars, Internet collections, and illustrations in children's books, such as the following:

- *The Spider Weaver: The Legend of Kente Cloth*, Julia Cairns illustrator

- *Charles Harper's Birds and Words*, by Charles Harper

MORE >

- *The Quilt*, by Ann Jonas
- Frank Lloyd Wright, well-known American architect and artist whose geometric artwork is readily available in libraries, catalogs, and on the Internet

☐ appropriate art media for children to use to re-create the selected artists' styles, such as colored pencils, markers, watercolors, and collage materials

CHILD'S LEVEL

This activity is most appropriate for older preschool and kindergarten children who are moving into the descriptive level of geometric thinking.

WHAT TO LOOK FOR

- Children will talk about the artwork and try to employ similar design features in their own work.
- Some children will talk about the artwork but make something that is completely different, which is fine.
- Younger children may just want to select some art materials to explore.

MODIFICATIONS FOR SPECIAL NEEDS OR SITUATIONS

For children with visual disabilities, look for art with strong contrast in color so that the design features are more distinct. Three-dimensional art, such as imprinted clay tiles, should also be considered.

MATHEMATICS CONTENT STANDARD CONNECTIONS

This activity aligns with the Geometry standard. If children form symmetrical designs or create patterns, it would also connect to the Algebra standard.

COMMENTS AND QUESTIONS RELATED TO MATHEMATICS PROCESS STANDARDS

Problem Solving: Look at how straight the lines are in this picture. How do you think the artist got his lines to be so straight?

Reasoning and Proof: Mike says he found thirteen circles in this picture, but Ali sees twelve circles. Mike, can you show Ali why you think there are thirteen circles?

Communication: Tell me how you used the rectangles in your picture.

Connections: Do you notice anything special about the lines in the spiderweb in this picture? (Connects to Algebra)

Representation: I see circles, triangles, and parallel lines that you used to represent the birds and trees in your picture.

Fold-Over Paintings

DESCRIPTION

Children are fascinated with the symmetrical designs they create with this activity. Start by folding dark-colored construction paper in half and then opening it. Children apply small amounts of white paint to one side of the paper, fold the paper over the paint, and rub the paper with their hands or a paint roller. As they open the paper, a symmetrical design appears. Children love describing what the various designs look like. Teachers should point out that the shapes are *flipped* because this is geometric vocabulary.

MATERIALS

☐ black or dark blue construction paper, 12 × 18 inches

☐ white tempera paint

☐ paint roller (optional)

CHILD'S LEVEL

This activity is appropriate for both preschool and kindergarten children.

WHAT TO LOOK FOR

- Children will eagerly apply the paint and marvel at the geometric designs they create.

- Many children will notice the symmetrical relationship between the two sides of the paper.

- Many children will name their artwork.

- Some children will experiment by applying paint to particular parts of the paper and observing the results.

MODIFICATIONS FOR SPECIAL NEEDS OR SITUATIONS

For most children, no modifications will be necessary. For children who are visually

MORE >

impaired, add sand or salt to the paint. After the paint has dried, the children can feel the symmetrical designs.

MATHEMATICS CONTENT STANDARD CONNECTIONS

Since this activity involves lines and shapes, it aligns to the Geometry standard. The creation of symmetrical patterns relates to both the Geometry and Algebra standards.

COMMENTS AND QUESTIONS RELATED TO MATHEMATICS PROCESS STANDARDS

Problem Solving: What do you see that is flipped on the two sides of your paper?

Reasoning and Proof: How can you prove that the shapes on this side of the paper are the same as the shapes on the other side, only flipped?

Communication: What did you have to do to make this symmetrical picture?

Connections: How many circles should I make on this side of the paper to end up with four circles when I open my paper? (Connects to Number and Operations)

Representation: Can you use a marker to copy this shape from your painting? Without looking, what do you think this shape looks like on the other side of the paper?

Reflective Symmetry

DESCRIPTION

Patterns and symmetry occur throughout nature. In mathematics, they are components of both geometry and algebra. In this activity, children look for reflective symmetry in seashells, leaves, crabs, butterflies, and other objects from nature. Teachers should encourage children to fold one side of the object over the other side if possible so that they can see that the shapes are the same. This transformation is called a *flip* in geometry. As an extension of this activity, children can experiment with flips by tracing a shape onto paper, flipping it, and then tracing it again. A symmetrical image should appear.

MATERIALS

☐ bivalve seashells, such as clams or scallops

☐ leaves pressed inside a book or ironed between wax paper to keep them from withering

☐ small plastic crabs, lobsters, insects, or spiders

☐ small plastic or paper butterflies

☐ paper and pencil or markers for tracing (optional)

CHILD'S LEVEL

This activity is most appropriate for older preschool and kindergarten children. While younger children may be interested in the materials, they may not yet be ready to focus on symmetry.

WHAT TO LOOK FOR

• Children will explore the materials and discuss how they look and feel.

• Some children will recognize the symmetrical design of the objects.

MORE >

- Some children will fold the sides of the objects together and notice they are the same.
- Some children will represent the objects by drawing them. They might also begin to draw other symmetrical figures.

MODIFICATIONS FOR SPECIAL NEEDS OR SITUATIONS

For children with visual disabilities, select or create objects with a strong tactile component. For example, the designs on plastic butterflies can be outlined in puffy paint. Larger objects, or objects with strong color contrast that show the symmetrical design on a larger scale, may also be helpful for some children..

MATHEMATICS CONTENT STANDARD CONNECTIONS

Due to its focus on patterns and symmetry, this activity connects to both Geometry and Algebra standards.

COMMENTS AND QUESTIONS RELATED TO MATHEMATICS PROCESS STANDARDS

Problem Solving: If I give you half of a heart shape to trace, what do you have to do to get a whole heart?

Reasoning and Proof: How can you tell for sure that both sides of the butterfly are the same shape?

Communication: Describe what you see on this side of the crab that is the same as on the other side.

Connections: Are there the same number of legs on each side of the spider? (Connects to Number and Operations)

Representation: Let's see if we can draw some symmetrical objects. We could also build symmetrical block structures.

Rotational Symmetry

DESCRIPTION

Many objects in nature are rotationally symmetrical. This means that as you turn them they pass through positions where they look the same as when in their original position. For example, if you hold a starfish so that one arm points upward and gradually rotate it, each time an arm points upward the starfish looks the same as when you started. Like the *flip* in the previous activity, the *turn* is one of the important transformations in geometry. In this activity, children explore rotationally symmetrical objects from nature. As an extension, children can make imprints of the objects in playdough or clay to further observe their symmetrical structure.

MATERIALS

☐ starfish

☐ plastic snowflakes

☐ daisies, sunflowers, or other flowers with a similar form

☐ eucalyptus pods

☐ playdough or clay (optional)

CHILD'S LEVEL

This activity is most appropriate for older preschool and kindergarten children. While younger children may be interested in the materials, they may not yet be ready to focus on symmetry.

WHAT TO LOOK FOR

• Children will rotate the objects as part of their explorations.

• Some children will notice that the objects look the same as they turn them.

• Some children will notice the symmetry when they press the objects into clay.

MORE >

MODIFICATIONS FOR SPECIAL NEEDS OR SITUATIONS

Select larger objects that can be easily handled for children with visual disabilities.

MATHEMATICS CONTENT STANDARD CONNECTIONS

Due to its focus on patterns and symmetry, this activity connects to both Geometry and Algebra standards.

COMMENTS AND QUESTIONS RELATED TO MATHEMATICS PROCESS STANDARDS

Problem Solving: How much do you have to turn the starfish before an arm points upward again?

Reasoning and Proof: Can you find any materials in the manipulative area that are rotationally symmetrical? How can you tell?

Communication: Can you describe the parts of the snowflake that are the same?

Connections: Let's put a sticker on this point of the snowflake. How many times can you turn it and still have it fit into the playdough mold you made? (Connects to Number and Operations)

Representation: Can you use this clay to show that the starfish is the same shape even after you turn it?

Kaleidoscopes

DESCRIPTION

Kaleidoscopes are a marvelous tool for children to use to observe rotational symmetry. The mirrors inside create a three-part symmetrical image centering around a point. The kaleidoscope also produces multiple copies of this image. As children turn the kaleidoscope, they can observe a vast array of symmetrical forms partially determined by the way they arrange objects in the kaleidoscope's base. From an educational standpoint, the most useful kaleidoscopes are those that allow children to directly place objects in the kaleidoscope, as opposed to kaleidoscopes that are sealed.

MATERIALS

☐ several kaleidoscopes designed so that children can place objects in their bases

☐ a variety of materials to place in the kaleidoscopes (shape cutouts, beads, small shells, etc.)

☐ pictures of images from kaleidoscopes downloadable from the Internet

☐ observational notebook, in which children can record or dictate their observations or draw the images they see in the kaleidoscope (optional)

CHILD'S LEVEL

This activity is most appropriate for older preschool or kindergarten children.

WHAT TO LOOK FOR

• Children will place objects in the kaleidoscopes and marvel at how they look.

MORE >

- Children will discover that the kaleidoscopes alter the images.
- Children will notice that the same image appears many times when viewed through a kaleidoscope.
- Some children will observe symmetry in the images created by the kaleidoscopes. Teachers can discuss the circular rotation of these images.

MODIFICATIONS FOR SPECIAL NEEDS AND SITUATIONS

For children with visual disabilities, images from kaleidoscopes downloaded from the Internet can be magnified. For blind children, provide rotationally symmetrical objects, such as those used in Rotational Symmetry (Activity 5.13), for them to feel.

MATHEMATICS CONTENT STANDARD CONNECTIONS

This activity aligns with the symmetry and patterning aspects of both Geometry and Algebra.

COMMENTS AND QUESTIONS RELATED TO MATHEMATICS PROCESS STANDARDS

Problem Solving: What do you think this circle will look like under the kaleidoscope?

Reasoning and Proof: Turn the kaleidoscope one full turn and see if you see the same image.

Communication: Describe what you see in the kaleidoscope.

Connections: How many triangles do you see in the kaleidoscope? (Connects to Number and Operations)

Representation: Would you like to draw what you see in the kaleidoscope?

Over, Under, Around, and Through— Gross-Motor Geometry

DESCRIPTION

Although many of us first think about shapes in connection with geometry, understanding positional terms is also an important component. In this activity, children have the opportunity to move over, under, around, through, next to, in front of, behind, above, and below familiar objects in the gross-motor area. Children take turns drawing "clue cards" that include both directions and illustrations about where to move. Teachers can help children interpret their clue cards and later use

MORE >

positional terms to describe where the child is located, such as, "You are above the balance beam." As an extension of this activity, teachers may choose to take digital photographs of the children and assemble them into a class book that describes where each child is located in the pictures.

MATERIALS

- ☐ gross-motor area equipment
- ☐ clue cards made by printing location directions on 5 × 7 inch cards and including illustrations made with silhouette stickers of children and pictures of gross-motor equipment cut from catalogs or downloaded from the Internet
- ☐ digital camera and class book (optional)

CHILD'S LEVEL

This activity is appropriate for all preschool and kindergarten children.

WHAT TO LOOK FOR

- Children will delight in drawing clue cards and moving into various positions throughout the gross-motor area.
- Some children will move to the correct object on their card but not into the correct position. Teachers can help them interpret the positioning aspect of the directions.
- Some children may need help finding the object in the gross-motor area that matches the picture on their card.

MODIFICATIONS FOR SPECIAL NEEDS OR SITUATIONS

Children who are challenged by motor planning may need extra help. The teacher can break down the steps needed to reach the desired object in the room. Children with balance and mobility challenges should, of course, be given cards that illustrate locations they can move to and occupy safely.

MATHEMATICS CONTENT STANDARD CONNECTIONS

This activity connects to the Geometry standard due to its emphasis on positional terms.

COMMENTS AND QUESTIONS RELATED TO MATHEMATICS PROCESS STANDARDS

Problem Solving: Where can you go so that you're on top of a big cube?

Reasoning and Proof: Your card said to get inside a cylinder. How did you know that the tunnel is a cylinder?

Communication: Tell me where to go so that I'm behind the climber. That's what my card says.

Connections: Your card says to stand behind the climbing cube. Will we still be able to see you, or is the cube taller than you are? (Connects to Measurement)

Representation: Show me what it looks like to be under the ladder climber.

Follow the Chicken's Path

DESCRIPTION

Some children's books create a story in which characters follow a clearly defined route through their environment. *Rosie's Walk* by Pat Hutchins is an example. As Rosie the hen, ominously followed by a fox, takes a walk around the farm, she moves over, under, around, and through various sites until she arrives safely home at the hen house. Children love recreating this story. Teachers can create simple props to designate key locations in the story and narrate while children reenact the events. Later, children may wish to create their own versions of the story and decide what objects Rosie should go over, under, around, or through. The positional terms used in this activity are an important aspect of the Geometry standard for young children.

MATERIALS

☐ simple props made from cardboard, paper, or fabric to represent the pond, haystack, windmill, fence, and beehives in the story

☐ a copy of the book *Rosie's Walk* by Pat Hutchins

CHILD'S LEVEL

This activity is appropriate for all preschool and kindergarten children.

WHAT TO LOOK FOR

• Some children will accurately follow all the directions in the story.

• Some children will go to the right place but misinterpret the directional term; for example, they may walk across the pond rather than around it.

• Some children will enjoy making up new directions for Rosie.

MORE >

MODIFICATIONS FOR SPECIAL NEEDS OR SITUATIONS

Children with language delays may benefit greatly from this activity; however, they may need extra help with the directions. Teachers can simplify the directions by focusing first on the object the child must go to and then on the child's position. Children with motor concerns may need assistive devices, such as steps or ramps, to help them climb. These should be set up ahead of time.

MATHEMATICS CONTENT STANDARD CONNECTIONS

This activity focuses on spatial sense and directionality, which are important aspects of the Geometry standard.

COMMENTS AND QUESTIONS RELATED TO MATHEMATICS PROCESS STANDARDS

Problem Solving: Can you show me how Rosie walks around the pond?

Reasoning and Proof: Do you think it would take more steps for Rosie to go around this side of the pond or the other side? How can we find out for sure?

Communication: Where does Rosie have to go to get inside her house?

Connections: How many steps does Rosie have to take to get all the way around the pond? (Connects to Number and Operations and Measurement)

Representation: Can you use these stepping stone cutouts to show the path you took when you were Rosie?

Building a Story—
Block Shapes and Symmetry

DESCRIPTION

Changes, Changes is another Pat Hutchins book that helps children connect with geometry. In this wordless picture book, two block people use colored table blocks to build a series of structures that are part of the story line. Children can use either blocks or paper cutouts of blocks to re-create or redesign the structures. The modeling draws their attention to both the shapes and their positions in the illustrations.

MATERIALS

☐ several copies of the book *Changes, Changes* by Pat Hutchins

☐ colored table blocks, similar to those used in the book, or cutouts of the block shapes made by tracing table blocks onto construction paper and cutting out the shapes

☐ white construction paper to form a base for the shapes

☐ glue

MORE >

CHILD'S LEVEL

This activity is most appropriate for older preschool and kindergarten children who are ready to model the block designs in the book; however, younger children will also enjoy talking about the shapes in the book.

WHAT TO LOOK FOR

- Some children will re-create the block structures with a high degree of accuracy.
- Some children will approximate the designs but have some inconsistencies.
- Some children will design new structures with the blocks or cutouts.
- Some children will create collages with the shape cutouts.

MODIFICATIONS FOR SPECIAL NEEDS OR SITUATIONS

For younger children or children with cognitive or perceptual challenges, modify the activity by having them place the blocks or cutouts directly on the picture. Teachers can tear apart a paperback version of the book, adhere magnetic tape to the back of the paper shapes, and tape a page from the book to a cookie sheet. When children place the shapes on the pictures, the magnets will hold them in place. For children with visual disabilities, teachers can use puffy paint to outline the block shapes in the pictures after the pages have been laminated. After the paint dries, children can feel the shapes and place the blocks over the matching outlines.

MATHEMATICS CONTENT STANDARD CONNECTIONS

This activity aligns directly with the Geometry standard.

COMMENTS AND QUESTIONS RELATED TO MATHEMATICS PROCESS STANDARDS

Problem Solving: I don't have a rectangular block that's as wide as the one in the picture. What blocks could I put together to make one?

Reasoning and Proof: How can we tell for sure that these two narrow rectangles will match the wider rectangle in the picture?

Communication: Can you explain to Kim how you made your square? There aren't any square blocks left.

Connections: What kind of shape did you use the most in your picture? (Connects to Number and Operations and Data Analysis)

Representation: Can you make this picture with the colored paper shapes?

Find the Missing Puppy

DESCRIPTION

Knowledge of geometry is critical for navigators and mapmakers who must accurately locate specific places and figure out how to move between them. This is one reason positioning and spatial awareness are important components of the Geometry standard. This activity gives young children some beginning experience in describing and finding specific locations. In later elementary school, they will begin to locate such positions on a grid or rectangular coordinate system.

Find the Missing Puppy activity can be played using a flat, cardboard house and a cutout image of a puppy or with an actual dollhouse and a toy puppy. Children take turns covering their eyes while the teacher or another child hides the puppy. The person who hid the puppy then gives clues to the children hoping to find it. The following are some examples:

1. The puppy is on the top floor. It is in the room on the right.
2. The puppy is on the bottom floor. It is in the middle room.

MORE >

3. The puppy is on the middle floor. It is in the smallest room.

MATERIALS

☐ cardboard doll house made from posterboard and markers

☐ lamination or clear contact paper to protect the house

☐ additional pieces of posterboard cut in sizes to cover each room and attached with tape to the side of each room after the house has been laminated

☐ cutout image of a puppy with a piece of magnetic tape on the reverse side, or a toy puppy

☐ magnetic tape cut in 1-inch strips and mounted in each room of the house to hold the puppy

CHILD'S LEVEL

This activity is appropriate for all preschool and kindergarten children.

WHAT TO LOOK FOR

• Some children will be able to locate the puppy after hearing the clues.

• Some children will be able to follow one of the clues but not both.

• Some children will have difficulty giving clues to other people.

• Some children will search randomly until they find the puppy.

MODIFICATIONS FOR SPECIAL NEEDS OR SITUATIONS

For younger children or for children with cognitive or language delays, give only one clue at a time. For children with visual disabilities, outline the rooms with puffy paint after the house has been laminated so they can feel the location of the rooms.

MATHEMATICS CONTENT STANDARD CONNECTIONS

This connects to both the Geometry and Measurement standards.

COMMENTS AND QUESTIONS RELATED TO MATHEMATICS PROCESS STANDARDS

Problem Solving: Can you find the puppy? It's on the middle floor in the biggest room.

Reasoning and Proof: How did you know the puppy would be in that room?

Communication: Tell Logan where to look for the puppy you hid.

Connections: Let's call the bottom floor the first floor, the middle floor the second floor, and the top floor the third floor. (Connects to Number and Operations)

Representation: Tomorrow we can build houses in the block area and play again.

Drawing What We've Built

DESCRIPTION

Children begin this activity by building a structure with wooden table blocks. Then they use markers on paper to draw it, converting their three-dimensional building into a two-dimensional representation. The process allows children to handle and explore geometric shapes and then reconsider the components of their structure as they re-create it on paper. You may want to take digital photos of the structures as well.

MATERIALS

☐ tray for each child to build on so they can reposition their structure when they draw it or save it for another time

☐ basket of table blocks for each child

☐ white construction paper, 8½ × 11 inches

☐ set of markers for each child

☐ digital camera (optional)

CHILD'S LEVEL

This activity is most appropriate for older preschool or kindergarten children who are beginning to create representational drawings. Younger children may want to build with the blocks, which is an excellent activity for them.

WHAT TO LOOK FOR

• Most children will eagerly build block structures, especially if they are to be photographed for a class book.

MORE >

- Some children will draw a recognizable representation of their structure.

- Some children will draw some of the shapes in their structure.

- Some children will need teacher help in the drawing phase. The teacher can isolate particular shapes and give guidance, such as "Look at this green shape. It has a straight line for each side."

MODIFICATIONS FOR SPECIAL NEEDS OR SITUATIONS

If some children become frustrated with the drawing part of this activity, teachers may elect to photograph the block structures. Later they can talk about the photos with the child.

MATHEMATICS CONTENT STANDARD CONNECTIONS

This activity aligns directly with the Geometry standard. Because it also includes a graphic representation, the activity also connects to Algebra.

COMMENTS AND QUESTIONS RELATED TO MATHEMATICS PROCESS STANDARDS

Problem Solving: Do you have to use straight lines or curved lines to draw this shape?

Reasoning and Proof: Did you include all of the blocks you used in your drawing? How can you tell?

Communication: What shapes will you need to draw when you make a picture of your building?

Connections: I see two sizes of rectangular blocks in your building. Where did you use the large rectangles, and where did you use the small ones? (Connects to Measurement)

Representation: We have to put the blocks away now, but we can get them out again tomorrow. If you want to build the same structure, you can use your drawing to help you remember how.

Building What We've Drawn

DESCRIPTION

Using their drawings or photographs from Drawing What We've Built (Activity 5.19), children can attempt to rebuild their original structures the next day or several days later. The activity shows children the relationship between construction drawings and the building process. Some children may have had blocks that were hidden behind other blocks in their original structure and were not represented in their drawing. This situation can prompt a discussion about the need to draw a building from various perspectives.

Following this activity, some children may wish to draw structures they intend to build in the block area prior to actually building them. These future architects can take their drawings with them to the block area. As they build, they can determine if all the necessary shapes were included in their drawing.

MATERIALS

☐ drawings or photographs of children's block structures

☐ wooden table blocks

☐ paper and drawing utensils for drawing new structures to build in the block area (optional)

MORE >

CHILD'S LEVEL

This activity is most appropriate for older preschool and kindergarten children; however, if photographs were taken of the buildings built by younger children, they may want to look at the photos and try to build their structures again.

WHAT TO LOOK FOR

- Some children will be able to re-create their previous block structure by looking at the drawing.

- Some children will use the same shapes as in their drawing but change the positioning of them.

- Some children will remember there were sides and a back to their previous building and realize they cannot see these perspectives in their drawing.

- Some children will want to create a new block structure.

MODIFICATIONS FOR SPECIAL NEEDS OR SITUATIONS

Some children may have difficulty moving from the two-dimensional drawing or photograph to building it in three dimensions with blocks. Teachers can help by breaking the activity into steps and helping children focus on one block at a time.

MATHEMATICS CONTENT STANDARD CONNECTIONS

This activity is directly related to the Geometry standard. Because it also involves working from a symbolic representation (drawing or photograph), it also connects to the Algebra standard.

COMMENTS AND QUESTIONS RELATED TO MATHEMATICS PROCESS STANDARDS

Problem Solving: Here's your drawing from yesterday. Do you think you can build the same building again?

Reasoning and Proof: Compare your building to your drawing. Is there anything missing?

Communication: What shapes will you need for the bottom of your building?

Connections: Is your building the same size as the drawing? (Connects to Measurement)

Representation: Yesterday you drew a model of your building. Can you build the same building from your drawing?

Geometry Treasure Hunt

> We saw a building with lots of windows. They were rectangles. There were 12 small rectangles inside the windows. There were triangles over the doors.
>
> Pedro and Julia

DESCRIPTION

Although we are constantly surrounded by geometric forms, we often don't notice or pay attention to them. This activity takes children on a geometry treasure hunt. Before embarking on a walk around the school neighborhood, each child is given a card with drawings of various geometric shapes. During the walk, children look for these shapes. Teachers can write down what children say about the shapes they see, as well as their location. A digital camera can help preserve the images for further discussion. The photographs along with the children's comments can be assembled into a class geometry book.

MATERIALS

- ☐ file cards, 5 × 7 inches, with drawings of standard geometric shapes for each child
- ☐ a notebook to write down children's comments
- ☐ a digital camera to photograph the sights

CHILD'S LEVEL

This activity is appropriate for all preschool and kindergarten children.

WHAT TO LOOK FOR

- Some children will quickly recognize shapes in the environment that match the shapes on their card.

MORE >

- Some children will at first need adults to point out some of the shapes.

MODIFICATIONS FOR SPECIAL NEEDS OR SITUATIONS

For younger children or children with cognitive delays, focus on one or two shapes, such as a circle or a rectangle. Point out the shape each time you see it. For children with visual disabilities, use puffy paint to outline the shapes on their card so they can feel them. Find some shapes ahead of time that the child will be able to feel during the walk.

MATHEMATICS CONTENT STANDARD CONNECTIONS

This activity aligns with the Geometry standard. Because it also involves working from a symbolic representation (drawing or photograph), the activity also connects to Algebra.

COMMENTS AND QUESTIONS RELATED TO MATHEMATICS PROCESS STANDARDS

Problem Solving: See if you can find all of the shapes on your card on our geometry treasure hunt.

Reasoning and Proof: How do you know the door is a rectangle?

Communication: Tell me what shapes you see in the bakery window.

Connections: Let's look at our geometry book and count how many rectangles we saw on our walk. (Connects to Number and Operations)

Representation: Can you make the shape of the church steeple with your hands?

Geometric Bubbles

DESCRIPTION

Geometric bubble wands take geometric exploration to a new level. These bubble wand frames form the edges, or outlines, of geometric solids, which are revealed when children dip the wands into bubble solution and create bubbles. Often the bubble film creates a secondary shape in the middle of the bubble wand; for example, the cube forms a clearly visible square in the center. Children also notice the lines moving from the corners of the cube to the corners of the central shape. The bubble film reveals some of the mathematical relationships that connect physics and geometry.

MATERIALS

☐ bubble wands showing the framework, or edges, of geometric solids, commercially available or make with pipe cleaners

☐ bubble solution

☐ container for the bubble solution that is deep and wide enough to submerge the wands

CHILD'S LEVEL

This activity is most appropriate for older preschool and kindergarten children. Younger children are often more interested in blowing the bubbles.

MORE >

WHAT TO LOOK FOR

• Children will immediately notice the geometric shapes created by the bubble wands, even if they can't name them.

• Children will notice the interior shapes in the bubble formations.

• Some children may name the three-dimensional geometric solids or the two-dimensional shapes formed by their sides (faces, in geometry).

• Some children will want to use the wands to blow bubbles.

MODIFICATIONS FOR SPECIAL NEEDS OR SITUATIONS

Some children may need help lowering the wands into the bubble solution. The activity will not work unless the wands are completely submerged.

MATHEMATICS CONTENT STANDARD CONNECTIONS

This activity connects to the Geometry standard. The nesting of shapes is also related to Measurement.

COMMENTS AND QUESTIONS RELATED TO MATHEMATICS PROCESS STANDARDS

Problem Solving: Find out what shapes each of these wands create.

Reasoning and Proof: Will this bubble wand always make a cube? Why?

Communication: What do you see in the bubble film on this wand?

Connections: How many lines do you see in the bubble? (Connects to Number and Operations)

Representation: Can you draw what the bubble cube looks like while your partner holds it?

Marshmallow Geometrics

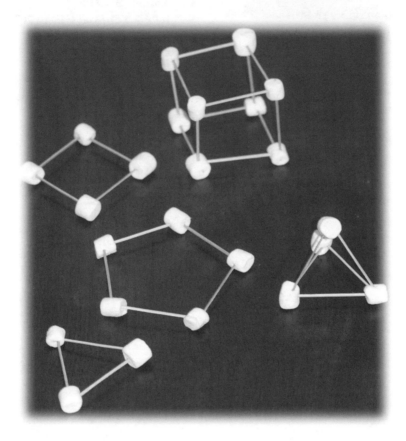

DESCRIPTION

Toothpicks and mini marshmallows provide the raw materials for children to explore both two- and three-dimensional geometric forms in this activity. After they have experimented with creating geometric shapes, children can expand their creations into architectural wonders.

MATERIALS

☐ mini marshmallows

☐ toothpicks or coffee stirrers

☐ models of geometric shapes and solids

CHILD'S LEVEL

This activity is most appropriate for older preschool and kindergarten children. Preschoolers may concentrate on creating two-dimensional shapes, while kindergartners may be ready to tackle geometric solids.

WHAT TO LOOK FOR

• Many children will be able to create two-dimensional shapes.

• Older children may expand their two-dimensional shapes into geometric solids.

• Children will talk about and compare the shapes they create.

MORE >

- Some children will expand their shapes into larger sculptures.

MODIFICATIONS FOR SPECIAL NEEDS OR SITUATIONS

For children with fine-motor challenges, large marshmallows and coffee stirrers can be substituted for small marshmallows and toothpicks.

MATHEMATICS CONTENT STANDARD CONNECTIONS

While this activity aligns with the Geometry standard, its emphasis on creating a model also connects it to Algebra.

COMMENTS AND QUESTIONS RELATED TO MATHEMATICS PROCESS STANDARDS

Problem Solving: What do you need to make a triangle?

Reasoning and Proof: Compare your cube to this model. Does it have the same points and edges?

Communication: What did you have to do to make the pyramid?

Connections: How many marshmallows do you need to make a cube? (Connects to Number and Operations)

Representation: Can you use the marshmallows and toothpicks to make these shapes?

The Wonderful World of Blocks

DESCRIPTION

Wooden blocks are arguably the best material ever created to support children's understanding of geometry. For this reason, they are showcased in this activity. Unfortunately, many preschool classrooms and even more kindergarten classrooms do not have wooden blocks, and those that do often have too few blocks to support children's creativity and learning.

The materials section of this activity describes the standard sizes and shapes of wooden blocks. The lengthy section on "What to Look For" explains that mathematical learning occurs when children have an adequate amount and variety of blocks as well as sufficient daily time to use them. Following this section are suggestions for teachers whose programs do not have and cannot afford commercial wooden blocks.

MORE >

MATERIALS

- ☐ Unit Block (A)
  - Size: 5½ in. long, 2¾ in. wide, 1⅜ in. thick
  - Minimum Amount: 50

- ☐ Half Unit Block (B)
  - Size: 2¾ in. long, 2¾ in. wide, 1⅜ in. thick
  - Minimum Amount: 20

- ☐ Double Unit Block (C)
  - Size: 11 in. long, 2¾ in. wide, 1⅜ in. thick
  - Minimum Amount: 40

- ☐ Quadruple Unit Block (D)
  - Size: 22 in. long, 2¾ in. wide, 1⅜ in. thick
  - Minimum Amount: 8

- ☐ Triangle Block (E)
  - Size: 5½ in. long, 2¾ in. wide, 1⅜ in. thick
  - Minimum Amount: 4

- ☐ Small Triangle Block (F)
  - Size: 2¾ in. long, 2¾ in. wide, 1⅜ in. thick
  - Minimum Amount: 8

- ☐ Large Cylinder Block (G)
  - Size: 5½ in. long, 2¾ in. diameter
  - Minimum Amount: 8

- ☐ Small Cylinder Block (H)
  - Size: 5½ in. long, 1⅜ in. diameter
  - Minimum Amount: 8

- ☐ Unit Arch Block (I)
  - Size: 5½ in. long, 2¾ in. wide, 1⅜ in. thick
  - Minimum Amount: 4

- ☐ Quarter Circle Block (J)
  - Size: 2¾ in. long, 2¾ in. wide, 1⅜ in. thick
  - Minimum Amount: 4

- ☐ Quarter Circle Arch Block (K)
  - Size: 5½ in. long, 2¾ in. wide, 1⅜ in. thick
  - Minimum Amount: 4

- ☐ Roof Board Block (L)
  - Size: 11 in. long, 5½ in. wide, ¼ in. thick
  - Minimum Amount: 4

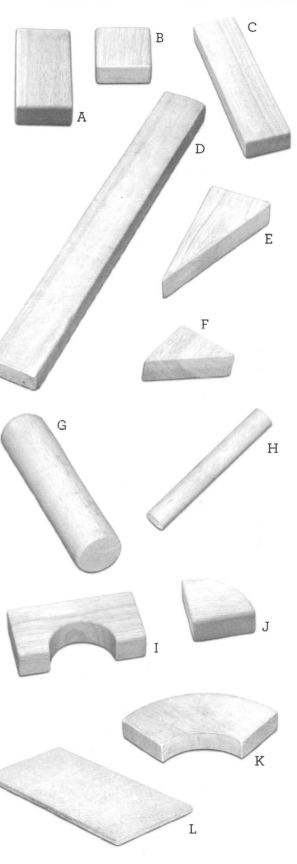

MORE >

CHILD'S LEVEL

This activity is appropriate for all preschool and kindergarten children.

WHAT TO LOOK FOR

- Children often start by placing blocks in flat, horizontal configurations.
- Children explore length (Measurement) by aligning rectangular and square blocks to form roads.
- Children may set identical rectangular blocks next to each other to create flat surfaces. In the process, they create a series of parallel lines where the edges of the blocks meet. They also explore concepts of area.
- Children may set square- and rectangular-faced blocks on their narrow sides to create fences and enclosures. In the process, they begin to explore concepts of perimeter. Where the blocks change direction, they can explore angles.
- Children will combine square- and rectangular-faced blocks with curved blocks to create circles and ellipses.
- Children will compare the lengths of blocks. They will discover that two half unit (square-faced) blocks are the same length as one unit block, and four half unit blocks are the same length as one double unit block.
- Children will discover that two of the triangular blocks can be put together to make a square. A square block and a triangular block form a house, or a pentagon.
- Children will sort the blocks by size and shape, particularly if the shelves are clearly marked.
- Children will explore the geometric properties related to balance. For example, they will find that a long rectangular block will balance securely on two cylindrical blocks, and they can build more blocks on top of this formation.
- Children will measure the span between blocks by trying to connect them with blocks of various sizes.

- Children will use positional terms, such as above, below, on top of, next to, under, and inside, in connection with the building process.

SUGGESTIONS FOR TEACHER-MADE BLOCKS

Cardboard Blocks

Dairy containers can be cleaned and used to make blocks. Use pairs of the same size of rectangular container, with one inserted inside the other and the bottoms facing out, to create various sizes of rectangular blocks. The blocks can be covered with contact paper or brown paper from grocery bags. Ask parents and friends to save the following sizes:

- half pints to make cubes
- pints to make blocks similar in size to unit blocks
- quarts to make blocks similar in size to double unit blocks

As children bring in their containers, the block area will grow.

Plastic or Metal Blocks

- Plastic food containers and cans with lids can be cleaned and covered to make curvilinear blocks.
- cocoa containers, such as Nesquik, to make elliptical solids
- coffee cans with lids to make cylinders
- spice cans to make small elliptical solids
- plastic spice jars to make small cylinders
- plastic peanut butter jars to make cylinders in various sizes (check about peanut allergies before using them in the classroom)

Wooden Blocks

Although they are not as heavy and well balanced as commercial hardwood blocks, substitute wooden blocks can be made from two by fours, which are used en masse to frame

MORE >

houses and other types of buildings. Although they are labeled two by four, the actual dimensions of these commercial boards is 1½ by 3½ inches. Some parents may be willing to donate a two by four, because they are not expensive. Building contractors and remodelers often have scrap pieces from two by fours that usually end up in a dumpster. They may be happy to save these pieces for your class. Once you've accumulated some lumber, the boards can be cut into sizes that are proportionate to traditional unit blocks, which are pictured earlier in this activity, but some modifications would be necessary to create the measurement equivalences of unit blocks that are such an important feature of them. Because two by fours are 3½ inches wide, lengths of 3½, 7, and 14 inches will correspond to half unit, unit, and double unit blocks, respectively. The wood will, of course, need to be sanded. It can be coated with polyurethane to protect the wood, guard against splinters, and make the blocks easier to clean. Do not use lumber that has been treated for outside use. It is not safe for children to handle.

MODIFICATIONS FOR SPECIAL NEEDS OR SITUATIONS

For children who may become overwhelmed in a large block area, start with two or three types of blocks, such as unit and double unit blocks, in a clearly delineated area.

MATHEMATICS CONTENT STANDARD CONNECTIONS

Block building is strongly related to Geometry, Measurement, Number and Operations, and Algebra (patterning).

COMMENTS AND QUESTIONS RELATED TO MATHEMATICS PROCESS STANDARDS

Problem Solving: We've run out of the long rectangular blocks. What could you use instead to build the structure you are thinking about?

Reasoning and Proof: How did you know that four of these unit blocks would be the same length as this long block?

Communication: What blocks did you use to create the high tower at the top of your building?

Connections: How can we tell if the bridge is tall enough for the car to go underneath? (Connects to Measurement)

Representation: Can you show how to support the roof? How many cylinders do you need?

CHAPTER 6

The Measurement Standard

Maryam, Jane, and Pooja worked diligently in the manipulative area hooking together interlocking blocks. As each finished her own strand, she joined it to the group's long chain. Soon the blocks stretched across the room.

"Look," said Pooja. "It's a snake!"

"It's a boa constrictor," added Jane.

"Let's measure it," said Maryam. She dragged a chair to the center of the room. "Get some more chairs," Maryam directed. Soon a line of chairs spanned a large length of the classroom. The girls placed the chairs adjacent to one another so that the front of one chair touched the back of the chair in front of it.

"Okay," said Maryam. "Let's put the snake on."

The girls lifted the snake across the chairs and stretched it out. It draped over the end of the last chair, so Pooja pushed it back, creating a loop in the chain.

"Now count the chairs," said Maryam. Together the girls counted, "One, two, three, four, five, six, seven, eight, nine."

"How long is your snake?" asked the teacher who had been observing from the book area.

"It's nine chairs long," Maryam proudly announced.

. . .

Measurement is the third area of mathematics designated by the National Council of Teachers of Mathematics as a curriculum target area for preschool and kindergarten (NCTM 2006). The Measurement standard encompasses aspects of their two other recommended curriculum focal areas, Number and Operations and Geometry. Even very young children make crude measurement comparisons, such as deciding which tricycle is the biggest or which bowl has the most cereal. Because young children are interested in measurement, already have some conceptual understanding of it, and will use measurement throughout life, it is considered an appropriate and important area for early mathematical study.

Teachers' Questions

How does the Measurement standard apply to young children?

For young children, the Measurement standard focuses on comparing objects and determining size relationships based on some identifiable, measurable attribute. While children begin by making gross, perceptual determinations of *more* and *less* or *big* and *little*, they gradually begin to seriate objects, such as aligning the bars on a glockenspiel from longest to shortest. Imposing order on objects based on measurable comparisons fascinates many children, as the popularity of nesting items attests. One teacher discovered the need for length-based order among her four- and five-year-olds when she added a bamboo xylophone to the music area. Although the instrument was designed to have varying lengths of bars placed in a random order, the teacher repeatedly discovered that the children had quietly rearranged them into a length-based order.

Eventually measurement by direct comparison leads to more logical and detailed measurement through the use of nonstandard and standard units (Clements and Sarama 2007). Young children need many experiences, however, before they fully understand unit-based measurement. For example, they typically do not realize that the units used to measure an item must be placed next to one another with no gaps. As the example at the beginning of the chapter indicates, they also do not initially understand that the object they are measuring must be straightened out, without curves or bends, if their measurement tool is straight.

What measurement concepts should teachers expect young children to understand?

Teachers should determine what children recognize as measurable attributes of objects, what language they use to describe their observations, and what strategies they use to solve measurement problems. In other words, what do children try to compare or measure, and how do they go about doing it?

Measurement begins with the physical knowledge children gain as they explore the attributes of objects. Through touching, lifting, pushing, dropping, and so forth, children determine key characteristics such as the following:

- A pumpkin is heavy. It is much harder to lift than a ball, even though the ball is just as big.

- Daddy's shoe is longer than my shoe.

- My big sister is taller than I am, but I'm taller than my baby brother.

As they make these initial comparisons, children inevitably harbor misconceptions based on their use of perceptions rather than logic (Piaget 1952). For example, children persist in their belief that a long, skinny glass holds more milk than a short, squat glass, even if they have just transferred the milk between the glasses themselves. The job of the teacher is not to try to correct these misconceptions, but rather to continue giving children many opportunities to physically explore materials and discuss their findings. These experiences cause children to eventually question their perceptually based responses and move toward more logical thinking.

Most preschool children measure by making direct comparisons, such as placing two shoes next to each other. Using an intermediate object for comparison purposes is another step along the lengthy developmental path to full understanding of measurement. With this in mind, the teacher might introduce an object for children to use in making length comparisons, such as shoe box lid to measure feet and shoe sizes in a shoe store set up in the dramatic play area. Kindergarten teachers and some preschool teachers may determine that their students are ready to use some sort of nonstandard unit to measure objects. Interlocking manipulative toys are useful for this purpose. When modeling language to describe measurement, teachers should be careful to refer to the unit, as in "Your hand measured ten beads long."

How do children develop an understanding of measurement concepts?

Experiences, especially when adults or peers comment on the experiences and pose questions, help children develop an understanding of measurement concepts. It is through the sharing of information that misconceptions come to light and are eventually replaced by more logical thinking. For example, children in Reggio Emilia, Italy, constructed the concept of a standard unit when measuring a table in their classroom (Morrow 1997). After deciding to use their own shoes to measure the table, the children discovered the shoes were not all the same size. This meant that the local carpenter, who was going to build a table identical to the one they were measuring, would not know what shoe to use to measure the new table-top. Meaningful experiences such as this, in which children can discuss and evaluate how to solve a real problem, lead to more advanced conceptual understanding. This is why the mathematics process standards are so important.

Teachers should also incorporate measurement into daily experiences in the classroom. For example, at lunch the teacher might ask, "Did I pour the same amount of milk in both of these glasses? What do I have to do to make them even?" In the block area, the teacher might comment, "Joe, your tower is taller than mine. How many blocks do I need to add to make my tower as tall as yours?" While both questions encourage children to make measurement comparisons, the second question introduces the idea of the block as a measurement unit. By incorporating measurement regularly, when it is of interest to children, teachers can help children solidify and expand their understanding of measurement.

How can teachers further support children's construction of measurement concepts?

In addition to taking advantage of natural learning opportunities within the classroom, teachers should plan intentionally for measurement learning opportunities. Measurement connects well with other areas of the curriculum. For example, some children's literature introduces measurement in a story format that children can reenact if interested. Because measurement is intricately linked to scientific inquiry, opportunities to compare and measure should be incorporated regularly into science experiences. Sensory table, cooking, art, and music activities also provide natural opportunities for children to engage in measurement. Examples of measurement activities throughout the curriculum are included in this chapter, along with important questions and comments for teachers to use to extend learning.

Can teachers directly teach measurement concepts?

While teachers cannot directly teach measurement concepts, they have a very important role to play in children's construction of these concepts.

First, teachers must plan appropriate activities to increase children's interest in measurement. When children show typical developmental misconceptions, teachers can interject comments or questions to cause disequilibrium. An example is Tower Race 2 (Activity 6.3), in which children create towers but use dissimilar units; therefore, the person using the smaller unit may roll more on the dice but end up with a shorter building. In trying to figure out why this is so, children must confront the disconcerting idea that the tower with bigger blocks has fewer units.

How can teachers modify measurement activities for children with disabilities?

While many children will not need any modifications for measurement activities, children with cognitive delays may need more time to make direct comparisons before moving on to using units when measuring. Teachers should design their activities to be open-ended so that children can use a variety of measurement strategies based on their level of thinking. For example, in Tower Race 2, the teacher might choose to use larger units for constructing the towers and smaller quantities on the die component of the activity for children who are working on quantifying very small amounts. This way, the child can still construct a tall tower while quantifying amounts that are understandable.

Many measurement activities take place within small groups. Teachers should serve as a facilitator for children who have more difficulty entering a group or cooperating with peers. For example, the teacher might say, "I promised to play the tower game, and here I am. Tommy is going to help me stack up my pieces." By providing a role for the child who may be left out, and by ensuring the success of the game through her presence, the teacher ensures that all children have the opportunity to participate.

Hide the Animal Game

DESCRIPTION

Young children delight in hiding things. This activity challenges them to find hiding places under boxes that differ in size for toy animals of various sizes. Measurement comparisons between the animals and the boxes are important if all of the animals are to have hiding places. For example, if a small animal is hidden under a large box, a large animal will have to be placed under a box that might be too small to hide it. The manipulative nature of this activity allows children to try placing various sizes of animals under different sizes of boxes, observe the discrepancies, and make adjustments.

MATERIALS

☐ 4–6 toy animals that vary in size

☐ 4–6 small boxes that correspond to the sizes of the animals

☐ a tray to hold the materials

CHILD'S LEVEL

This activity is most appropriate for preschool children who are experimenting with perceptual variations in size.

WHAT TO LOOK FOR

- Some children will randomly place the animals under boxes and then realize they must take account of the relative sizes of the animals and boxes.

- Some children will attempt to match the sizes of the animals to the sizes of the boxes.

- Some children will seriate the boxes and the animals.

- Children will use language related to size, such as "larger," "smaller," or "too big," as they play with the materials.

MORE >

MODIFICATIONS FOR SPECIAL NEEDS OR SITUATIONS

This activity is appropriate for all children; however, to avoid a choking hazard, teachers should carefully monitor the size of the materials with children who still put objects into their mouths.

MATHEMATICS CONTENT STANDARD CONNECTIONS

This activity aligns with the Measurement standard. Because children will be putting animals and boxes in a one-to-one correspondence relationship, it is also connected to Number and Operations.

COMMENTS AND QUESTIONS RELATED TO MATHEMATICS PROCESS STANDARDS

Problem Solving: Can you find a box to hide each of these animals?

Reasoning and Proof: Why isn't there a box left that is big enough to hide this animal?

Communication: How did you decide where to put the pig?

Connections: Do you have enough boxes for each animal to have one? (Connects to Number and Operations)

Representation: Can you show me an animal that will fit under this box?

Tower Race 1

DESCRIPTION

In this construction game, children take turns rolling one die or two and adding an equivalent number of construction pieces to their tower. The construction units are all the same size. Players try to build the tallest building possible without knocking it over. The game allows children to build on their understanding of measurement because the amount of units they can select has a direct effect on the size of their building. They can also compare units to determine how much higher another player's tower is.

MATERIALS

□ construction-related manipulative pieces of the same size, such as Duplo blocks, 1-inch cubes, or table blocks

□ 1 die or 2 dice

□ a basket to hold the manipulative pieces

□ a tray for each child to build on

CHILD'S LEVEL

This activity is appropriate for both preschool and kindergarten children. Younger children may focus more on size comparisons, while older children may be more interested in quantifying the heights of the buildings and making unit comparisons.

WHAT TO LOOK FOR

• Children will roll the dice to determine how many units to add to their buildings.

• Children will compare the heights of their towers.

• Some children will determine how many units taller one tower is than another.

MORE >

- Children will select a quantification strategy (global, one-to-one correspondence, or counting) commensurate with their level of thinking.
- Some children will add two dice together by counting all the dots or counting on from one of the sets.

MODIFICATIONS FOR SPECIAL NEEDS OR SITUATIONS

For children with fine-motor concerns, use blocks that hook together securely and can be fastened to a base plate. For younger children or children with cognitive delays, use one die with one to three dots per side. For children with visual disabilities, use raised dots on the dice that they can feel.

MATHEMATICS CONTENT STANDARD CONNECTIONS

This activity employs a consistent unit of measure (the building pieces) and therefore connects to the Measurement standard. In addition, due to its focus on the creation and comparison of sets, quantification, and addition, it also connects to the Number and Operations standard.

COMMENTS AND QUESTIONS RELATED TO MATHEMATICS PROCESS STANDARDS

Problem Solving: How many blocks do you get to add to your tower this time? Will that be enough to make it higher than my tower?

Reasoning and Proof: How do you know how many blocks higher your tower is than Ann's?

Communication: How many more blocks do you think you can add to your tower before it falls over?

Connections: Which color of blocks did you use the most in your tower? (Connects to Data Analysis and Number and Operations)

Representation: Can you show me a tower that is five units shorter than your tower?

Tower Race 2

DESCRIPTION

This activity is a follow-up to the previous activity, Tower Race 1 (Activity 6.2). This time the players use units that differ in size. This disparity causes children to think about the relationship between the size of the measurement unit and the number of units required to reach a particular height. Some interesting dilemmas may occur in this game. At first it may seem advantageous to use the larger units, because the tower grows quickly, but this may become a problem when the tower begins to teeter due to its height.

MATERIALS

☐ 2 sets of stacking materials, 1 of which has smaller pieces than the other

☐ 1 die or 2 dice

☐ tray for each child to build on

☐ 2 baskets, 1 for each set of stacking materials

CHILD'S LEVEL

This activity is most appropriate for older preschool or kindergarten children who may be better able to focus on both the size of the units and their relationship to the size of the towers.

WHAT TO LOOK FOR

• Children will roll the dice to determine how many units to add to their buildings.

• Children will compare the heights of their towers.

• Children will realize that the same number of units does not result in towers of the same height due to the discrepancy in the size of the units.

• Some children will revise the rules so they can switch the size of the units they use when it is to their benefit.

MORE >

MODIFICATIONS FOR SPECIAL NEEDS OR SITUATIONS

As with the previous activity, for children with fine-motor concerns, select units that easily hook together so children can successfully construct their building.

MATHEMATICS CONTENT STANDARD CONNECTIONS

This game connects to both Measurement and Number and Operations. It is a more complex measurement activity than Tower Race 1 due to its focus on the size of the measurement unit.

COMMENTS AND QUESTIONS RELATED TO MATHEMATICS PROCESS STANDARDS

Problem Solving: If you roll a five on the die, will your tower catch up to Ben's?

Reasoning and Proof: Your towers are just about the same height. Do they have the same number of pieces? How can you tell?

Communication: Can you explain to Erin why you have more pieces in your tower even though hers is taller?

Connections: What would happen if you alternated big and small building pieces? (Connects to Algebra)

Representation: Show me what a tower would look like if you used the same number of large blocks as there are small blocks in this tower.

Pinecone Potpourri

Some animals eat
pine nuts from the pinecone.

DESCRIPTION

There are many sizes and varieties of pinecones. Cones from the cypress family, which includes junipers and arborvitae, are usually small, with many less than an inch long. At the other end of the spectrum, western white pines may have cones that are ten inches long. Cones can be collected on nature walks, purchased at craft shops, or ordered over the Internet. They make an interesting study for the science center and lead children to naturally compare sizes.

MATERIALS

☐ assortment of pinecones that vary in size

☐ standard measuring tool, such as a ruler

☐ nonstandard measuring tool, such as unifix cubes

CHILD'S LEVEL

This activity is appropriate for both preschool and kindergarten children. Younger children are usually interested in more general size comparisons; they may seriate the pinecones, or arrange them in order by length. Older preschool or kindergarten children may be interested in using standard or nonstandard measurement tools to actually measure the length of the pinecones.

WHAT TO LOOK FOR

• Children will examine the pinecones and compare their lengths.

• Children will begin to use measurement language, such as longer, shorter, bigger, smaller, and largest.

• Some children will arrange the pinecones by size (seriation).

• Some children will use measurement tools to determine how long the pinecones are.

MORE >

MODIFICATIONS FOR SPECIAL NEEDS OR SITUATIONS

Remove the smallest pinecones for children who still put objects into their mouths.

MATHEMATICS CONTENT STANDARD CONNECTIONS

This activity aligns with the Measurement standard.

COMMENTS AND QUESTIONS RELATED TO MATHEMATICS PROCESS STANDARDS

Problem Solving: Can you find two pinecones that are almost the same size?

Reasoning and Proof: How can we tell for sure how long this pinecone is?

Communication: What is similar about these pinecones? What is different?

Connections: How many of these tiny pinecones (or unifix cubes) would it take to be as long as this big pinecone? (Connects to Number and Operations)

Representation: Can you show me how the pinecones would look if they went from longest to shortest?

Hoops—Measuring Circles and Sound

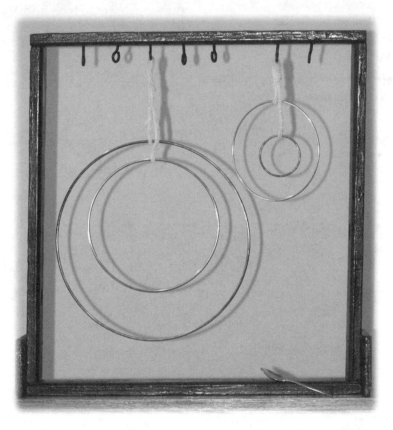

DESCRIPTION

This activity focuses children's attention on the relationship between the sizes of brass hoops and the sounds they create. It, therefore, connects the areas of mathematics (measurement), music, and science (physics). Several sizes of inexpensive brass craft hoops are suspended with string from a frame or peg-board divider. Children use a spoon to play them and quickly discover the larger hoop has a different (and lower) sound than the smaller hoops. As the hoops become smaller, their pitch becomes higher. Older children can use measuring tape or string to measure the diameter (distance across) and circumference (distance around) of the hoops.

MATERIALS

- several sizes of brass hoops, available in craft or fabric stores
- frame or peg-board divider with hooks to hold the hoops

MORE >

□ string to suspend the hoops from the frame

□ metal spoon to strike the hoops and create sounds

□ measuring tape or string to measure the hoops

CHILD'S LEVEL

All children will be interested in making sounds with the hoops. Younger children can compare the relative size of the hoop to the sound it makes, while older preschool and kindergarten children can actually measure the hoops.

WHAT TO LOOK FOR

• Children will play the hoops and notice they make different sounds.

• Children will compare the sizes of the hoops and the sounds they make.

• Children will begin to use measurement terms, such as small, large, and biggest, to compare the hoops.

• Some children will be interested in measuring the diameter and circumference of the hoops.

MODIFICATIONS FOR SPECIAL NEEDS OR SITUATIONS

No modifications are anticipated for this activity.

MATHEMATICS CONTENT STANDARD CONNECTIONS

This standard connects to Measurement. If children use a unit measure, such as unifix cubes, to measure the hoops, then it would also connect to Number and Operations. If children play patterns on the hoops, which they often do, then it also aligns with Algebra.

COMMENTS AND QUESTIONS RELATED TO MATHEMATICS PROCESS STANDARDS

Problem Solving: How long would the piece of metal have to be to make each of these hoops?

Reasoning and Proof: Is the diameter of this hoop longer or shorter than the circumference? Will the diameter of the little hoop also be shorter than its circumference?

Communication: Which hoops should I play if I want the song to be high like a bird singing?

Connections: Can you play a pattern on the hoops? (Connects to Algebra)

Representation: Can you arrange the hoops in order by size? How does it sound when you play them in size order?

Soda Shop

DESCRIPTION

For this activity, children use one cup measures to fill large, medium, and small glasses with colored water. The activity appeals to a wide range of children. Younger children make perceptual comparisons of the glasses and find they can fill the smallest glass quickest, perhaps with only one cupful of water. Older preschool children can quantify how many cups it takes to fill each size glass. Kindergarten children may wish to compare how many half cup measures versus one cup measures it takes to fill each glass.

MATERIALS

☐ water table, or plastic washtubs, filled with water colored with red food coloring

☐ 3 sizes of plastic glasses for each child using the area

☐ 1 cup measure for each child

☐ ½ cup measure for each child (optional)

CHILD'S LEVEL

This activity is appropriate for all preschool and kindergarten children.

WHAT TO LOOK FOR

• Younger children will eagerly fill the glasses. They may pour a small glass into a larger glass or attempt to pour a larger glass into a smaller one. Observing the results helps them understand size differences.

• Some children will count how many cups it takes to fill each of the glasses.

• Some children will notice that it takes fewer cups to fill the smaller glass than the larger glasses.

MODIFICATIONS FOR SPECIAL NEEDS OR SITUATIONS

Keep a close watch on children who may try to drink the colored water.

MORE >

MATHEMATICS CONTENT STANDARD CONNECTIONS

This activity deals with the measurement of volume and therefore aligns with the Measurement standard. Because some children will quantify the number of cups they use to fill a glass, it also coordinates with the Number and Operations standard.

COMMENTS AND QUESTIONS RELATED TO MATHEMATICS PROCESS STANDARDS

Problem Solving: Which glass do you think will hold the most water? How can you find out?

Reasoning and Proof: How can you prove that the smaller glass holds less water than the big glass?

Communication: Can I use this big glass to fill this little glass? What will happen?

Connections: How many half cups did you use to fill the big glass? Did you use more half cups or whole cups? (Connects to Number and Operations)

Representation: Can you put the glasses in order by size?

Ramp Race 1—Fast and Slow

DESCRIPTION

Racing toy cars is a natural interest of young children. In this activity, they change the slopes of two adjacent ramps and observe how this affects the speed of the cars. Older kindergarten children can time the cars with a stopwatch.

MATERIALS

☐ ramp frame made as follows:

1. Cut 2 3-foot lengths of 2 × 4 inch wood.

2. Drill 3 1-inch holes, evenly spaced, in each piece of wood.

3. Cut 1-inch wooden dowels into 3 pieces, each 2 feet long.

4. Sand the wood and glue the dowels into the holes to form a vertical ladder.

5. Cut 2 8-inch lengths of 2 × 4 inch wood. Glue and nail these strips to the bottom of each side of the ladder frame to support it.

☐ ramp boards made as follows:

1. Purchase 2 pieces of light-weight wood, ¼-inch thick and 4 feet long, to form the ramps.

2. Glue a strip of wood across the width of each board approximately 2 inches from the top of the board. This allows the boards to be hooked over the dowels on the frame.

☐ 2 identical toy cars

☐ stopwatch (optional)

MORE >

CHILD'S LEVEL

This activity is most appropriate for older preschool or kindergarten children who can easily adjust the ramps.

WHAT TO LOOK FOR

- Children will adjust the slopes of the ramps and notice that the car moves faster on the steeper of the two ramps.

- Some children will be interested in timing the cars, either with a stopwatch or by simply counting until they reach the bottom of the ramps.

MODIFICATIONS FOR SPECIAL NEEDS OR SITUATIONS

For children with visual disabilities, place an object such as a metal baking pan at the bottom of each ramp so the car makes a sound when it reaches the bottom.

MATHEMATICS CONTENT STANDARD CONNECTIONS

This activity focuses on the relative measurement of speed and, therefore, aligns to the Measurement standard. If children quantify the time it takes for the cars to reach the bottom of the ramps, it also aligns to Number and Operations. The activity connects to the Physical Sciences standard as well.

COMMENTS AND QUESTIONS RELATED TO MATHEMATICS PROCESS STANDARDS

Problem Solving: Which car do you think will win the race? Why?

Reasoning and Proof: How do you know the car on the steeper ramp will go faster?

Communication: What did you see when the two cars went down the ramps?

Connections: Let's see how many times we can clap before the car reaches the bottom. (Connects to Number and Operations)

Representation: Can you build some ramps in the block area? Then we can race cars again when we go inside.

Ramp Race 2— How Far Will It Go?

DESCRIPTION

This activity is an extension of the previous activity, Ramp Race 1—Fast and Slow (Activity 6.7). This time the focus is on how the slope of the ramp affects the distance the cars travel. Lines are created on the ground at the base of the ramps with tape or chalk, depending on the surface, and spaced twelve inches apart. Children can use the lines to measure how far the cars travel.

MATERIALS

☐ ramp materials from the activity Ramp Race 1—Fast and Slow (Activity 6.7)

☐ chalk or tape to create measurement lines 12 inches apart at the base of the frame

☐ data sheets to indicate the relative height of the ramp and record the distance the car traveled

RAMP RACE	
RAMP HEIGHT	DISTANCE TRAVELED
SHORT	
MEDIUM	
HIGH	

CHILD'S LEVEL

This activity is most appropriate for older preschool and kindergarten children.

WHAT TO LOOK FOR

• Children will initially use a global, or perceptual, strategy to determine how far the car has traveled.

• Some children will count the chalk or tape lines to determine the distance the car has traveled.

MORE >

- Some children will use the lines as relative distance markers but not count them.
- Some children will use the data sheets to record measurement data.

MODIFICATIONS FOR SPECIAL NEEDS OR SITUATIONS

For children with visual disabilities, use tape rather than chalk lines so they can feel the distance the car has traveled.

MATHEMATICS CONTENT STANDARD CONNECTIONS

This activity focuses on the measurement of distance and, therefore, connects to the Measurement standard. If children quantify the lines, it also aligns with the Number and Operations standard. If the data sheets are used, it connects to the Data Analysis standard.

COMMENTS AND QUESTIONS RELATED TO MATHEMATICS PROCESS STANDARDS

Problem Solving: Let's find out how far the cars go on each ramp. How can these lines help us?

Reasoning and Proof: How can you prove that the car on the highest ramp went the farthest?

Communication: How did you know the car on the low ramp would only go as far as one line?

Connections: By looking at your data sheet, can you predict how far your car will go on this ramp? (Connects to Data Analysis and Probability)

Representation: Use your data sheet to mark how many lines your car crossed. The data can help us remember that on the middle ramp, the car went past three lines.

How Tall Is My Pony?

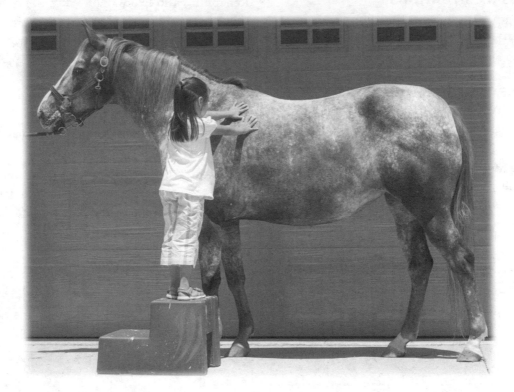

DESCRIPTION

Traditionally, horses and ponies have been measured in hands. This was a convenient unit to use before measurement became standardized. The horse was measured from the ground to the top of its withers, the shoulder area at the base of a horse's neck. The person measuring the horse turned his hands sideways and used them as a measurement tool. Today horses are still measured using hands, but the unit has been standardized to four inches.

Because many children are interested in horses and ponies, this activity gives them the opportunity to use their own hands to measure a drawing of a pony mounted to the wall. In the process, they are likely to arrive at different measurements, which can lead to an interesting discussion. Did Bobby put his hands closer together than Megan when he measured the pony? Is everyone's hand the same size? At some point, a standard four-inch hand can be introduced.

MATERIALS

☐ side view of a pony, from a poster or an enlarged version of the photograph in appendix C, mounted to the wall

☐ large piece of paper to record the measurements

☐ standard hand measure, drawn on a 4-inch-wide card

MORE >

CHILD'S LEVEL

This activity is most appropriate for older preschool or kindergarten children who are more likely to show interest in measuring with a unit.

WHAT TO LOOK FOR

- Children will be interested in measuring the pony and will need to be shown how high to measure.

- Most children will not place their hands next to each other when measuring. They need time and experience to figure out why this is important.

- Some children will notice that their hands are not all the same size.

- Children will compare the sizes of their hands to the standard hand unit.

MODIFICATIONS FOR SPECIAL NEEDS OR SITUATIONS

For children with visual disabilities, outline the pony in puffy paint. After the paint dries, they will be able to find the height of the withers by feel.

MATHEMATICS CONTENT STANDARD CONNECTIONS

This standard aligns to both the Measurement and Data Analysis standards due to its focus on a unit of measure and the recording and analysis of children's measurement data.

COMMENTS AND QUESTIONS RELATED TO MATHEMATICS PROCESS STANDARDS

Problem Solving: You can use your hands, turned sideways, to measure the pony up to here (point). Let's find out how tall it is.

Reasoning and Proof: Why do you think you and Charlie got different heights for the pony?

Communication: Let's talk about all the different heights we recorded for the pony. Did the pony change? What are your ideas for why our measurements are different?

Connections: How many hands tall did you count for the pony? (Connects to Number and Operations)

Representation: Show us how you measured the pony.

How Big Is a Foot?

DESCRIPTION

In this activity, the teacher traces each child's foot onto tagboard and helps cut it out. Children can use the cutout images of their feet to measure objects and distances in the room. The teacher can help children record the results and lead discussions about their findings. At some point, children can compare the size of their feet to a model cutout of a foot that is twelve inches long.

MATERIALS

☐ cutout of a foot for each child made by tracing each child's foot onto tagboard and cutting it out

☐ standard foot template made the same way but 12 inches long

☐ measurement sheets to offer suggestions of objects or distances to measure in the classroom

☐ ruler (optional)

CHILD'S LEVEL

This activity is most appropriate for older preschool and kindergarten children.

WHAT TO LOOK FOR

• Children will use their foot templates to measure but will leave space between the places where they set them.

• Some children will figure out that their foot units need to touch one another when they measure or the results will not be consistent or accurate.

MORE >

• Children may at first be surprised when they get a smaller measurement number while using the larger, twelve-inch foot template.

MODIFICATIONS FOR SPECIAL NEEDS OR SITUATIONS

No modification is anticipated for this activity.

MATHEMATICS CONTENT STANDARD CONNECTIONS

This activity connects to Measurement due to its use of a measurement unit. It also aligns with Number and Operations because units are quantified and with Data Analysis through the use and comparison of data collections sheets.

COMMENTS AND QUESTIONS RELATED TO MATHEMATICS PROCESS STANDARDS

Problem Solving: Use your foot cutout to measure how far it is between the sink and the stove in the dramatic play area. Can we fit the table in between?

Reasoning and Proof: What made you decide the table wouldn't fit between the sink and the stove?

Communication: Why was the table four feet long when Andy measured it but only three feet long when Sophie measured it?

Connections: Does it take more of your foot templates to go across the table or more of the twelve-inch foot template? (Connects to Number and Operations)

Representation: Show me how it looks when you measure the table with your foot template and when you measure it with a ruler.

Inchworm Measurements

The __doll__ was __10__ inches long.

DESCRIPTION

Young children do not yet understand that the units used to measure length must be contiguous (touch each other) or the measurement will not be accurate. Interlocking toy inchworms can give children experience measuring length using discrete units that touch one another. The children's book *Inch by Inch* by Leo Lionni connects well with this activity and inspires children to do their own measuring with the inchworms.

MATERIALS

□ interlocking inchworms, commercially available or made by adhering Velcro to the sides of 1-inch cubes and gluing "worms" made from foam strips to the tops

□ measurement fill-in strips, such as the following:

The _____ was _____ inches long.

□ a copy of the book *Inch by Inch* by Leo Lionni (optional)

CHILD'S LEVEL

This activity is most appropriate for older preschool and kindergarten children.

WHAT TO LOOK FOR

• Children will hook the inchworms together to measure objects but may not start measuring at the edge of the object.

MORE >

- Children may place their inchworms at a slant when measuring across an object.
- Some children will count the number of inchworms they use; others will use the connected strip as a unit of one.

MODIFICATIONS FOR SPECIAL NEEDS OR SITUATIONS

Children with fine-motor challenges may find the Velcro cubes easier to use than the commercial inchworms. Younger children or children with cognitive delays may need help filling in the measurement fill-in sheets, or the sheets can be omitted.

MATHEMATICS CONTENT STANDARD CONNECTIONS

This activity aligns with the Measurement standard. Because many children will also quantify units (inchworms), it also connects to Number and Operations.

COMMENTS AND QUESTIONS RELATED TO MATHEMATICS PROCESS STANDARDS

Problem Solving: How many inchworms tall is this doll?

Reasoning and Proof: If the row of inchworms goes across the table like this (from the bottom left corner to the top right corner, or diagonally), will it still reach?

Communication: What did you have to do to measure around the ball?

Connections: Did it take more inchworms to measure the length of the fire truck or the dump truck? (Connects to Number and Operations)

Representation: You can use this fill-in sheet to write down the number of inchworms you used.

How Big Is My Building?

DESCRIPTION

Once they have had some initial experience with measuring, many children become interested in measuring their own block structures. At first, materials with discrete units, such as the inchworms in Inchworm Measurements (Activity 6.11), are best to use because they help children understand the concept of a uniform unit. Later, teachers can show children how these units are organized and quantified on a standard measurement tool, such as a ruler or yardstick.

MATERIALS

☐ interlocking manipulative material, such as interlocking inchworms or unifix cubes

☐ classroom area with building materials, such as the manipulative or block areas

☐ standard measuring materials, such as tape measures or yardsticks

CHILD'S LEVEL

This activity is most appropriate for older preschool and kindergarten children.

WHAT TO LOOK FOR

• Children will link measuring units together to measure their buildings.

• Children may be surprised at how many units it takes to measure a tall building, which is a good time to introduce a standard measure, such as a tape measure, that already has the units connected.

MORE >

MODIFICATIONS FOR SPECIAL NEEDS OR SITUATIONS

For children with fine-motor challenges, use blocks that are easier to hook together, such as magnetic blocks, for the measurement units.

MATHEMATICS CONTENT STANDARD CONNECTIONS

Like many measurement activities, this activity aligns to both Measurement and Number and Operations standards. Children experiment with an important measurement concept, the use of units of the same size to measure objects. Since children quantify the units as part of the measurement process, the activity also connects to Number and Operations.

COMMENTS AND QUESTIONS RELATED TO MATHEMATICS PROCESS STANDARDS

Problem Solving: What would you like to use to measure your block building?

Reasoning and Proof: This block is six inchworms long. If we put two of these blocks together, how long will it be?

Communication: Tell me what parts of your building you want to measure. Then we can decide what tools to use.

Connections: I see you made a field for the cows. How many blocks long is each side of the field? (Connects to Number and Operations)

Representation: Stand next to your building. I'll take a picture so we can tell if it is as tall as you are.

T-Rex Footprint

DESCRIPTION

For generations young children have been fascinated by dinosaurs. In this activity, the teacher makes a paper footprint the size of a Tyrannosaurus rex foot. The children first estimate how many of their feet will fit into the T-rex footprint. Then the teacher traces around the children's feet to determine the answer.

MATERIALS

☐ large paper cutout, approximately 3-feet across, to represent the footprint of a Tyrannosaurus rex

☐ chart paper to record children's estimates

CHILD'S LEVEL

Estimations such as this are most appropriate for older preschool and kindergarten children; however, all children enjoy comparing the size of their feet to T-rex's foot.

WHAT TO LOOK FOR

• Children may wish to stand inside the dinosaur footprint before estimating how many of their feet will fit inside.

• Children will be eager to find out how many of their feet fit inside the footprint.

MORE >

MODIFICATIONS FOR SPECIAL NEEDS OR SITUATIONS

For children with visual disabilities who may have trouble seeing the outlines of the feet, teachers can tape cutouts of the children's feet (see Activity 6.10: How Big Is a Foot?) onto the dinosaur print rather than tracing around their feet. Children who have trouble seeing can feel the cutouts when quantifying them.

MATHEMATICS CONTENT STANDARD CONNECTIONS

This activity helps children gain a general concept of the measurement of area. It, therefore, connects to the Measurement standard. Because children will also estimate and quantify the number of their feet that fit inside the dinosaur print, this activity also connects to the Number and Operations standard.

COMMENTS AND QUESTIONS RELATED TO MATHEMATICS PROCESS STANDARDS

Problem Solving: How many of your feet do you think will fit into this T-rex footprint?

Reasoning and Proof: How can we find out whose estimate was the closest to the actual number of our feet that fit inside the dinosaur print?

Communication: Is there another way we can find how many feet are inside the footprint besides counting the outlines? (The people could be counted.)

Connections: If we do this activity again and use the teacher's feet, will there be more, fewer, or the same number of feet inside the dinosaur print? (Connects to Number and Operations)

Representation: Is there a way we can show which feet have been counted so we don't count them again?

Weighing Mini-Pumpkins

DESCRIPTION

Although young children have some concept of weight and may use labels, such as heavy and light, understanding how a scale measures weight is difficult for them to comprehend. Teachers often introduce the concept of weight with a balance scale so children can see the reaction of the scale when an object is placed on one of its sides. Children do notice that one side of the scale goes up and one side goes down. The surprise for teachers comes when they ask the child which side is heavier. Children almost always respond that the side that is higher is heavier, probably because they associate height with weight.

This activity offers opportunities for children to begin to correct their misconceptions about measuring weight. A small pumpkin or pumpkin-shaped gourd is placed on one side of the scale. Children then add weighted units, such as buckeyes, to the other side of the scale and wait for the scale to respond. When a weight equivalent to the weight of the pumpkin is reached, the sides of the scale are, again, balanced and even. Children can count the number of buckeyes necessary to equal the weight of the pumpkin. Repeated opportunities are needed for children to construct the relationship between weight and the behavior of the scale. Teachers can help by commenting on what they see, such as:

• The side with the pumpkin always goes down, doesn't it?

• It took sixteen buckeyes to balance the scale! The pumpkin must weigh as much as sixteen buckeyes.

MORE >

MATERIALS

☐ balance scale

☐ pumpkin or gourd

☐ basket of buckeyes, wooden cubes, or other items that are similar in size and weight to one another

CHILD'S LEVEL

This activity is most appropriate for older preschool and kindergarten children due to the abstract nature of measuring weight. Because they cannot "see" the weight of an object, they must instead observe the response of an intermediary tool such as a scale.

WHAT TO LOOK FOR

• Children will notice that the pumpkin lowers one side of the scale.

• Children may mislabel which side of the scale is heavier.

• Children will observe the behavior of the scale as they add buckeyes or other items.

MODIFICATIONS FOR SPECIAL NEEDS OR SITUATIONS

No modifications are anticipated for this activity. Teachers must, of course, use materials that are not a choking hazard for children who may still put things into their mouths.

MATHEMATICS CONTENT STANDARDS CONNECTIONS

This activity connects to both Measurement and Number and Operations standards because children must quantify the materials on the scale.

COMMENTS AND QUESTIONS RELATED TO MATHEMATICS PROCESS STANDARDS

Problem Solving: Watch what happens when you add buckeyes to this side of the scale.

Reasoning and Proof: What happened to change the scale?

Communication: Tell me what you did to get the scale to balance.

Connections: How many cubes balanced the pumpkin? (Connects to Number and Operations)

Representation: Let's keep a chart to compare how many buckeyes and how many cubes balance the scale.

How Much Time?

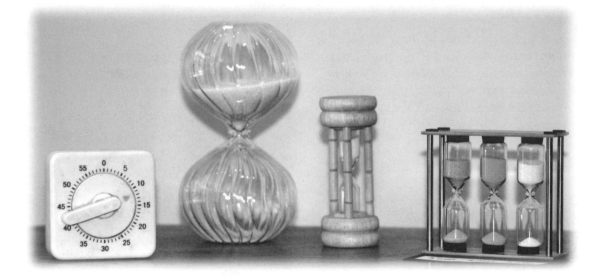

DESCRIPTION

Measurement of time is a very abstract concept for children. They can see the length of a block or feel the weight of a pumpkin, but they cannot see or feel time. Children have some concept of the passage of time based on routines in their daily life, such as during the school day, and they know time is measured by the adults in their world. Daddy may say they need to get to school by 8 a.m., or the teacher may indicate that each child can have a ten-minute turn on the computer.

Old-fashioned timekeepers, such as an hourglass or egg timer, allow children to relate a particular unit of time to something they can see. In this activity, suggestions are made for using several types of timers.

MATERIALS

☐ windup timer with bell

☐ wooden craft sticks

☐ egg timer

☐ hourglass

☐ clock with large Arabic numerals

CHILD'S LEVEL

Due to the abstract nature of time, this activity is most appropriate for older preschool or kindergarten children.

TYPES OF ACTIVITIES

Activity A—Windup Timer

Many teachers use a windup timer with a bell to manage turn taking. For children who are waiting for a turn, teachers can turn their waiting time into a measurement activity. When the timer is at the five-minute mark, give the child who is waiting five craft sticks. Help the child watch the dial on the timer. Each time another minute is reached by the countdown, the child can put one stick into a jar. When the bell rings, five minutes have passed and the last stick goes into the jar.

MORE >

Activity B—Egg Timer

Traditional egg timers have two small glass funnels that connect at their narrow ends, forming a conduit for a dry material, such as sand, to drip through. They are usually calibrated so the last of the sand reaches the bottom funnel in three minutes, which is the time needed to soft boil an egg. Teachers can use the egg timers in conjunction with other cooking activities. For example, when making pudding, each child can stir until the timer runs out. The other children at the table can help watch the timer and tell the teacher when the three minutes are up.

Activity C—Hourglass

Hourglasses are similar to egg timers, but they are usually much larger. They are calibrated so the last of the sand reaches the bottom when one hour has passed. In kindergarten, the teacher may appoint a daily timekeeper. At a given time, the timekeeper can carefully turn over the hourglass, and the teacher can set it in a safe place. The job of the timekeeper is to periodically monitor the hourglass and notify the teacher when the sand has reached the bottom. The teacher may plan this activity so it starts and ends on the hour. Then the teacher can show the children the position of the hour hand on a clock at the beginning and end of the hour.

WHAT TO LOOK FOR

- Younger children will find the egg timer easier to watch and relate to as a unit of time because it moves faster.

- Older children will begin to understand that an hour is much longer than a minute.

- Children will begin to perceive how long five minutes is through repeated use of the windup timer.

MODIFICATIONS FOR SPECIAL NEEDS OR SITUATIONS

For children with visual disabilities, place a dark background behind the egg timer or hourglass to make white sand easier to see.

MATHEMATICS CONTENT STANDARD CONNECTIONS

This activity aligns with the Measurement standard.

COMMENTS AND QUESTIONS RELATED TO MATHEMATICS PROCESS STANDARDS

Problem Solving: If I set the timer for six minutes instead of five minutes, how many sticks will you have put into the jar when the bell rings?

Reasoning and Proof: How can we tell that six minutes is longer than five minutes?

Communication: Tell us what the clock looks like now that the sand in the hourglass is all in the bottom.

Connections: How many sticks did you put in the jar before the timer rang? (Connects to Number and Operations)

Representation: What does the hourglass look like when half an hour has passed? What does it look like when one hour has passed? What does it look like when you first turn it over?

Making Playdough— The Many Ways To Measure

DESCRIPTION

This activity is positioned last in the chapter because it encompasses most of the measurement concepts highlighted in the preceding activities. Children will need to use volume measurers, such as a cup and a tablespoon, when making the dough. An egg timer can measure elapsed time during the cooking process—first while children stir the mixture, next while the teacher cooks the dough in an electric skillet, and finally when they are all waiting for the dough to cool.

After the playdough has cooled, children can begin playing with it. As their creations unfold, teachers can introduce various types of measurement if the children are interested.

For example, children often create long coils, or "snakes," with the dough. They may want to measure these snakes using a unit measure, such as the interlocking inchworms (see Inchworm Measurements, Activity 6.11). Other children may create spheres, or balls. Circumference can be measured with an intermediary object, such as a string, and the string can then be measured with the inchworms, paperclips, or some other unit material. Playdough also has weight. Children may want to place their creations on a balance scale and determine how many weighted units, such as wooden cubes, it takes to balance the playdough.

MORE >

MATERIALS

☐ Playdough Recipe

- 2 cups flour

- 2 cups water

- 1 cup salt

- 3 tbsp cream of tartar

- 2 tbsp oil

- Mix all ingredients.

- Heat in electric skillet until batter clumps together.

- Cool and knead.

☐ large mixing bowl

☐ large spoon for stirring

☐ measuring cup and tablespoon

☐ egg timer

CHILD'S LEVEL

Both preschool and kindergarten children enjoy participating in this activity. Teachers can vary the conversation, as well as the type and amount of measurement concepts incorporated into the activity, depending on the ages and experience levels of the children.

WHAT TO LOOK FOR

- All children will want some role in the measuring of the ingredients for the playdough.

- Many children will be interested in the timers.

- Some children will want to measure their creations.

MODIFICATIONS FOR SPECIAL NEEDS OR SITUATIONS

This activity is appropriate for all children.

MATHEMATICS CONTENT STANDARD CONNECTIONS

This activity connects to the Measurement standard. Because children must quantify units of measurement, this activity also connects to Number and Operations.

COMMENTS AND QUESTIONS RELATED TO MATHEMATICS PROCESS STANDARDS

Problem Solving: How can you find out how long your snake is?

Reasoning and Proof: Did we put more water or more oil into the bowl? How do you know?

Communication: What did you find out about how heavy your playdough is?

Connections: If you cut your playdough pizza in half, how many pieces will your have? (Connects to Number and Operations)

Representation: How many cups of flour does the recipe chart say we need?

CHAPTER 7

The Data Analysis and Probability Standard

"What kind of shoe are you wearing today?" This was the title of a large graph made with columns for tie, Velcro, buckle, boots, and slip-on. The kindergarten teacher introduced the graph on Monday at group time and planned to leave it in the classroom for the rest of the week. The children were very excited to use the graph. In fact, the teacher observed Olivia directing Kate's attention to the graph on Tuesday and again on Wednesday. The teacher overheard comments from Olivia, such as, "I wore the Velcro shoes that had the most votes yesterday, but today I'm wearing boots." The teacher wisely asked Olivia if her vote today would make a difference in the graph. Olivia thought for a moment. As she moved her name card from the Velcro column to the boots column, she proudly declared that Velcro and boots are now the same.

At group time, the teacher asked children to estimate how many buckeye nuts were inside a small, clear jar. The group of children ranged in ages from three to five years. Bonnie, age three, guessed the same number of buckeyes as her age, as did Rachel. Marisela, age four, estimated twelve, which was as high as she could rote count. Daniel, age four and a half, estimated ten; Aloke, age five, estimated 100. There were actually seventeen buckeyes in the jar. The children all agreed that counting was the best way to find out how many buckeyes were really in the jar.

· · ·

When teachers intentionally introduce the ideas of graphing and estimation, children readily become interested in problems such as those posed in the anecdotes above. Their experiences in classroom situations help children develop the broad base of mathematical understanding necessary for success in school and future careers.

Teachers' Questions

How does the Data Analysis and Probability standard apply to young children?

Young children are interested in data and probability and deal with these concepts on a daily basis. In addition, the Data Analysis and Probability standard supports the Number and Operations, Measurement, and Algebra standards. How many children came to school today? Are there more boys or girls? Are there enough cookies for every child to have two? Which pudding flavor got the most votes? What is the probability, or chance, that it will snow today? All of these questions connect to Number and Operations. Dealing with important data encourages young children to think and problem solve. For example, they might help graph the pudding votes and then decide which flavor has the most votes by looking for the highest column or by counting the votes. This connects number to measurement. Finally, problem solving is the heart of the Algebra standard. Graphing and estimation activities directly relate to problem solving.

Does sorting and classifying belong in the Algebra standard or the Data Analysis and Probability standard?

Sorting and classifying belong in both standards. As previously noted in chapter 4 on the Algebra standard, sorting and classifying are closely related to later patterning relationships and contribute to children's understanding of equality. Both are essential components of Algebra. Data Analysis takes sorting and classifying a step further by connecting it to Number and Operations. As children sort the data, they classify it according to attributes, and they quantify it; therefore, Data Analysis supports children's growing understanding of algebraic and numeric concepts.

How do class graphs support the Data Analysis standard?

Before data can be analyzed, it must be organized. The representations used in graphing activities help children organize, visualize, and analyze their data. Before graphing can begin, data must be sorted into categories. Predetermined columns on teacher-constructed graphs help children with this organizing process. In order for the data to have meaning, it must connect directly to something children can visualize and understand. The graphs in this chapter represent items of particular interest to children, such as the Shoe Fastener Graph (Activity 7.7) showing the type of shoes they are wearing or the Favorite Ice Cream Graph (Activity 7.6) showing their favorite kind of ice cream. The graphic representation of this information includes the name tag of the child it relates to. This makes the information relevant to children and helps them quantify data that otherwise would be difficult to envision.

What mathematical concepts do children construct through the use of class graphs?

The use of class graphs provides opportunities for children to think about classification, one-to-one correspondence, quantification, set comparisons, addition, and subtraction. Questions such as "How many people ride the bus, walk, or ride in a car to school?" inspire children to think deeply about important mathematical concepts. Children intently watch as each child's selection is transferred into the appropriate column on the graph. They see that all children who make the same choice are grouped together. Graphing strongly supports classification concepts. Children also see there is one bar on the graph for each child's vote. This reinforces concepts of one-to-one correspondence.

Children are eager to quantify as the graphs emerge. They want to know how many votes their column has. They look to see which column has the most. They chuckle about columns that have few or no votes, and they become excited if one column begins catching up with another.

Children tackle difficult concepts of addition and subtraction on graphs because they are eager to solve problems. If two columns have the same number of votes, it becomes important to speculate about how the addition of the votes of two absent children could affect the outcome. What is the likelihood that both children will vote for the same choice? If a column is catching up to their column, children will wrestle with subtraction strategies to find out how far ahead they are. Comparing the final tallies is also of interest. Children eagerly relate to their parents or friends how many more votes one group has than another. It is amazing how long children will persist with difficult problems when the results really matter to them.

What are some important criteria to consider when creating class graphs?

Always graph from bottom to top. Children are accustomed to making height comparisons of familiar things, such as block towers, people, buildings, or animals. Many children become confused if the graph starts at the top and goes down, because the columns all appear to be the same height.

Use clear pictures and/or words at the bottom of each column to indicate which votes will go in each one. Such attention to detail assures data is organized, collected accurately, and understandable.

Children are more interested in graphs if they can remember how each person voted. Therefore, teachers should print the children's names on slips of paper to fit onto the graph or let the children write their own name in their own way. It is important to make the slips of paper all the same size so that the graphing data remain consistent.

Be sure the name tags are carefully aligned. Otherwise, a column with fewer votes may look taller than a column with more votes. The graph can be marked in a grid manner to make placement easier. Using a dry erase marker, children can also write directly onto a graph that has been laminated.

Allow enough space in each column to record all the possible votes. Sometimes a large number of children select the same item!

Select a topic that is truly interesting to the children in the group. Children will not be motivated to think about mathematical concepts if the activity does not appeal to them. Graphs that correlate with a topic of interest are often effective. Children truly want to know which flavor of pudding they will make or how many children like a specific book.

Graphs for younger preschool children should be very personal. Graphing whether you are a boy or a girl or your age are good choices for them.

Older preschool children and kindergarten children more easily understand abstract choices. Graphs such as your favorite animal at the zoo, type of shoe fastener, and favorite character from a book are more easily understood by them.

What are some pitfalls to consider?

Teachers should avoid asking the entire group for a show of hands when voting. Younger children often vote for every choice, and older children might vote for the "winning" choice or for the same choice as a friend.

We want children to make independent decisions for the graph. Votes can be collected throughout the day, recorded on the graph, and presented at large group time. Children can be responsible for placing their name on a graph, such as in the Shoe Fastener Graph (Activity 7.7), in which choices may change as they wear a different type of shoe to school.

Be aware of ramifications of the topic you select. Voting for what you ate at Thanksgiving isolates children who do not celebrate that holiday for cultural or socioeconomic reasons. A vacation graph may make children who do not take vacations feel self-conscious.

Avoid cultural stereotyping. In a published curriculum discovered by the authors, children were asked to imagine they are a Navajo and to vote for whether they would rather herd sheep, make jewelry, or weave rugs. These selections suggest they are the only things Navajo people do. The same is true for assumptions about other cultural groups.

Avoid highlighting a "winning" choice on the graph. Older preschool and kindergarten children naturally gravitate toward competition and focus on winning and losing. Children should make autonomous choices when voting and focus on the mathematical concepts embedded in the graphing activity rather than on winning. The teacher's attitude and approach help avoid this pitfall.

How can teachers support children's math skills through their use of graphs?

Teachers can direct their comments and questions toward important mathematical concepts, such as on-to-one correspondence, counting, and set comparison. They can also use their questions to focus on processing standards. Children will notice a name is added to the graph for each child's vote. Teachers can reinforce this one-to-one correspondence relationship by periodically reading from the graph. For example, the teacher might say, "Let's see, so far Wendy, Tina, and Andre have voted for chocolate pudding." At that point, it is also natural to emphasize counting, as in, "That's one, two, three—three votes so far for chocolate." As the graphing process continues, teachers can draw children into a mathematical conversation. Questions such as "Which kind of pudding has the most votes so far? How do you know? Does everyone agree?" encourages children to problem solve, communicate, and employ reasoning and proof, which are three important mathematical process standards. Finally, teachers can draw attention to arithmetic operations. Questions such as "How many more votes does vanilla pudding have than strawberry?" start thinking about addition and subtraction as children count and compare one column with another.

How can teachers incorporate probability concepts into their teaching?

Well-timed questions encourage children to think about probability. While teachers don't expect children to know the answer right away or even at all, they hope children will begin to *think* about probability. Sometimes a teachable moment presents itself. For example, a teacher plays a board game and her mover is fifteen spaces ahead of the child. This is a teachable moment, and she asks, "Do you think you are likely to catch up to me on your next turn?" The question may cause the child to consider the relationship between the fifteen spaces on the path and the highest amount he can possibly roll on his next turn. What is the probability of getting fifteen on a pair of dice?

Teachers must also think ahead to questions that focus on probability. A class Author Study Graph (Activity 7.8) that records the results of voting for a favorite book in an author study is a good example. If a teacher anticipates one or more children will be absent on the day of the graphing activity, she could plan a question. The teacher might say, "*Rosie's Walk* has the most votes right now, but *Titch* is just three votes behind. How likely is it that all three children will vote for *Titch*?" Children may know at least one child likes *Rosie's Walk* the best, so it is impossible for *Titch* to catch up. They may consider other possibilities as well.

Why is estimation important?

"Estimation skills and understanding enhance the abilities of children to deal with everyday quantitative situations," according to NCTM. NCTM includes estimation as one of the standards for kindergarten through grade twelve. This standard focuses on estimation as a way to help develop "flexibility in working with numbers and measurement, and an awareness of reasonable results" (NCTM 1989, 38).

Estimation is a useful tool for choosing the best answer. Estimation also enhances the probability of choosing the most logical answer. For this reason, estimation is included in this chapter. Many children make errors in math calculations later in school because they fail to consider the *improbability* of their answers. Estimation activities for young children may help eliminate such errors for children in the primary grades. Children who make estimates and verify and refine them build a foundation for later experiences with problems.

Is estimation merely guessing?

Estimation is more than guessing; it is based on logic and previous knowledge. We want children to become familiar with the concept of using what they already know to make estimates, rather than making a wild guess. Their first estimates are likely to be guesses, unrefined and egocentric. Many preschool children initially estimate a quantity of objects to be the same as their age. Kindergarten children often like very large numbers, and their estimates reflect this when they respond to questions of quantity by saying "a zillion." They are also likely to be swayed by their peers and may select the same amount as a friend or the same number as the majority of the class. For this reason, teachers may want to solicit estimates from children individually, rather than during group time. Repeated experiences give children opportunities to consider the probability of their answer, and their estimates become more accurate. For example, if the small jar holds thirteen acorns, then the large jar will probably hold more.

When do children become more logical in estimation?

Children use more logical thinking strategies to estimate after they have had numerous experiences comparing their estimates to actual quantities. They also become more logical in their thinking when they are confronted with answers different from their own. Young children profit from many opportunities to solve problems using their own thinking strategies, but they also benefit when they hear another person's point of view. This forces children to rethink and defend their own point of view, sometimes leading to disequilibrium or new learning.

How can teachers incorporate estimation into the curriculum?

Teachers can plan interesting estimation activities as well as stimulate interest in estimation as part of natural experiences throughout the day. Specific activities planned by the teacher may highlight estimation as a possible method of determining quantity. Activities that coordinate with the rest of the curriculum or build on interests of the children are particularly effective. For example, if a class has recently visited a pumpkin farm, the children might be interested in estimating how many grooves are on a pumpkin. Other opportunities for estimation arise as children use materials in the classroom. For example, the teacher may suggest that children estimate how many marbles will sink a boat in the sensory table, how many seeds are in an apple or orange at lunch, or how many pieces of tape are needed to secure two pieces of paper together.

Recycling Game

DESCRIPTION

This activity encourages children to collect and sort the "trash" spilled onto a photo of a park or urban environment. Children roll the dice and collect trash from the environment. They not only quantify and compare the different types of trash, but also begin to sort it into categories as they observe the similarities and differences. Does this can have print like these others, or does it go with the soft drink group? Do all the large boxes get separated from the small boxes, or do they all go together? Well-timed questions by teachers encourage children to analyze the data and think about probability. For example, teachers might ask children questions, such as the following:

- How will you sort the trash you have collected?
- Will you collect all the boxes first or collect a little of each?
- What is the likelihood that you will collect more newspaper than cans on your last turn?
- Do you have more boxes or more cans?
- Will you collect more trash if you roll a pair of dice?

MATERIALS

☐ posterboard about 16 × 16 inches or large enough for a 3-inch border around the illustration

MORE >

- ☐ illustration of a pristine environment in a rural, suburban, or urban setting glued to the posterboard and laminated for durability (teachers can take a photo of the playground or other school grounds and enlarge it for use with the game)

- ☐ 2 or 3 small novelty trash cans, 6 inches high, or desk trash cans (available at office supply stores)

- ☐ 25–50 assorted small counters, such as cans and boxes found at novelty or party stores and catalogs

- ☐ 1–6 die or a pair of dice

- ☐ 1-inch graph paper for recording quantities of each type of trash collected

CHILD'S LEVEL

This activity is most appropriate for children who can quantify to at least six. The use of dice is most appropriate for older preschool and kindergarten children who can combine the quantities of dots on a pair of dice.

WHAT TO LOOK FOR

- Children may roll the die and take a corresponding amount of trash to put into their trash cans.

- Children may sort the trash into groups by attributes, such as type, size, or material, and place it into piles.

- Children may use the small trash items to form a graph on the table by making columns of trash sorted by attributes.

- Children will use the graph paper to align items by category.

- Children may count or compare quantities of different types of trash.

MODIFICATIONS FOR SPECIAL NEEDS OR SITUATIONS

Depending on individual needs, teachers can substitute a large die or spinner, empty food containers like small cans or empty individual cereal boxes, and crumpled newspaper pieces, along with a small bathroom or kitchen trash can. Try using one with a flip lid or a step to press for opening the lid. The larger items will be more easily distinguished from each other. The quantities of dots on the die or spinner can be adjusted for developmental levels. Intriguing "trash" may attract some children who avoid other traditional math activities. Kindergarten children can use the graph paper for recording the results of sorting the collection of trash.

MATHEMATICS CONTENT STANDARD CONNECTIONS

Sorting the trash into categories aligns with the Data Analysis and Probability standard. As children roll the die or dice and take an equivalent amount of trash, they are applying concepts of the Number and Operations standard. Because children model a problem using concrete materials, they also employ Algebra.

COMMENTS AND QUESTIONS RELATED TO MATHEMATICS PROCESS STANDARDS

Problem Solving: How many more pieces of trash do you have to collect to clean the area?

Reasoning and Proof: Do you have more boxes or more cans? How can you tell?

Communication: How would you like to sort the trash?

Connections: Did you collect the same amount of cans as you did boxes? How do you know? (Connects to Number and Operations)

Representation: Use the graph paper to show how many pieces of each kind of trash you collected. How will you remember how many pieces of each you had?

Animal Families

DESCRIPTION

Many teachers include toy animals as accessories in the block area. This activity shows a particular way to organize such materials to encourage mathematical thinking and problem solving in young children. The setup includes animals for children to group based on common attributes or by animal families. Children often struggle to understand the concept that objects can belong to more than one category. For example, the cow may be viewed as belonging to the set of animals, the set of black and white animals, the set of animals with spots, and the set of cows. Children make errors in thinking when asked if there are more cows or more animals. They focus attention on one attribute at a time and often answer by indicating "more cows." The use of concrete materials and intentional teaching strategies helps children construct important relationships, which are the foundation of mathematics.

MATERIALS

- ☐ 5 or more plastic animal families, each with at least 1 adult and 2 babies
- ☐ 1 additional adult and other babies to add in subsequent weeks

CHILD'S LEVEL

This activity is appropriate for preschool children of all ages. Younger children may play with the animals in a pretend play manner for an extended period of time and eventually become more interested in questions posed by the teacher.

MORE >

WHAT TO LOOK FOR

- Children will group the baby animals with the corresponding adult animals.

- Children will quantify the number of baby animals and adult animals in each family.

- Some children will count to quantify how many animals, adult animals, or baby animals they have.

- Some children will group the animals by size, color, spots, horns, etc.

MODIFICATIONS FOR SPECIAL NEEDS OR SITUATIONS

Children with cognitive or language delays may need more time to explore the animals in a pretend manner. They may also need assistance learning the names and signs for the animals or using an augmentative language device programmed with the appropriate vocabulary. The activity can be made more challenging by increasing the types of animals available.

MATHEMATICS CONTENT STANDARD CONNECTIONS

As children group animal families, they analyze the data they have collected; therefore, the activity connects to the Data Analysis standard. This activity also aligns with Number and Operations because it incorporates concepts of one-to-one correspondence, counting, set comparisons, addition, and subtraction. Some children may think about Measurement as they use the blocks to build enclosures for the animals. For example, they might ask, "Will the cows need a larger pen than the sheep?" Since the activity also allows children to model a mathematical problem, it incorporates aspects of the Algebra standard.

COMMENTS AND QUESTIONS RELATED TO MATHEMATICS PROCESS STANDARDS

Problem Solving: Do all of the mother animals have the same number of babies?

Reasoning and Proof: Yarick, you say you have more cows than farm animals. How did you figure that out?

Communication: Can you tell me which animals go together?

Connections: How many more baby animals do you need to have three in each family? (Connects to Number and Operations)

Representation: What would you do if you had only three pens for the animals? Which ones would you put together?

Personal Graph for Snack

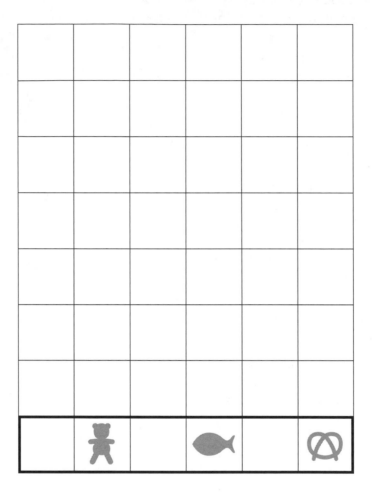

DESCRIPTION

In this activity, children receive a small bag containing safe snack food, such as various cereals, crackers, and pretzels. Teachers make decisions about which foods to include based on their knowledge of children's allergies and the school policy about food. The children use one-inch graph paper to record their quantities of food in their own way. Be sure to tell children they will get to eat the snack after they make the graph!

MATERIALS

☐ individual bags of food containing the following:

• 2–5 goldfish crackers

• 2–5 teddy bear crackers

• 2–5 pretzels

☐ 1-inch graph paper with illustrations of the food at the bottom of each column

☐ pencil, marker, or crayon

MORE >

CHILD'S LEVEL

This graphing activity is most appropriate for kindergarten children who have had experiences with group graphing activities.

WHAT TO LOOK FOR

- Some children may make a line in an appropriate number of squares on the graph paper to indicate the quantity of food they ate in each category.

- Some children will fill in the appropriate number of spaces in each column on the graph paper to indicate the quantity of food they ate in each category.

- Some children will draw a picture of each food item in an appropriate number of spaces in each column on the graph paper.

- Some children will use numerals to record the quantity of food they ate in each category.

- Some children may place the food on the graph to determine how many of each type they have.

MODIFICATIONS FOR SPECIAL NEEDS OR SITUATIONS

For children with cognitive delays, reduce the amount of food in each category and limit the categories to two. More food can be added after the math portion of the activity.

MATHEMATICS CONTENT STANDARD CONNECTIONS

The individual graphs help children organize and interpret data, which is the focus of the Data Analysis and Probability standard. Because children create and compare sets of food, the activity also aligns to Number and Operations.

COMMENTS AND QUESTIONS RELATED TO MATHEMATICS PROCESS STANDARDS

Problem Solving: Which food do you have the least of?

Reasoning and Proof: How can I tell from your graph how much of each food you have?

Communication: Tomorrow Dena wants to have the same amount of teddy bears as you had. Can you tell her how many you have?

Connections: Which column on your graph is the tallest? (Connects to Measurement)

Representation: How can you represent the food in your bag on this paper so we can remember what was in the bag after you eat snack?

Seashell Collection

DESCRIPTION

Many children are interested in exploring a collection of shells. Teachers can find an inexpensive basket filled with shells at a dollar store or craft store. Some teachers will be lucky enough to live in a place where they can collect the shells. Display the shells in a basket or on a tray that is divided into four or five sections. Begin with a smaller collection and add to it in subsequent weeks; this encourages children to more closely observe similarities and differences and to sort the shells in a variety of ways. Shells sold in a craft store may not differ much in color, but they have numerous other characteristics such as ridges, spiral or flat shapes, stripes or not, etc.

MATERIALS

- ☐ 25–30 shells in 3 types, with large and small shells in each type
- ☐ other shells to add to the collection after initial exploration by children (add a new type of shell perhaps)
- ☐ basket for holding shells
- ☐ divided container for sorting the shells

CHILD'S LEVEL

Preschool and kindergarten children will enjoy this collection.

WHAT TO LOOK FOR

- • Children usually focus on the type of shell when they initially sort them.

MORE >

- Children may sort by any attribute they perceive from their observations.

- Some children will quantify types of shells.

- Some children will compare how many shells are in each group.

MODIFICATIONS FOR SPECIAL NEEDS OR SITUATIONS

Do not include small shells for groups in which children still put things into their mouths.

MATHEMATICS CONTENT STANDARD CONNECTIONS

Sorting and classifying are elements of both Data Analysis and Probability and Algebra, so this activity aligns directly with both standards.

COMMENTS AND QUESTIONS RELATED TO MATHEMATICS PROCESS STANDARDS

Problem Solving: Is there another type of shell that could go with this one?

Reasoning and Proof: Do you have more spiral shells or more flat shells? How can you tell?

Communication: How did you decide these shells go together?

Connections: Can you sort the shells by their shapes? (Connects to Geometry)

Representation: This tray has five sections, but you only used three of them. How would you sort the shells if you had to use all of the sections?

Apple Tasting Graph

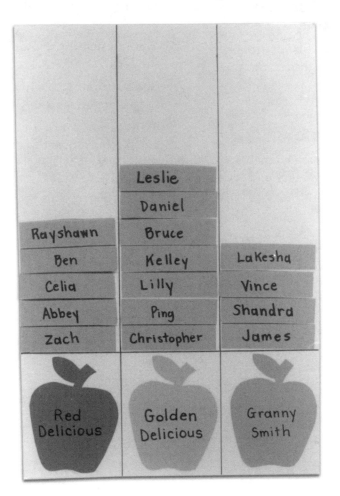

DESCRIPTION

Most children are familiar with apples. In this activity, children taste three types and colors of apples, such as Granny Smith, Red Delicious, and Golden Delicious. The results of which apple children think tastes the best are recorded on a graph and kept in the classroom. Children often return to confirm the results or check for new votes. Teachers can use the graph in large or small group settings as a catalyst for discussions related to Data Analysis and Probability.

MATERIALS

- ☐ 3 different types and colors of apples
- ☐ red, yellow, and green strips of paper mounted on white posterboard to form the columns of the graph
- ☐ illustration of each type of apple at the bottom of each column
- ☐ name tag for each child

MORE >

CHILD'S LEVEL

Older preschool and kindergarten children are intrigued with taste differences and are excited about this graph. Younger children, on the other hand, often have difficulty selecting a favorite apple. Their interest lies in eating the apples, but this graph may be less appealing to them.

WHAT TO LOOK FOR

- Children may want to vote for more than one apple.

- Children may count to quantify how many votes each type of apple received.

- Children may compare column heights to determine whether there are more, fewer, or the same number of votes for each apple.

- A few children may subtract to determine how many more votes one column has than another.

MODIFICATIONS FOR SPECIAL NEEDS OR SITUATIONS

No modifications are anticipated for this activity.

MATHEMATICS CONTENT STANDARD CONNECTIONS

Although the focus of this activity is collecting, recording, and reviewing data, which aligns to the Data Analysis standard, it also incorporates elements of Number and Operations. Children quantify the number of votes, compare sets, and sometimes use addition and subtraction to do so. If children use the height of the columns to compare sets, they engage in aspects of the Measurement standard as well. Because the activity offers opportunities for problem solving, Algebra is involved.

COMMENTS AND QUESTIONS RELATED TO MATHEMATICS PROCESS STANDARDS

Problem Solving: How many votes do Golden Delicious apples have?

Reasoning and Proof: Which is the most popular kind of apple? How do you know?

Communication: How can we tell the afternoon class how many people voted for each type of apple?

Connections: Which column is the highest? Does it have the most votes? (Connects to Measurement)

Representation: What would happen if two more people vote for Granny Smith apples?

Favorite Ice Cream Graph

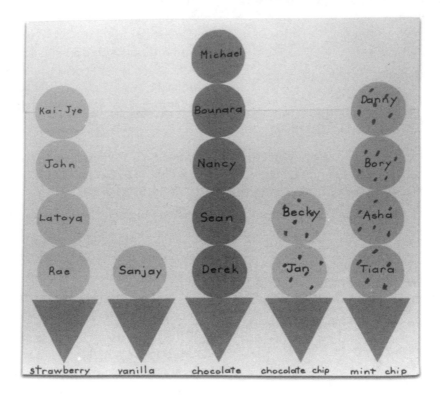

DESCRIPTION

For this graphing activity, each child chooses one of several predetermined flavors of ice cream. The selections are then graphed. Instead of bars, this graph uses circles so that the columns look like giant ice cream cones. Teachers determine the selection of ice cream flavors; otherwise there might be too many choices. Chocolate, vanilla, strawberry, mint, and cookies and cream are some suggestions.

MATERIALS

☐ posterboard or paper, 18 × 16 inches or a size large enough to accommodate all of the children's decisions, laminated for durability

☐ brown construction paper cones to form the base of each column (write the name of each flavor below the cone

☐ name tags made from construction paper circles in colors to represent the ice cream flavors

☐ tape to attach the name tags to the chart

CHILD'S LEVEL

Both preschool and kindergarten children like talking about ice cream. For younger preschoolers, this activity should follow an ice cream tasting experience to make it more concrete. Teachers may want to ask children individually for their votes and compile the

MORE >

data on the graph at a later time. Kindergarten children often want to vote the same as their friends or for the "winning" choice.

WHAT TO LOOK FOR

- Children may count to quantify how many votes each flavor of ice cream received.
- Children may compare the quantity of votes received by each flavor.
- Children may determine how many more votes a flavor needs to equal the votes of a different flavor.

MODIFICATIONS FOR SPECIAL NEEDS OR SITUATIONS

For children with visual disabilities, the name tags could be made of felt, foam, and other textured materials with braille or raised print used for the names. The cones could be made of sandpaper. The textured graph could be read by a child with a visual disability and is appealing to all children.

MATHEMATICS CONTENT STANDARD CONNECTIONS

This activity aligns directly to the Data Analysis and Probability standard because children are organizing and interpreting data. Because children are quantifying and comparing the amount of votes each flavor received, it is also connected to Number and Operations. Some children may employ Measurement to compare the columns.

COMMENTS AND QUESTIONS RELATED TO MATHEMATICS PROCESS STANDARDS

Problem Solving: Which flavor has the fewest votes?

Reasoning and Proof: Are there more votes for all ice cream flavors or more votes for chocolate?

Communication: Kam, tell Damian which flavor you think has the most votes.

Connections: How many more votes does mint need to have the same as strawberry? (Connects to Number and Operations)

Representation: If the teachers vote for vanilla, will that change the results?

Shoe Fastener Graph

buckles	shoelaces	velcro	no fasteners
		Elizabeth	
		Jamie	
	Anna	Sammy	
	Latoya	Ketan	
Katrina	James	Andre	Dong-Wan
Deaira	Virgil	Mittoo	Nancy

DESCRIPTION

Children seem to be very interested in their shoes. For this graph, they are asked how their shoes fasten. The graph is made on a magnetic whiteboard, and the name tags have magnetic tape on the back. This allows children to change the graph each day if they wear different shoes. Each day children check the data collected to see if their vote or the votes of others changes the results. Teachers assess the types of shoes worn by children and determine which ones to use on the graph. One column should be included for "no fasteners" or "slip-on" as a category of shoes.

MATERIALS

☐ magnetic whiteboard, posterboard, or paper large enough to accommodate all of the children's decisions

☐ small buckle, shoelace bow, and piece of Velcro to identify each column

☐ name tag for each child with magnetic tape attached to the back for the whiteboard or cellophane tape for attaching paper name tags

CHILD'S LEVEL

This is a good beginning graph for preschool children who are very interested in their own shoes. Kindergarten children also like this graph and enjoy comparing the results of the data collection, which regularly changes as children wear different shoes. Some children might decide to wear particular shoes to influence the results of the data on the graph!

MORE >

WHAT TO LOOK FOR

- Children may count to quantify how many children have each type of fastener.

- Children may compare column heights to determine whether there are more, fewer, or the same number of name tags for each type of shoe fastener.

- Some children will subtract to determine how many more votes one type of shoe fastener received than another.

MODIFICATIONS FOR SPECIAL NEEDS OR SITUATIONS

The shoe fasteners on the graph are three-dimensional, making the graph accessible to all children. Name tags can be made using a braille machine or raised print.

MATHEMATICS CONTENT STANDARD CONNECTIONS

Although the graph itself, which is a collection of data, directly aligns with Data Analysis and Probability, most children will also want to compare the number of votes for each type of shoe. This relates to the Number and Operations standard. Some children may add or subtract to quantify how many more votes are needed to make columns equal.

COMMENTS AND QUESTIONS RELATED TO MATHEMATICS PROCESS STANDARDS

Problem Solving: What is the most common type of shoe fastener in the class today?

Reasoning and Proof: How will you know which type of shoe fastener had the fewest votes?

Communication: Are more people wearing shoes with shoelaces or slip-ons today?

Connections: Two columns are the same height. Do they have the same number of votes? (Connects to Measurement)

Representation: How many children will need to wear shoes with Velcro fasteners to make that column have the most votes?

Author Study Graph

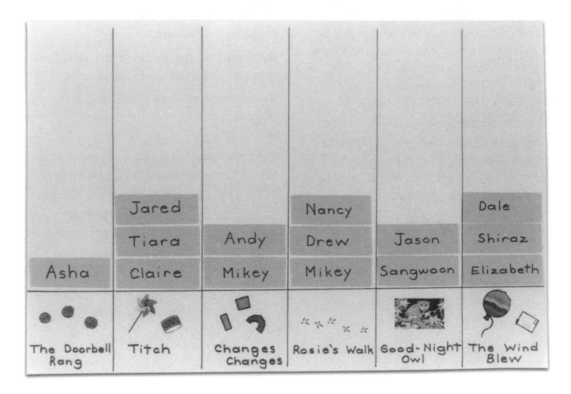

DESCRIPTION

This graph is a concluding activity for a unit on author Pat Hutchins that includes her books *The Doorbell Rang; Titch; Changes, Changes; Rosie's Walk; Good-Night, Owl!;* and *The Wind Blew.* The children vote for their favorite book. This is sometimes difficult for children who may have liked several or all of the books. Voting for only one choice is an important concept of Data Analysis and Probability.

MATERIALS

☐ posterboard or paper, 18 × 12 inches or a size large enough to accommodate all of the children's decisions, laminated for durability

☐ illustrations to represent each book placed at the bottom of each column

☐ name tag for each child in the class

CHILD'S LEVEL

This topic is more abstract than topics related directly to children, such as shoe fasteners used for the Shoe Fastener Graph (Activity 7.7). Therefore, this graph is more appropriate for older preschool and kindergarten children and should follow other activities that involve more concrete graphs.

WHAT TO LOOK FOR

• Children may count to quantify how many votes each book received.

MORE >

- Children may not realize that a column with no votes has less than a column with one vote.

- Children may compare column heights to determine whether there are more, fewer, or the same number of votes for each book.

- A few children may subtract to determine how many more votes one column has than another.

MODIFICATIONS FOR SPECIAL NEEDS OR SITUATIONS

For children with visual disabilities, consider using a tactile representation for each book, such as foam cutouts of a cookie, child, hen, owl, and umbrella. The name tags can be written in braille or raised print.

MATHEMATICS CONTENT STANDARD CONNECTIONS

This activity aligns primarily with Data Analysis and Probability as children organize and interpret data. It also includes elements of the Measurement standard. Children may think about the application of number to measurement when they use the height of the columns to compare votes.

COMMENTS AND QUESTIONS RELATED TO MATHEMATICS PROCESS STANDARDS

Problem Solving: Did any of the books receive the same number of votes?

Reasoning and Proof: How many more votes does *Titch* have than *The Doorbell Rang*? How do you know?

Communication: Let's write a note to the afternoon class to tell them the results of our vote. What should I write down so we remember how many votes each book received?

Connections: Which column is the highest? Does it also have the most votes? (Connects to Measurement and Number and Operations)

Representation: If you vote for *Changes, Changes,* will that book have the most votes?

Recording Permission Slips

Zoo Permission Slips

Yes	Not Yet
Shiraz	
Andy	
Mikey	
Elizabeth	
Drew	Sangwoon
Claire	Dale
Molly	Jason
Nancy	Asha
Tiara	Jared
Thisara	Daniel

DESCRIPTION

This graph has a practical purpose. It records data about who has or has not yet returned field trip permission slips. The data changes as permission slips are brought to school. Teachers can use a cookie sheet with magnetic properties and name tags with magnetic tape on the back to collect the data. Children are responsible for placing their name tag on the graph. Perhaps one or two children could be assigned the job of counting and recording data each day. Teachers might pair more capable peers together with children who are struggling with mathematical concepts. Peer modeling is a good way to further learning for all children.

MATERIALS

☐ magnetic cookie sheet, posterboard, or paper large enough to accommodate all of the children's decisions

☐ illustration of a completed permission form to mark 1 column

☐ name tag for each child, with either magnetic or cellophane tape on the back to attach the tag to the graph

CHILD'S LEVEL

Field trips are a part of many preschool and kindergarten programs, and collecting permission slips is a significant part of

MORE >

the process. Therefore, both preschool and kindergarten children are interested in this graph.

WHAT TO LOOK FOR

- Many children will be interested in counting how many permission slips have or have not been returned.

- Children will compare the quantities of permission slips returned to the quantity not yet returned.

- Some children will count the name tags in both columns to verify that everyone has recorded his or her result.

- Many children will eagerly return to the graph every day to see the results.

MODIFICATIONS FOR SPECIAL NEEDS OR SITUATIONS

No modifications are anticipated for this activity. Children's names can be written in braille if appropriate.

MATHEMATICS CONTENT STANDARD CONNECTIONS

This activity aligns with both Data Analysis and Probability and Number and Operations. Children collect the data and quantify the results of the data collection. Because children are creating a mathematical model on the graph, it also aligns with Algebra.

COMMENTS AND QUESTIONS RELATED TO MATHEMATICS PROCESS STANDARDS

Problem Solving: How many permission slips have been brought back so far?

Reasoning and Proof: How many permission slips will we have when everyone has returned his or her permission slip?

Communication: If two more children bring their permission slips today, will the columns be equal?

Connections: How tall is the column for children who have returned their permission slips? (Connects to Measurement)

Representation: Max and Elena, be sure to write how many children have returned their permission slips and how many have not.

Lunch Menu Graph

Choose your favorite fruit.		
Yannick		
Bonnie		
Sally		
MaryBeth		
Claire	Stephen	
Jeffery	Bobby	
Evan	Peter	
Cathy	Charlie	Tamara
Megan	Brenda	Kurt

for example. Teachers work together with the food staff to narrow the choices to two or three per category.

Example (see photo)

Main Course: pizza, chicken nuggets, macaroni and cheese

Vegetable: green beans, carrots, spinach

Fruit: oranges, apples, peaches

A label is placed at the bottom of each column with the name and picture of the food choice. At the top of each graph, include a sentence, such as "What is your favorite fruit?" Teachers may write the names of children on slips of paper, or children may do so. The name tags should all be the same size in order to accurately align them on the columns of the graph and compare quantities in each column.

MATERIALS

☐ Three pieces of posterboard or paper, one for each graph, 18 × 12 inches or a size large enough to accommodate all of the children's decisions, laminated for durability

☐ illustrations to represent the food choices at the bottom of each column, as pictured

☐ three sets of name tags for each child in the class

DESCRIPTION

Teachers sometimes have the opportunity to collaborate with the food preparation staff at school. When this is possible, children may occasionally choose the food for lunch or snack. One way to record this information is by graphing the results. For this activity, several graphs are needed—one each for main course, vegetable, and fruit choices,

CHILD'S LEVEL

All children are interested in choices when it comes to food. Most preschool and kindergarten children eagerly wait their turn to vote for their choice and keep tabs on the results of the voting. Children do not have to participate, but most of them want to vote and influence the choices for lunch or snack.

MORE >

WHAT TO LOOK FOR

• Children will discuss and debate which food to vote for.

• Children will compare the heights of the columns to determine which food has the most or fewest votes.

• Some children will count the votes in each column and compare amounts.

MODIFICATIONS FOR SPECIAL NEEDS OR SITUATIONS

The choice of food in each category can be written using a braille machine for children who are blind. The choices can also be programmed into an augmentative language device for children with communication disorders.

MATHEMATICS CONTENT STANDARD CONNECTIONS

These graphs directly align with the Data Analysis and Probability standard. Children also compare quantities of votes and may add and subtract to determine which column has the most votes. This aligns with Number and Operations. If children use the height of the columns to compare quantities, they apply concepts of the Measurement standard to the graph.

COMMENTS AND QUESTIONS RELATED TO MATHEMATICS PROCESS STANDARDS

Problem Solving: How will we know which foods to tell the kitchen staff to prepare?

Reasoning and Proof: Do you think your favorite fruit is the choice with the most votes? How many votes did each fruit receive?

Communication: We have to tell the kitchen staff which foods to cook. How will we know what to tell them?

Connections: Is it very likely that chicken nuggets will catch up to fish when the three children who are absent return? Fish is three votes ahead. (Connects to Data Analysis and Probability)

Representation: What will the graph look like if I vote for macaroni and cheese? Will that change the final result?

How Many Bears?

DESCRIPTION

For this activity, children estimate how many papa bear counters will fit into three different sizes of nesting cups. The teacher can ask estimation questions as the children play. Children may construct the relationship between the size of the container and how many bears it will hold.

MATERIALS

☐ 3 small nesting cups

☐ 10 papa teddy bear counters

CHILD'S LEVEL

This activity is appropriate for younger preschool children. The papa bear counters are too large to be a choking hazard. They are of high interest to young children, and the quantity each cup holds is under five.

WHAT TO LOOK FOR

• Some children will estimate the quantity of bears that will fit into each cup.

• Experienced children will estimate that a different quantity will fit into different sizes of cups.

• Some children will initially play with the bears in a pretend play manner.

• Some children may stack or nest the cups.

• Some children will fill each cup with the bears.

MODIFICATIONS FOR SPECIAL NEEDS OR SITUATIONS

Modifications are not necessary for this activity. The materials are large enough for most children to handle. Color is not a deciding factor in the activity.

MATHEMATICS CONTENT STANDARD CONNECTIONS

This activity connects to the standards of Data Analysis and Probability, Number and Operations, and Measurement. Although the design of the activity focuses on estimation, a component of Data Analysis and Probability,

MORE >

children must also consider the size of the bears and cups and quantities of bears in each cup to verify their estimates.

COMMENTS AND QUESTIONS RELATED TO MATHEMATICS PROCESS STANDARDS

Problem Solving: Will more than one bear fit in this cup?

Reasoning and Proof: Do you think the red cup will hold just as many bears as the yellow cup? How can we tell?

Communication: Which cup holds the most bears?

Connections: How many bears do you have altogether? (Connects to Number and Operations)

Representation: If you wanted to divide the bears equally in the cups, what would that look like?

Buckeyes or Acorns

DESCRIPTION

This is a more complex estimation activity in which children must guess the quantities of two different materials, buckeyes and acorns, which are sealed in two identical containers. The jars are placed in the science area during the day for children to examine. They may record their estimates on the paper provided. The teacher introduces the estimation activity during a whole group experience and records the results. The activity allows children to compare how the size of the objects placed in a container affects the number that will fit. They learn to vary their estimates accordingly.

MATERIALS

☐ 2 small, clear containers, such as peanut butter jars, each with either a buckeye or acorn glued to the top

☐ sufficient quantities of buckeyes and acorns to fill each jar (fewer than 20 in each)

☐ paper and pencil for recording estimates

CHILD'S LEVEL

This activity is appropriate for older preschool and kindergarten children, because they must estimate without manipulating the materials. This requires more abstract thinking. This activity is best introduced after

MORE >

children have had numerous experiences estimating the quantity of one type of object in a single container.

WHAT TO LOOK FOR

- Some children will record their estimations on the paper provided in the science area.

- Children may estimate that each jar holds the same amount because the jars are the same size.

- Some children may focus on the size of the buckeye compared to the size of the acorn and estimate that the jar of buckeyes must contain fewer than the jar of acorns.

- Some children may change their estimations after repeated explorations and conversations with the teacher or other children.

MODIFICATIONS FOR SPECIAL NEEDS OR SITUATIONS

For younger or less experienced children, introduce the activity using one jar containing only acorns.

MATHEMATICS CONTENT STANDARD CONNECTIONS

Estimation activities align with the Data Analysis and Probability standard and also Number and Operations as children develop an understanding that counting is the way to verify an estimate.

COMMENTS AND QUESTIONS RELATED TO MATHEMATICS PROCESS STANDARDS

Problem Solving: Do you estimate that more buckeyes or more acorns are in the jars?

Reasoning and Proof: You think there are twelve buckeyes in the jar. How will you find out if your estimate is accurate?

Communication: Dani, tell Jackson how to estimate how many buckeyes are in the jar.

Connections: Which are bigger, buckeyes or acorns? Since the buckeyes are bigger, will there be more or fewer buckeyes than acorns in the jar? (Connects to Measurement)

Representation: What will you write on the paper as your estimate?

Lunchtime Guesses

DESCRIPTION

This estimation activity can be planned by the teacher or may occur naturally as children eat lunch or snack. The teacher asks the children to estimate how many seeds might be inside an apple. The responses can be recorded and compared to the estimates of children at other tables or to estimates on different days. Children can verify the estimates after the apples have been cut open. They may want to repeat this activity on other occasions and compare the results. This activity combines science and math and gives children the opportunity to make an educated guess when they cannot see the actual objects they are estimating. By comparing the quantity of seeds in different apples, children discover the contents of materials that appear to be identical may not be exactly the same.

MATERIALS

☐ several apples, so that small groups of children each have an apple to work with

☐ paper and pencil for recording the children's estimates and for recording the actual quantity of seeds

CHILD'S LEVEL

This activity is appropriate for preschool children because the quantity of seeds is typically fewer than 8. Kindergarten children also find the activity interesting.

WHAT TO LOOK FOR

• Some children will at first guess their age.

• Some children will be unable to venture an estimate because the seeds are not visible.

MORE >

- Kindergarten children may estimate a large yet unrealistic number because they are interested in large numbers.

- In subsequent estimations of seeds in an apple, many children will estimate the same amount as the first experience. They are using what they know from a previous experience.

MODIFICATIONS FOR SPECIAL NEEDS OR SITUATIONS

Cut open and count seeds in apples and other fruits before introducing the idea of estimation. This gives children with a cognitive delay an opportunity to build concrete experiences before tackling this more abstract estimation activity. Older or more experienced children would benefit from additional estimation activities using several varieties of apples.

MATHEMATICS CONTENT STANDARD CONNECTIONS

Estimation combines concepts of Data Analysis and Probability as well as Number and Operations. Many children will begin to consider the probability that all apples contain approximately the same quantity of seeds. Children will necessarily need to count to quantify the actual amount of seeds in the apple after they make their estimations.

COMMENTS AND QUESTIONS RELATED TO MATHEMATICS PROCESS STANDARDS

Problem Solving: How many seeds were in your apple the last time you estimated? Do you think there will be more, fewer, or the same amount of seeds this time?

Reasoning and Proof: How will you find out if your apple has just as many seeds as my apple?

Communication: I want to know how many seeds are in Phoebe's apple. Will you go ask her and come back and tell me?

Connections: Does your apple have more seeds than you thought or fewer seeds? (Connects to Data Analysis and Probability and Number and Operations)

Representation: How did we record the estimation of seeds the last time?

Sink the Boat

DESCRIPTION

Estimation can occur anywhere in the classroom, including the sensory table. In this activity, children estimate how many marbles it will take to sink small boats and then carry out the experiment. This activity combines math and science and helps children construct the relationship between the weight of the marbles and how many it takes to sink the boat. Children learn that estimates can be revised based on observations. They consider the probability of whether one more marble will sink the boat or whether placing the marbles on one side of the boat is likely or unlikely to sink the boat.

MATERIALS

☐ sensory table or small dishpan filled with enough water to allow the boats to float

☐ approximately 50 black or dark marbles (dark marbles show up better in the water)

☐ small plastic or rubber boats (2 per child)

☐ 1 ladle for each child participating in the activity

CHILD'S LEVEL

This activity is appropriate for preschool and kindergarten children. It is not appropriate for children who may still put objects into their mouths.

WHAT TO LOOK FOR

• Some children may ladle the marbles into the boats without regard to estimation.

• Some children may communicate to each other about their estimates of how many marbles will sink the boat.

• Children will check to see if their estimates are accurate.

• Some children will revise their estimates based on their prior observations as they experiment with other boats.

MORE >

MODIFICATIONS FOR SPECIAL NEEDS OR SITUATIONS

Children with communication disorders can use an augmentative language device or sign language to communicate their directions. Older or more experienced children may be encouraged to record their estimates before trying out the solution and compare the estimates to the result of their explorations.

MATHEMATICS CONTENT STANDARD CONNECTIONS

Estimation is one component of the Data Analysis and Probability standard in this activity. Children are very motivated to think about the probability of the next marble sinking the boat. This activity also aligns with both Number and Operations and Algebra standards. Children design a problem that they solve using concrete materials, and they want to test the accuracy of their estimates by counting the marbles they use.

COMMENTS AND QUESTIONS RELATED TO MATHEMATICS PROCESS STANDARDS

Problem Solving: How many marbles do you think will sink this boat?

Reasoning and Proof: Your boat is still floating. How many more marbles do you estimate you will need to add to sink the boat?

Communication: What is happening to the boat as you add more marbles?

Connections: Are all the boats the same size? Would it take more marbles to sink a larger boat? (Connects to Measurement)

Representation: Take as many marbles as you estimate you will need to sink two boats.

Shopping Cart Bonanza

DESCRIPTION

For this game, each player has a small shopping cart. Children take turns rolling a die and selecting tiny plastic foods to put into their carts. They may group the foods together, sorting by types of foods, foods they like or not, or other attributes they observe. One alternative is to use a single, larger shopping cart shared by all players. Novelty shopping carts and food items are available in several sizes.

MATERIALS

☐ 2 novelty shopping carts (approximately 3 inches long)

☐ tiny plastic foods

☐ basket to hold the foods

☐ 1–3 or 1–6 die, depending on the quantities of groceries available

CHILD'S LEVEL

Both preschool and kindergarten children will enjoy playing this game. Younger children may want an individual shopping cart; whereas, kindergarten children may enjoy shopping together and using a pair of dice.

WHAT TO LOOK FOR

• Some children will divide the food into the carts without using the die.

• Children will roll the die and take an equivalent quantity of foods.

• Children may sort the food before beginning the game or at the end of the game.

MODIFICATIONS FOR SPECIAL NEEDS OR SITUATIONS

For children with cognitive delays, use a toy shopping cart, empty boxes and cans of food,

MORE >

and a large foam die. Increase the quantity of foods and use a pair of dice or a ten-sided die for more experienced children. Provide a shopping list for children to use as they collect food. They can quantify how many they have of each food item.

MATHEMATICS CONTENT STANDARD CONNECTIONS

This activity aligns with the Data Analysis and Probability standard and incorporates elements of Number and Operations as children sort the food they collect and quantify how much of each food they have. They may also compare quantities of each type of food they collect and record the amount using numerals, hash marks, or drawings.

COMMENTS AND QUESTIONS RELATED TO MATHEMATICS PROCESS STANDARDS

Problem Solving: How many pieces of food do you want to collect?

Reasoning and Proof: Do you have more cans of food or more boxes of food?

Communication: How many more cans of food do I need to have the same as you?

Connections: Have you each collected the same amount of food? (Connects to Number and Operations)

Representation: What will it look like if you divide the foods equally before you begin playing and then pretend you are unloading the groceries at home?

CHAPTER 8

Assessment and Planning

It was mid-March, and Jaumall was checking his preschool students' classroom records prior to the upcoming spring break. He planned to use some of his time off to design new math materials targeted toward specific children in the class. Jaumall first looked at Mickey's file. Mickey, four years and eight months old, had cognitive and language delays. Jaumall scanned a checklist of quantification and counting skills he kept for each child in his class. He was pleased to see a strong developmental trend on Mickey's checklist.

When Mickey had started preschool in the fall, he was unable to give any response when shown quantities of two or three items and asked which had more. After about three weeks, he had started to employ a global quantification strategy. For example, when Jaumall suggested Mickey take one toy animal for each car on his three-car block train, Mickey grabbed a handful. Mickey continued this strategy in play situations until after winter break, when he began to match one new object to each object in his original set. At this point, when Jaumall set out four toy cars, Mickey carefully placed one driver in each car. When Mickey played games with other children that involved a die and counters, he set one counter on each dot on the large die before placing it in his pile of counters. Jaumall noted that Mickey played math games almost every day. He clearly enjoyed them. Jaumall also noticed a new development. Mickey had started subitizing when he rolled a one or a two on the die; in other words, he could tell quantities of one or two just by looking. For quantities above two, he still used one-to-one correspondence.

Jaumall read through his anecdotal notes for Mickey. Mickey had started to repeat count strings of one through five, especially when singing counting songs at circle time. More significantly, Mickey pointed and counted when he saw two objects. "Great," Jaumall said to himself. "We can use a die with one to four dots per side this spring. That will allow us to model counting sets up to four. Mickey should move from using one-to-one correspondence to counting sets of four by the end of the year. If we can get him into a good summer program, he should be able to transition into kindergarten with his peers in the fall."

In the room next door, Jaumall's colleague Karen was examining her kindergartners' records. Karen also had a quantification checklist she used for her class that included addition and subtraction strategies. Karen looked at Juanita's checklist. "Just as I thought," mused Karen. "She's not being challenged enough." Juanita's checklist indicated that in January, at the beginning of the third grading period, she was adding by counting on from one of the addends. Now, however, Juanita no longer needed to do that. She either knew by memory or quickly mentally calculated all of the addition combinations. During choice time, Juanita was no longer choosing math games. An anecdotal note written by a teacher assistant indicated Juanita thought those games were boring.

After reviewing the rest of the class records, Karen identified four children who seemed ready to work on problems that involved groupings of tens—beginning place value. "This will be fun," Karen thought. "We'll see what they figure out using the place value blocks. I think they can also try using two ten-sided dice. That will give them lots of opportunities to think about larger numbers."

• • •

Ongoing assessment of all students is critical in mathematics. It allows the teacher to quickly discover concepts children have mastered and those that are presenting difficulties. This, in turn, enables the teacher to develop materials and activities that help children solidify important concepts, develop new strategies for solving mathematical problems, and continue moving forward in their development. Assessment should not be onerous for either children or their teacher; rather, it should be an ongoing part of regular classroom experiences. As NCTM advises, "Assessment should support the learning of important mathematics and furnish useful information to both teachers and students" (NCTM 2000, 22).

Teachers' Questions

What assessment methods can teachers use to chart learning and guide planning?

Teachers can keep anecdotal records of children's learning, design check-lists to quickly summarize learning in specific areas, and rely on curriculum-based assessments for monitoring ongoing progress. Through regular anecdotal record keeping, teachers can capture important learning episodes while they are in progress or shortly thereafter. Because much crucial learning for young children occurs during play, anecdotal notes enable teachers to remember exactly what occurred and to chart growth.

Checklists offer a quick method for busy teachers to record key areas of learning. They can be aligned to developmental levels of thinking, such as the Kamii/Piaget stages of quantification (Kamii 1982), the Gelman/Gallistel counting principles (Gelman and Gallistel 1978), or the van Hiele stages of geometric reasoning (van Hiele 1999). Carefully designed checklists allow teachers to quickly notice developmental trends across the class and with individual children and alter planning accordingly.

Although anecdotal records and checklists provide teachers with a great deal of useful knowledge about children's mathematical development, sometimes crucial information is missed. For this reason, curriculum-based measures are a third important component of classroom assessment. These short assessments are directly tied to the curriculum and can, therefore, be used as both learning activities and mathematical assessments, thereby meeting the NCTM recommendation that assessment be part of the learning process (NCTM 2000, 22–24).

What information should be included in anecdotal records?

Anecdotal records should reflect the date when the observation occurred, the learning situation, and exactly what the child said or did. Interpretations can be made later. The date is obviously important because it helps teachers chart growth over time. The learning situation is also critical information. Teachers may discover that particular children show increased mathematical thinking in particular areas of the classroom, such as in the dramatic play area or the gross-motor room. This information can help teachers develop more complex math activities for those areas, and also provide ideas for math activities that may interest the children in other areas of the classroom. Finally, it is critically important to record exactly what the child said or did. This informs the teacher of the level of the child's mathematical thinking, the strategies the child uses to solve mathematical problems, and the child's use of mathematical processes, such as representation and communication.

What are some effective methods for recording anecdotes?

Some teachers develop anecdotal note-taking forms that can be placed around the classroom within easy reach. Others record anecdotal notes in a notebook that includes a section for each child. Tech-savvy teachers may chose to record notes on a handheld device for future transference into a computer file. Teachers should obviously select whatever method or combination of methods is most useful for them. The important thing is to record anecdotes regularly and to store them in such a way that they can be analyzed later.

Early childhood classrooms are busy places, so teachers may find time slipping away with none leftover for recording anecdotal records. For this reason, it may be helpful to devise a system to ensure records are kept for all children. For example, in a class of twenty children, the teacher might decide to focus on five children each day of the week in terms of anecdotal note taking. Naturally, even in a situation such as this, the teacher will want to record key learning among other children. On the other hand, deliberately focusing on particular children ensures that quiet children who seldom demand attention also receive the teacher's attention.

How can checklists help teachers chart growth?

Checklists provide a convenient way to measure growth over time by focusing on important developmental indicators. In contrast, anecdotal records capture a broader expanse of learning. Because they are usually designed to record very specific information, checklists chart the emergence and solidification of important mathematical concepts and reasoning. A quick glance at a mathematical checklist can refresh the teacher's mind as to what concepts he wants to focus on with a particular child, perhaps during math time in kindergarten or on the child's scheduled observation day in preschool.

What is portfolio assessment?

Portfolio assessment combines anecdotal records and checklists with actual examples of the child's work in various areas over time. Portfolios provide the most complete picture of a child's learning. In addition to work samples, some teachers include photographs that may capture a child's strategy and solution to a particular mathematical problem. For example, photographs can quickly record how children sort and classify collections of objects; create patterns with a variety of materials; combine geometric shapes to compose new shapes; or model a mathematical problem through drawing, reenacting a scenario, or using manipulative materials. Some teachers assemble each child's work in a folder or notebook to present to the parents at the end of the year. Portfolio assessment is highly recommended for some children with disabilities or other challenges who may not be able to adequately demonstrate their learning through traditional assessment procedures (Salend 2008, 512–16).

What is curriculum-based assessment?

Curriculum-based assessments are brief measurement tools that are aligned with classroom curriculum in order to provide teachers with ongoing information on students' development (Shinn and Bamonto 1998). These assessments can be used by teachers to guide their planning and instructional decisions. Young children are often difficult to assess using traditional testing methods. If children are not interested in the assessment, they may refuse to cooperate. If children become bored, they may lose attention. In addition, teachers often complain that the data they receive from annual standardized tests does not provide the ongoing information they need to guide instruction. Curriculum-based assessments are designed to accommodate the developmental interests and attention spans of children while furnishing teachers with important, ongoing information about learning that is directly related to the curriculum. Frequently, the assessment itself may be devised as a learning activity. For example, the teacher might play a carefully designed quantification game with children and use the information for curriculum-based assessment.

Number and Operations— Quantification Anecdote

BACKGROUND

It was the beginning of the school year. Audrey's kindergarten teacher had noticed her interest in the interactive literacy chart that accompanied the song "Ten in the Bed" (Activity 3.2), which the class had been singing daily. There were felt teddy bears children could place into a bed on the chart. During the first weeks of school, Audrey seemed to have no idea how to decide how many teddy bears to put into the bed. Although she counted by rote to twelve, she did not show an understanding of cardinality; therefore, when the teacher asked her how many bears she had, Audrey could not answer. Audrey watched intently each day as her classmates put bears onto the chart, counted to see how many bears they had, and argued with one another over whether they had put the correct number of bears into the bed for the verse they were about to sing.

ANECDOTE

Child: Audrey
Date: September 15
Area: Literacy
Notes: Audrey went quietly by herself to the "Ten in the Bed" chart during choice time. She picked up the bears one at a time and counted to ten as she placed them in the bed. She quietly sang the first verse of the song. Then she removed one bear. She carefully pointed to each remaining bear while counting to nine. Then she sang the verse with "nine in the bed." Audrey removed one more bear and counted the remaining bears. Melanie joined her and asked how many bears there were, to which Audrey replied eight. The two girls then sang the verse "eight in the bed." Melanie removed one bear and the girls counted the bears to seven. . . .

INTERPRETING THE ANECDOTE

Audrey shows tremendous growth in her understanding of counting and quantification in this anecdote. Her careful pointing to the teddy bears while she counts them demonstrates that she now understands she can pair the sequence of counting words (which she already knew) to objects she wants to quantify. This shows application of the one-to-one correspondence principle in counting. Audrey also demonstrates an understanding of cardinality when Melanie asks her how many bears there are on the chart. Having just counted the bears, Audrey answers Melanie by repeating the last number she had said when she was counting the bears. This shows she understands that the last number tag represents the entire set of bears. Finally, Audrey continues to count and sing when another child joins her, which shows she no longer needs to hang back and watch when other children are around. She is confident enough in her counting skills to participate with a peer.

GUIDES FOR FUTURE PLANNING

This anecdote verifies that the interactive chart and counting song are leading to important mathematical learning, at least in Audrey's case. There may be other children

MORE >

in the class who have also recently learned to count in order to quantify. The teacher will want to continue to reinforce this newly acquired understanding, perhaps by creating a chart to go along with another counting song. The chart also enables children to use the teddy bears to model subtracting by one. The teacher will want to watch carefully to see if some children can now subtract by one without needing to re-count the bears each time.

Audrey needs opportunities to apply her newly acquired counting skills to other quantification situations. Directing her to a math game in which children roll a die and then take a corresponding number of counters would give her plenty of practice in counting, first as she quantifies the dots on the die and again when she takes the required number of counters. Because Audrey seems comfortable in the literacy area, adding a selection of counting books would seem appropriate. Audrey can already count to twelve, so the teacher might wish to include books that go up to fifteen or twenty.

Number and Operations— Arithmetic Operations Anecdote

BACKGROUND

This anecdote took place in a preschool classroom during spring quarter. The teacher had incorporated math games, such as those in chapters 2 and 3, as a regular component of her math curriculum. Therefore, the children had had many experiences quantifying dots on a die or spinner and creating an equivalent set with counters or by moving along a path. In preschool classes such as this, it is not unusual to see preschool children transitioning into addition. In this anecdote, the teacher recorded information on two children, both four and a half years old.

ANECDOTE

Child: Beth and Andre
Date: April 5
Area: Math Game Table
Notes: Beth and Andre played a farm long path game together. They used two standard dice. Andre rolled a five and a three on the dice. He counted the five dots and moved five spaces, then he counted the three dots and moved three spaces. Beth rolled a two and a six on the dice. She counted all the dots together and then moved eight spaces. Andre took another turn. This time he rolled a three and a four. He counted the three dots and moved three spaces; then he counted the four dots and moved four spaces. Beth said to Andre, "You don't have to count the dice like that. You can just count them all together." Beth rolled a five and a four. She counted all nine dots and moved nine spaces. Andre took another turn. He rolled a three and a two. He counted the

three dots and moved three spaces; then he counted the two dots and moved two spaces. Andre continued to quantify the dice separately throughout the game. Beth continued to count all the dots together before moving. Neither made any quantification errors.

INTERPRETING THE ANECDOTE

Both of the children in this anecdote reflect the counting stage of quantification. They immediately count to find out how many dots are on the dice and then move an equivalent number of spaces. They are very secure counters, understanding that they can use counting to quantify both the dots on the dice and the spaces on the game board. The game board spaces are less concrete for children to quantify, because they must count forward from a designated space each time they take a turn rather than counting all the visible spaces on the board.

Beth is clearly transitioning into addition. She understands that she can count all the dots on the dice together to get the total amount and applies this strategy consistently. Andre, on the other hand, still views each individual die as a complete set of dots rather than the two dice together as the complete set. For this reason, he needs to quantify the dice separately and move separately for each amount. Beth has challenged his thinking, both by modeling her count all strategy and by telling him directly that he doesn't need to count the dice separately. Andre is clearly not ready to take her word for it. He continues to follow his own reliable strategy.

MORE >

Children usually do not change their thinking immediately when a peer challenges them; however, the modeling and the dialogue may cause them to think about what they are doing, what the other child is doing, and how the two strategies compare. Piaget called this *disequilibrium*. The child may continue to pursue the same strategy as before but is nonetheless thinking hard about the inconsistencies between the strategies. In the case of Andre, a follow-up anecdote two weeks later showed him counting all the dots together on two dice before moving the total number of spaces along the path. This is a major step forward in thinking for Andre because he figured out why a counting all strategy would work. This is very different from a child who counts all the dots to get the total just because the teacher tells him to use that strategy. In the latter case, the child is simply following a rule given to him by the teacher rather than constructing the concept that two sets can be combined into a new set that can be counted to get the total.

GUIDES FOR FUTURE PLANNING

Games that encourage children to combine sets, such as the one in this anecdote, will continue to be excellent curriculum materials for these two children for some time to come. As the children continue to add sets, they will eventually begin to remember some of the combinations and no longer need to count to find the total. When the teacher joins in the play of the game, he can model a more advanced counting strategy, *counting on*, by counting forward from one of the sets. For example, if the teacher rolled a three and a four on the dice, he might point to the die with three dots and say, "three" then say, "four, five, six, seven," while pointing to the dots on the second die.

Algebra Anecdote

BACKGROUND

This anecdote occurred at a child care center during the summer. All of the children had recently turned five years old and would be heading to kindergarten in the fall. The teacher had introduced patterning several weeks earlier during group time. He used stamps of a chicken and a fox, two characters in a book the class had been reading, to create an alternating pattern. At first, the children did not seem to recognize the pattern. Nevertheless, as soon as they began chanting and clapping "chick-en fox, chick-en fox," they caught on. Soon they were noticing patterns throughout the classroom—the stripes on the curtains, the floor tiles in the bathroom, the stripes on the flag, and so on. The teacher encouraged the children to begin creating patterns with manipulative materials, art materials, and musical instruments. The following anecdote was one of the results.

ANECDOTE

Child: Molly and Ismail
Date: July 8
Area: Manipulative
Notes: At going home time, Molly showed me a repeating pattern she had constructed with one-inch colored cubes: red-blue, red-blue, etc., for five repetitions. Then the school receptionist announced over the intercom that Molly's carpool was waiting for her. Molly looked very disappointed. "Now I can't show my pattern to my friends," she said.

"Don't worry, Molly," said Ismail. "I can copy your pattern on this paper." Ismail brought a piece of graph paper from the art center and began to color in the boxes to match Molly's pattern. He colored ten boxes in the red-blue pattern. Then he put the paper in Molly's cubby.

INTERPRETING THE ANECDOTE

This anecdote falls under the Algebra standard for two reasons: (1) it involves patterning, and (2) it reflects two ways to model a mathematical idea. Both children demonstrate an understanding of the concept of an alternating pattern—Molly, by creating one with colored cubes, and Ismail, by copying it. It is particularly impressive that Ismail realizes he can represent the same pattern using different materials.

GUIDES FOR FUTURE PLANNING

The teacher will undoubtedly want Molly and Ismail to share their patterning experience with the class. Ismail could describe how he decided to represent the block pattern using graph paper, which might lead to further discussion about other ways to represent Molly's pattern. During the coming days, the teacher can encourage children to create patterns for one another and represent them using a variety of materials. For example, if a child made a pattern out of beads, the teacher might ask if someone could represent the same pattern using paint at the easel. The teacher will also want to introduce more difficult patterns, such as some of the examples in chapter 4.

MORE >

Geometry Anecdote

BACKGROUND

Books have a role throughout the early childhood classroom. They can serve many purposes when not confined solely to the book area. In this case, the teacher has included several books in the block area because they provide interesting illustrations of block structures or real buildings. A four-and-a-half-year-old boy has used one of the books as a model to construct a symmetrical block structure. The anecdote illustrates the importance of integrating geometry throughout the classroom.

ANECDOTE

Child: Takuo
Date: January 30
Area: Blocks
Notes: Takuo used a combination of unit blocks and table blocks to reconstruct an illustration from the Pat Hutchins book *Changes, Changes*. Although he did not have the necessary blocks to match the colors in the book, the shapes matched perfectly. Takuo built his reproduction vertically. He did not attempt to simply lay the blocks on top of the drawing. At the top of the building, Takuo needed a rectangular table block to match the illustration but couldn't find one. Instead, he combined two triangular blocks to form the rectangle. Takuo was proud of his accomplishment and asked me to take a photograph of his building.

INTERPRETING THE ANECDOTE

In this anecdote, Takuo demonstrates an understanding of important geometric concepts in several ways. First, he clearly recognizes and can match geometric shapes, even when the colors do not match. He is able to correctly re-create a rather complex symmetrical pattern. In addition, he has constructed his model vertically, thereby demonstrating an understanding of balance and spatial awareness. Finally, Takuo shows he can compose a new geometric shape, a rectangular solid, by combining two triangular forms. The information in this anecdote would place this child in van Hiele's *descriptive level* of geometric understanding.

GUIDES FOR FUTURE PLANNING

The addition of books to the block area combined with the availability of several types of blocks has clearly enabled this child to demonstrate strong geometric awareness. Obviously the teacher will want to continue to supply materials such as this in the future. Taking a photograph of Takuo's building project is an excellent way to make important learning outcomes visible to the child. In this case, the photograph will preserve the concept of moving from a drawing to an actual three-dimensional representation. The teacher may want to take this idea a step further by encouraging Takuo to create his own drawings and then reproduce them with the blocks.

Measurement Anecdote

BACKGROUND

Measurement activities often grow out of children's natural explorations. They want to reach as far as they can, build the tallest building possible, or fit into a small box. Preschool children seem to have a proclivity for chaining together as many interlocking manipulative pieces as possible. Sometimes teachers may wish that children would build more complex forms rather than long strands of interconnecting pieces. On further reflection, the teacher may decide these chains or strands represent children's natural desire to span distances. Whatever the reason, children's interest in linking together longer chains of materials can be guided by attentive teachers into learning about measurement. The following anecdote illustrates a child's quest to reach the sky, or at least the ceiling. She is three years and eight months old.

ANECDOTE

Child: Carina
Date: February 5
Area: Manipulative
Notes: Carina was busy hooking together interlocking plastic cylinders. The teacher glanced over several times and noticed the tower growing taller. Then Carina stood up and extended the cylinder column toward the ceiling. Not satisfied, she sat back down and added more pieces to her tower. The teacher commented that Carina's tower was getting tall.

"I'm trying to reach the ceiling," Carina replied.

"That's a long way to reach," the teacher said.

"Yes," replied Carina.

Carina worked for approximately forty-five minutes on her cylinder tower. Periodically, she would stand up and extend it toward the ceiling. Then she would sit back down and return to her work. On the umpteenth attempt, Carina was delighted to finally touch the ceiling with the cylinders. The teacher took a photograph to document the result of Carina's diligent effort. Then the teacher asked Carina if she wanted to find out how many cylinders it had taken to reach the ceiling. Together they counted thirty-seven pieces.

INTERPRETING THE ANECDOTE

Carina's goal is simple, and challenging to achieve. She wants to span the distance from herself to the ceiling to find a way to touch something she cannot reach without the aid of a tool. The teacher wisely stays out of the way while Carina pursues this goal. It is only when Carina has satisfied her quest that the teacher introduces the possibility of quantifying the distance.

In this case, Carina uses a nonstandard unit to bridge the distance to the ceiling. We cannot assume from this anecdote that she realizes the importance of a uniform size for the unit; it is merely a tool of convenience. On the other hand, Carina does understand adding units that initially stretch across the floor can extend the vertical reach of her measurement tool. The teacher selects just the right moment to stretch Carina's thinking by introducing the idea of quantifying the units. This builds her understanding of measurement.

MORE >

GUIDES FOR FUTURE PLANNING

Carina's measurement adventure sparked interest throughout the classroom. After all, it's not every day that a child reaches the ceiling. The teacher can capture this enthusiasm by planning more measurement activities with the class, perhaps through questions such as the following:

• What else would you like to reach?

• How far do you think it is across our classroom?

• How many blocks would it take to reach Marty's office?

• Do we have enough blocks to reach the next classroom?

As the children select and pursue answers to questions like these, the teacher's goals should be to help them construct the concept of a uniform (though probably nonstandard) unit for measurement and the idea that this unit can be quantified. Many different manipulative materials should be provided. Children may discover it is better to use larger units when measuring longer distances and smaller units for shorter distances.

Data Analysis Anecdote

BACKGROUND

This anecdote took place in a beginning kindergarten class. The children had all attended the same preschool during the previous year. Most of the children had opportunities to vote on issues that were important to them and record the results on a class bar graph throughout their preschool experience (chapter 7). The kindergarten teacher was curious about how the children would individually handle the concept of graphing.

The children were each given a bag containing goldfish crackers, vanilla teddy bear crackers, and chocolate teddy bear crackers. There were one to five crackers of each type in the bags. The children were encouraged to represent on one-inch graph paper what was in their bags so everyone could remember what each child had received after all the crackers had been eaten; however, the children were not told how to make the graph.

The following six examples are representative of the varying ways the children represented their crackers. All six children constructed mathematical concepts that enabled them to symbolically represent the crackers; nevertheless, many different levels of understanding with regard to graphing concepts are evident.

ANECDOTES AND INTERPRETING THE ANECDOTES

Anecdote 1

Philip lined up his crackers in the appropriate columns. He put one cracker in each box in consecutive order from bottom to top. Philip then drew a vertical line through the boxes to show how high each row was. He drew his lines correctly through the columns containing two or three crackers, but he made a long line to the top of the page for the column containing five bears.

Interpretation: Philip is able to correctly represent the quantities of crackers on his graph when using the actual crackers, but representing them with a line is more challenging. He is able to correctly represent small quantities of two and three but reverts to a more global representation for the larger quantity of five. Children can often handle more difficult concepts when they involve small quantities but revert to earlier thinking strategies for larger quantities. In this case, Philip used either one-to-one correspondence or counting to quantify and represent two and three crackers, and used a global representation for the five crackers.

Anecdote 2

Kenan colored in blocks to correspond to the number of each type of cracker in his bag. He used the same color of marker as the color of the cracker; however, he did not line up the blocks in columns.

Interpretation: Kenan has constructed the concepts of one-to-one correspondence and classification when graphing, as shown by his representation of crackers based on color. He does not yet understand the idea of grouping data in columns for comparison.

Anecdote 3

Danny lined up his crackers, one per box, in the appropriate columns. He put hash marks at the top of each column to indicate how many crackers had been in each row.

MORE >

Interpretation: Danny understands the concept of grouping his data in columns, but he may not yet realize that the number of boxes used in each column also quantifies the data. He therefore supplies hash marks to record the amounts of each type of cracker.

Anecdote 4

Anthony correctly graphed his crackers in appropriate columns. Rather than just coloring in a corresponding number of boxes, he drew a picture of the type of cracker he wanted represented in each box.

Interpretation: Although Anthony has correctly graphed his data, he may not yet realize that coloring in the boxes in the appropriate column provides enough information to tell another person which type of cracker is meant. He therefore feels the need to actually draw each cracker being represented.

Anecdote 5

Heidi also correctly graphed her crackers, but like Anthony drew a picture of each type of cracker rather than just coloring in the boxes. Heidi also wrote the appropriate numeral at the top of each column to indicate the quantity.

Interpretation: Heidi shows that she can correctly use a numeric symbol to represent quantity. Like Anthony, she may not yet realize that she does not need to draw actual pictures on her graph in order to convey all the necessary information.

Anecdote 6

Ping graphed her crackers by coloring in the appropriate number of boxes in each column. She used only one color of marker for the graph. While coloring in her boxes, Ping told the teacher that she did not need to change the color of marker to tell how many of each type of cracker she had. She could tell that by looking at the symbols at the bottom of the columns.

Interpretation: Ping shows the most advanced conceptual understanding of graphing in this group. She correctly organizes her data in columns and realizes this provides all the information necessary to tell how many of each type of cracker she has. Ping is the only child in the class who realized this.

GUIDES FOR FUTURE PLANNING

These anecdotes show the variety of ways in which kindergarten children understand and represent data. Kindergarten children are usually quite sociable and enjoy comparing information with one another. The teacher will likely decide to continue with regular group graphing on topics of interest, because children can work at somewhat higher levels when they are part of a group. Also, group graphs allow the teacher to pose important mathematical questions that can be determined from the graph, such as which group has the most, which has the fewest, and how many more or fewer one group has than another.

Periodically providing children with opportunities to graph individually is also a good idea. Individual graphs allow the teacher to monitor each child's progress in understanding and representing data. The experience allows children to share not only their mathematical outcomes but also the reasoning they used to come up with the results. This sharing of information helps more advanced children solidify their understanding of mathematical concepts and less advanced children stretch their thinking. All can feel successful.

Quantification Checklist

BACKGROUND

The quantification checklist used in this vignette can be found in appendix D. It is designed to capture the child's level of quantification, as described by Kamii (Kamii 1982); application of three key counting principles developed by Gelman and Gallistel (Gelman and Gallistel 1978); and emergent addition skills by Kamii (Kamii 2000). It is especially useful for documenting the results of quantification games (chapters 2 and 3).

When a child decides to play with the materials in a quantification game, two outcomes are possible: (1) the child may play imaginatively with the pieces or (2) the child may attempt to play the game. If the latter is the case, the child will attempt to make sets. In the first set of columns on the checklist, the teacher can document "outcome" as either *free play* or *makes sets*. If the child attempts to make sets, some strategy will be needed, which will determine the child's level of quantification. In the second set of columns, the teacher can document whether the child uses a *global*, *one-to-one correspondence*, or *counting* strategy to determine how many counters to take or how many spaces to move along a path. If a child selects counting as his or her strategy, then we know the child understands cardinality, or the concept that the last number used when counting represents the entire set. We do not know, however, whether or not the child says the number words correctly or counts each object one and only one time.

The next set of columns allows the teacher to document that information. First, the teacher can record the highest number the child counts to correctly, or in *stable order*. Children often *skip* over an object when counting or *re-count* an object they have already counted. These are typical and developmen-tally appropriate errors that happen using the one-to-one correspondence counting principle. Finally, some children will have advanced to the point of combining two sets when playing games, such as by rolling two dice. The final set of columns on the checklist allow teachers to document whether the child *counts all* the objects together to determine the total, counts or *adds on* from the first set, or knows some addition *combinations* without counting. Terms and definitions used in the checklist can be found in appendix E.

INTERPRETING THE CHECKLIST

From this checklist, we can quickly tell Nancy's progression in quantification over the first six weeks of school. In the beginning, she used *one-to-one correspondence* to construct an equivalent set when playing a spinner and counter game like the Strawberry Picking Game (Activity 2.1). Two weeks later she used the more advanced strategy of *counting* when playing the same game. Nancy continued to use counting to quantify sets of other math materials for sets up to four; however, for sets of five and six she reverted back to the one-to-one correspondence level of quantification.

GUIDES FOR FUTURE PLANNING

Nancy seems interested in math materials and is progressing in her use of counting to quantify and create equivalent sets. Reverting to the one-to-one correspondence level may indicate she does not know the counting words for five and six or she is overwhelmed by these larger quantities. She needs more experience with games that use a 1–6 die or spinner. One could predict that she will soon count quantities to six after modeling her teacher or a peer when playing these games.

MORE >

Child: Nancy

Figure 8.7: Individual Quantification Checklist

DATE	MATERIAL	OUTCOME		STRATEGY				ERRORS		ADDITION			COMMENTS
		FREE PLAY	MAKES SETS	GLOBAL	1:1	COUNTS	STABLE ORDER TO	SKIPS	RE-COUNTS	COUNTS ALL	ADDS ON	KNOWS COMBINA-TIONS	
9/15	Strawberry Picking Game (Activity 2.1)		X to 3		X								
9/30	Strawberry Picking Game (Activity 2.1)		X to 3			X	3						
10/17	Spiderwebs (Activity 2.8)		X to 3			X	3						
11/3	Nature Game (Activity 2.3)		X to 4	X 5 and 6		X to 4	4						Rolls 1–6 die. Makes correct sets for 1–4. Puts in handful for 5–6.

Group Quantification Checklist

BACKGROUND

Checklists, such as Quantification Checklist (Assessment Example 8.7), can also be used for groups. Classroom checklists are particularly useful when a teacher wants to document all children using the same material or when an activity has been planned for a special area, such as the gross-motor room. The following checklist shows how three different children responded to the same mathematics-oriented literacy chart. A blank Group Quantification Checklist can be found in appendix F.

INTERPRETING THE CHECKLIST

From this group checklist, the teacher can determine a range of mathematical outcomes for the interactive chart. At this point, Mikey enjoys playing with the teddy bears but cannot yet make sets to accompany the song; however, he does like to count along with the other children, and he is likely learning the counting words from these experiences.

Anna counts to decide how many bears to place on the chart for each verse of the song. While she has stable order counting to ten, she skips some of the bears when she counts them. Latoya also counts to determine how many bears to put on the chart. She does not show any counting errors in this example.

GUIDES FOR FUTURE PLANNING

A range of children are enjoying using the chart. Children, such as Anna and Latoya, are gaining practice with counting, while Mikey is learning from them. It would be good to leave the chart out for a while longer and then replace it with a similar chart. Mikey and other children on his level might benefit from a chart that went up to five rather than all the way to ten. He might begin to make sets with the smaller numbers. Finally, additional materials such as die and counter games (chapters 2 and 3) and counting books could be introduced to expand counting and quantification experiences for these children.

MORE >

Figure 8.8: Class Quantification Checklist

Material: "Ten in the Bed" Chart (Activity 3.2)

CHILD	OUTCOME		STRATEGY			ERRORS			ADDITION			COMMENTS
	FREE PLAY	MAKES SETS	GLOBAL	1:1	COUNTS	STABLE ORDER TO	SKIPS	RE-COUNTS	COUNTS ALL	ADDS ON	KNOWS COMBINA-TIONS	
Mikey	X											Counts when others play. No attempts to make sets.
Anna		X			X		X					
Latoya		X			X							No errors.

Checklist for Sorting and Classifying

BACKGROUND

The development of concepts for sorting and classifying is a critical component of the Algebra standard for preschool and kindergarten children (chapter 4). A simple checklist, such as the one included in appendix G, can help teachers monitor development of these concepts throughout the year. The following example shows how a four-year-old child demonstrates sorting and classifying during the first months of school, as recorded on a checklist.

INTERPRETING THE CHECKLIST

This checklist provides valuable information for the teacher. It shows that Sanjay can sort a variety of objects, and he is not limited to one attribute per collection. In each case, he sorts the items by either two or three different attributes over time.

GUIDES FOR FUTURE PLANNING

Sanjay is responding well to the collections for sorting and classifying in his classroom. Because he clearly recognizes a variety of attributes, the teacher might use the same collections to model patterning. In addition, she might combine graphing with a class collection. For example, when introducing a seashell collection into the science area, she might ask Sanjay and some other children to graph how many of each type of shell there are. They could also graph other attributes of the collection, such as size, shape, or color.

MORE >

Figure 8.9: Individual Assessment Form for Collections

Child: Nancy

COLLECTION	SORTS BY, DATE					
Hat Collection (Activity 4.10)	type 9/15	size 9/20				
Clothespin and Clip Collection (Activity 4.11)	color 10/15	size 10/17	type 10/23			
Key Collection (Activity 4.12)	size 11/15	size 11/18				

Curriculum-Based Assessment

BACKGROUND

It was nearing the end of the first quarter of preschool, and James would soon be holding parent-teacher conferences. Although he had a variety of assessments on each child, including anecdotal and checklist records, he wanted to have a current and consistent record of the children's quantification knowledge to share with parents during conferences. Because his curriculum incorporated many math games, James decided to use a quantification game for his curriculum-based assessment. As it had recently snowed for the first time that year, James designed a snowman game to play with each child. Children would take turns with him drawing cards that had from one to five snowmen stickers on them, and they would be asked to take as many plastic snowmen counters as they had stickers on their cards. James also devised a simple scoring sheet to record the data for each child. He planned to check for quantification level, counting skills, and the child's ability to compare sets.

SAMPLE SCORING SHEET

Name: Sammy Date: 12/3	SCORE	COMMENTS
CARD 1—QUANTIFICATION Ask the child to take as many snowmen as there are stickers on the card.	0 1 2 ③ 4 **Score 0** if the child does not take any snowmen **Score 1** for global **Score 2** for 1:1 **Score 3** for counts **Score 4** counts & is correct	Sammy counted the 4 stickers correctly but took 5 snowmen.
CARD 1—COUNTING Ask the child how many snowmen he has all together.	0 1 ② 3 4 **Score 1 point** for each: ① stable order 1 1:1 principle ① cardinality 1 correct answer	Sammy skipped 1 snowman; he counted 4 and told me he had 4.
CARD 1—COMPARING SETS Ask the child who has more snowmen, or if you have the same.	0 1 ② 3 4 **Score 0** for no attempt **Score 1** for global strategy **Score 2** for 1:1 strategy **Score 3** for counting strategy ***Score 1** extra pt. for correct answer	Sammy initially just looked at the snowmen and said he had more. Then he lined up the snowmen and realized we had the same.

MORE >

INTERPRETING THE CURRICULUM-BASED MEASURE

When James meets with Sammy's parents, he will be able to show them how much their three-year-old son already understands about mathematics. First, he is at the counting level of quantification, which indicates he understands the purpose of counting. While Sammy makes some typical one-to-one correspondence errors when he counts objects, he demonstrates stable order counting and understanding of cardinality. Finally, when Sammy compares sets, he initially responds by relying on his perceptions, but then he rechecks his thinking by placing the objects in the two sets into a one-to-one correspondence relationship. The parent conference will give James an opportunity to explain what these math terms and concepts mean and to describe the likely learning trajectory for Sammy during the rest of the year. With this knowledge, the parents may be able to reinforce Sammy's mathematical understanding at home.

GUIDES FOR FUTURE PLANNING

The data from this curriculum-based measure shows that games such as the one used for this measurement tool are at the right instructional level for Sammy. He can use the knowledge he already has to play the games and then gradually move forward in his thinking, such as by applying his counting skills to set comparison problems. If James finds other children in the class are not challenged by the curriculum-based measure, he can design more complex games for them, such as a path game with two dice to combine together.

Portfolio Assessment

BACKGROUND

Portfolio assessments give teachers and parents a broad perspective of a child's learning because they include information from a variety of sources and chart development over time. Because they can capture learning that children may not be able to demonstrate on traditional assessments, portfolios are especially useful for children who have disabilities and children who are learning English as a second language. According to Loris Malaguzzi, founder of the highly esteemed Reggio Emilia schools in Italy, all children have many languages in which to express themselves, including art, music, play, and movement (Edwards et al. 1998). Because portfolios often include photographs, work samples, and even recordings, learning in the various mathematical content standards that might otherwise be lost can, instead, be preserved and analyzed. Portfolios may be compiled in scrapbook form and given to parents at the end of the school year.

The following examples show elements related to mathematical learning taken from the portfolio of a preschool child who was just beginning to learn English at the beginning of the school year. For purposes of this assessment example, the child's name will be Lin.

ANECDOTES AND CHECKLISTS

Anecdotes and checklists can be important components of portfolio assessments that teachers keep for their own information; however, teachers need to select which information they choose to include in a portfolio given to parents. Generally, information that is positive and shows progression over time is most appropriate. Teachers may choose to maintain anecdotal records and checklists just for themselves, and include summaries, photographs, and work samples in the portfolios they give to parents, as was the case with Lin's portfolio.

PHOTOGRAPHS

A photograph taken on the first day of school (figure 1) shows Lin already playing a simple quantification game, the Strawberry Picking Game (Activity 2.1), part of the Number and Operations standard. Although she does not yet speak much English, she is able to demonstrate her mathematical knowledge with the die and strawberry counters and play the game with another child. A second first day photo (figure 2) shows Lin painting a symmetrical picture at the easel, thereby documenting this component of the Geometry standard.

As the year progresses, photographs capture Lin sorting animal pegs simultaneously by color and type of animal, playing a drum pattern to represent thunder during music time, and creating and extending patterns with picture cards (figure 3). Her interest in symmetry is repeatedly captured as she carefully examines a symmetrical leaf rubbing, models a symmetrical cat mask she designed and constructed (figure 4), shows symmetrical happy and sad puppets she made, and wears a symmetrical necklace she strung with colored pasta. These are components of both the Algebra and Geometry standards. Lin's understanding of measurement is documented in photographs of her using a sewing pattern to cut out pants for a costume (figure 5) and holding up burlap to measure pants for a friend (figure 6).

MORE >

Figure 1

Figure 2

Figure 3

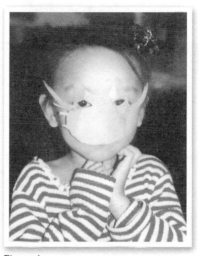

Figure 4

Figure 5

Figure 6

MORE >

WORK SAMPLES

Work samples included in Lin's portfolio document further her work in mathematics during this preschool year. Not surprisingly, there are many art examples that reflect symmetry: drawings of faces, people, and animals; nonrepresentational marker drawings with a strong sense of both shape and symmetry (figure 7); and fold-over paintings, which create symmetrical images. Of particular interest from the Algebra and Measurement areas is a drawing of cats nested within cats (figure 8). Another art sample shows a house created by gluing on paper cutouts of geometric shapes (figure 9). A work sample taken from near the end of the school year shows Lin's attempts at writing addition combinations using mathematical notation (figure 10). Because this would not have been introduced in preschool, she may have learned this notation at home. Although numerals are sometimes reversed and signs missing, the work sample shows her mathematical thinking:

- In the top example, she knows that $5 + 5 = 10$ but gets an answer of twelve when she adds one more. She then writes that $6 + 6$ (numerals reversed) $= 12$.

- In the middle example, she appears to indicate that six and seven are thirteen, although two numerals are reversed and the plus sign is in the wrong place. (She has also written the name of her teacher.)

- In the bottom example, Lin seems to indicate that $5 + 5 = 8 + 1 + 1$, because the $1 + 1 = 2$. She also writes $6 + 6 = 12$.

Lin's use of standard and nonstandard conventions in notating her mathematical thinking are strongly reminiscent of her writing examples, which include letterlike forms, phonemic spelling, and standard spelling. These occur elsewhere in her portfolio.

Taken as a whole, Lin's portfolio demonstrates substantial learning and understanding in Number and Operations, Algebra, Geometry, and Measurement. How did she arrive at such strong conceptual understanding in these areas? A final sample from her portfolio gives a clue. Figure 11 shows Lin using art to play with ideas of symmetry, representation through geometric forms, and the graphics of letters and numbers early in the school year. The portfolio documents Lin playing with math concepts in the manipulative area, art, and music. It substantiates the substantial learning that occurs in a play-based preschool environment.

MORE >

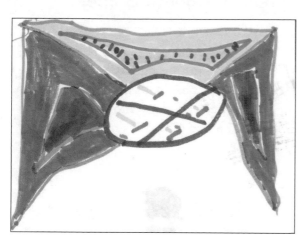

Figure 7

Figure 8

house

Figure 9

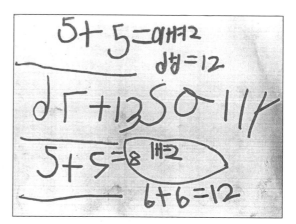

Figure 10

Figure 11

Appendix A: General Instructions for Board Games

There are three types of board games—grid, short path, and long path. Grid games are the easiest for young children, and long path games are the most challenging. Short path games provide a bridge between the other two types. They are more challenging than the grid games but not as complex as long path games. Teachers may include all three types of games throughout the year.

Grid Games

- Bingo-type cards without letters and numbers used in combination with die or spinner and intriguing counters

- Two game boards made from poster board with stickers, clip art, or rubber stamp impressions to form the grid

- Each grid board has 8–20 spaces

- In most cases a 1–3 die will be used for grid games. A 1–6 die may be most appropriate for a grid game with multiple counters as the cover up pieces

- Counters should fit the size of the grid space (not too large or too small)

- Do not use more than one picture in each grid space

- Grid boards should be laminated or covered with clear contact paper for durability

Short Path Games

- Poster board for game board

- Each game has two paths, either on the same poster board or two separate boards

- Each path is created by using circles, squares or other simple shapes to form the path

- Each path has 10–12 spaces (not including the ending point)

- Each path is straight

- The path may contain an illustration for the beginning and ending point

- Collection pieces, if desired, may be added for interest

- Environmental print may be added if desired

- One mover for each player (can be the same type)

- The movers should not be larger than the spaces on the path

MORE >

- In most cases a 1–3 die is shared by the players

- The game board(s) should be laminated or covered with clear contact paper for durability

Long Path Games

- Poster board for creating the game board (approximately 22 × 22 inches)

- Path made with circles, squares, or other simple shapes (about 1 inch each)

- 25–50 or more spaces to form the path (can be more for kindergarten)

- Path configuration and number of spaces match level of difficulty of the game

  – Simple: 90 degree straight path S formation (fewest number of spaces)

  – More complex: curved S formation (30 spaces or more)

  – Most complex: irregular path configuration (40–50 spaces or more)

- Illustration for beginning and ending point

- Environmental print if desired

- Trap or bonus spaces if desired

- Different mover for each player

- 1–6 die, shared by players, for simplest path configuration

- Pair of dice, shared by players, for more complex game

- Collection pieces, if desired, to add interest

- The movers should not be larger than spaces on the path

- The spaces should not touch each other or be too close together

- Do not connect the spaces on the path with a line

- The spaces should not be too far apart

- The game is aesthetically appealing, free of too much print or illustrations, smudges, pencil marks, etc.

- The game board should be laminated or covered with clear contact paper for durability

Appendix B: Sample Letter to Parents

Dear Parents,

It is your child's turn to have the Math Suitcase for the weekend. The games in the suitcase are similar to those you see in the classroom. Please send it back on Monday so that I may prepare it for the next child's turn. You will find an inventory of the pieces for the games inside the suitcase.

What should you do to help your child play the games?

You or an older sibling can play the games with your child. Grandmas and grandpas might like to play too. Although there aren't any rules for how to play the games, there are some guidelines for how to begin playing the games. Children will play the games in a variety of ways, and that is okay. They will learn math concepts by playing the games and especially by watching you make decisions on your turn. They will make mistakes, and that is okay too. These mistakes are a part of learning. You don't need to correct the mistakes when they happen. Watch for changes in your child's thinking as he or she gains experience with math games.

Grid Game: two game boards, a 1–3 die, and marble chips for cover-up pieces

These game boards might look like Bingo cards to you. For this game, each player takes one gird game card. You will each take turns rolling the die to determine how many cover-up pieces to take. For example, if a player rolls the die and gets 2 dots, that player takes 2 marble chips and places one on each space of the grid board. Some children may grab a small handful rather than counting the dots on the die. Some children may point to a dot and take a marble chip, point to the next dot and take another marble chip. Some children may count the dots and take the same number of marble chips to place on each picture on the grid. You can count the dots on your turn, but you don't need to correct the child on his or her turn.

Path Game: one game board, two movers, and a 1–6 die

This game probably looks like board games you have seen before, but it doesn't come with a set of rules. Players try to get from the beginning of the path to the end of the path by taking turns rolling the die and moving along the path. As they are learning, some children may hop to the end of the path without rolling the die. Some children may roll the die but skip spaces as they move on the path. Some children may re-count the space they occupy each time they take a turn. Some children may miscount the dots on the die or miscount the spaces as they move on the path. These errors in thinking are all part of learning. Developing math concepts takes time and experience. Children

MORE >

lose confidence in their math abilities if we constantly correct the mistakes they make. They may begin to think that only adults can solve math problems. You can model counting the dots and moving on the path when it is your turn.

What can you do if your child makes errors while playing the games?

- You can ignore the mistakes in many instances. They are part of learning about mathematics, just like children may say "bana" for banana when learning to talk.

- Play accurately on your turn. Use your tone of voice to emphasize the counting words as you count the dots on the die. "One, two, three. I have three dots, so I will take three marble chips."

- Describe what you are doing on your turn. "Let's see, I have six dots on the die, and I am going to move my person ahead six spaces on the path toward the end." Emphasize advancing forward on the path.

Here are some questions you can ask your child to help further math knowledge.
(Ask them sparingly or your child may not want to play the game!)

- How did you know how many marble chips to take?

- How many more spaces until you reach the end of the path?

- If you roll two dots on the die, will you cover the rest of the spaces on the grid?

- What do I have to roll to reach the end of the path?

- How many more marble chips do you need to fill the rest of your grid board?

I hope you enjoy playing math games with your child. Please let me know if you have questions about the games or about how to play with your child.

Appendix C: Pony Photograph

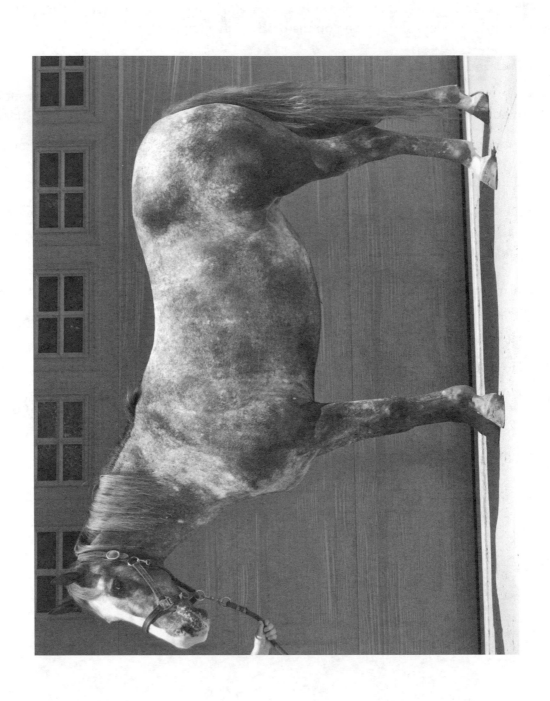

More Than Counting: Standards-Based Math Activities for Young Thinkers in Preschool and Kindergarten, Standards Edition, by Sally Moomaw and Brenda Hieronymus, © 2011. Redleaf Press grants permission to photocopy this page for classroom use.

Appendix D: Individual Assessment Form for Number Concepts

Child:

DATE	MATERIAL	OUTCOME		STRATEGY			ERRORS				ADDITION			COMMENTS
		FREE PLAY	MAKES SETS	GLOBAL	1:1	COUNTS	STABLE ORDER TD	SKIPS	RE-COUNTS	COUNTS ALL	ADDS ON	KNOWS COMBINA-TIONS		

More Than Counting: Standards-Based Math Activities for Young Thinkers in Preschool and Kindergarten, Standards Edition, by Sally Moomaw and Brenda Hieronymus, © 2011. Redleaf Press grants permission to photocopy this page for classroom use.

Appendix E: Terms and Definitions for Number Concepts Assessment

TERM	DEFINITION	EXAMPLE
free play	Imaginative play, not necessarily involving math	A child hops the squirrel counters randomly around the grid board and pretends they are collecting nuts.
makes sets	Attempts to construct sets of a particular quantity	A child rolls the die and takes the same number of counters as dots on the die or moves the same number of spaces along a path (see chapters 2 and 3).
global	Takes a handful or fills in randomly with boundaries	A child rolls the die and then grabs a handful of counters.
1:1	Uses one-to-one correspondence to take an equivalent amount	A child takes a game piece each time she points to a dot on the die or places one counter on each sticker of a grid game (see chapters 2 and 3).
counts	Uses counting to decide how many to take	A child counts the dots on the die and then counts a corresponding number of game pieces or moves a corresponding number of spaces along a path (see chapters 2 and 3).
stable order	Says number words in the correct order	A child counts 1, 2, 3, 4 in the same order each time. After 4, the number words vary: 1, 2, 3, 4, 8, 6; 1, 2, 3, 4, 6, 9; 1, 2, 3, 4, 9, 8.
skips	Skips over some objects when counting	A child points to the stars faster than he counts. * * * * * * * 1 2 3 4 5
re-counts	Counts some objects more than once	A child counts the stars in the first row then the stars in the second row and then some from the first row again.
counts all	Combines two dice by counting all the dots	A child counts all the dots on one die and continues counting all the dots on a second die.
adds on	Knows the quantity of the first set and counts on without re-counting the first set	A child rolls a 3 and a 6. Recognizing the 3, she counts on: 4, 5, 6, 7, 8, 9.
combinations	Remembers some addition combinations	Most children remember "doubles" first, for example, $1 + 1 = 2$; $2 + 2 = 4$; $3 + 3 = 6$.

Appendix F: Class Assessment Form for Number and Operations

Material:

CHILD	OUTCOME		STRATEGY			ERRORS			ADDITION			COMMENTS
	FREE PLAY	MAKES SETS	GLOBAL	1:1	COUNTS	STABLE ORDER TO	SKIPS	RE-COUNTS	COUNTS ALL	ADDS ON	KNOWS COMBINA-TIONS	

More Than Counting: Standards-Based Math Activities for Young Thinkers in Preschool and Kindergarten, Standards Edition, by Sally Moomaw and Brenda Hieronymus, © 2011.
Redleaf Press grants permission to photocopy this page for classroom use.

Child:

COLLECTION	SORTS BY, DATE				

References

CHAPTER 1

Florida Department of Education. 2007. http://www.floridastandards.org/Standards/FLStandardSearch.aspx, accessed October 24, 2009.

Klibanoff, Raquel S., Susan C. Levine, Janellen Huttenlocher, Marina Vasilyeva, and Larry V. Hedges. 2006. Preschooler Children's Mathematical Knowledge: The Effect of Teacher "Math Talk." *Developmental Psychology* 42 (1): 56–69.

National Council of Teachers of Mathematics (NCTM). 1989. *Curriculum and Evaluation Standards for School Mathematics*. Reston, VA: NCTM.

National Council of Teachers of Mathematics (NCTM). 2000. *Principles and Standards for School Mathematics*. 4th ed. Reston, VA: NCTM.

National Council of Teachers of Mathematics (NCTM). 2006. *Curriculum Focal Points for Prekindergarten through Grade 8 Mathematics*. Reston, VA: NCTM.

National Mathematics Advisory Panel. 2008. *Foundations for Success: The Final Report of the National Mathematics Advisory Panel*. Washington, DC: U.S. Department of Education.

National Research Council. 2009. *Mathematics Learning in Early Childhood: Paths toward Excellence and Equity*. Committee on Early Childhood, Christopher T. Cross, Taniesha A. Woods, and Heidi Schweingruber, eds. Center for Education, Division of Behavioral and Social Sciences and Education. Washington, DC: The National Academies Press.

Salend, Spencer J. 2008. *Creating Inclusive Classrooms: Effective and Reflective Practices*. 6th ed. Upper Saddle River, NJ: Pearson Merrill Prentice Hall.

CHAPTER 2

Gelman, Rochel, and C. R. Gallistel. 1978. *The Child's Understanding of Number*. Cambridge, MA: Harvard University Press.

Kamii, Constance. 1982. *Number in Preschool and Kindergarten: Educational Implications of Piaget's Theory*. Washington, DC: National Association for the Education of Young Children.

National Council of Teachers of Mathematics (NCTM). 2006. *Curriculum Focal Points for Prekindergarten through Grade 8 Mathematics*. Reston, VA: NCTM.

CHAPTER 3

Baroody, Arthur J. 1987. The Development of Counting Strategies for Single-Digit Addition. *Journal for Research in Mathematics Education* 18 (2): 141–57.

Clements, Douglas H., and Julie Sarama. 2007. Early Childhood Mathematics Learning. In *Second Handbook of Research on Mathematics Teaching and Learning: A Project of the National Council of Teachers of Mathematics,* ed. Frank K. Lester Jr. Charlotte, NC: Information Age Publishing.

Kamii, Constance, with Leslie Baker Housman. 2000. *Young Children Reinvent Arithmetic: Implications of Piaget's theory.* 2nd ed. New York: Teachers College Press.

National Council of Teachers of Mathematics (NCTM). 2000. *Principles and Standards for School Mathematics.* 4th ed. Reston, VA: NCTM.

CHAPTER 4

Moomaw, Sally. 1997. *More Than Singing: Discovering Music in Preschool and Kindergarten.* St. Paul, MN: Redleaf Press.

National Council of Teachers of Mathematics (NCTM). 2000. *Principles and Standards for School Mathematics.* 4th ed. Reston, VA: NCTM.

CHAPTER 5

Clements, Douglas H., and Julie Sarama. 2007. Early Childhood Mathematics Learning. In *Second Handbook of Research on Mathematics Teaching and Learning: A Project of the National Council of Teachers of Mathematics,* ed. Frank K. Lester Jr. Charlotte, NC: Information Age Publishing.

National Council of Teachers of Mathematics (NCTM). 2000. *Principles and Standards for School Mathematics.* 4th ed. Reston, VA: NCTM.

National Council of Teachers of Mathematics (NCTM). 2006. *Curriculum Focal Points for Prekindergarten through Grade 8 Mathematics.* Reston, VA: NCTM.

van Hiele, Pierre M. 1999. Developing Geometric Thinking through Activities That Begin with Play. *Teaching Children Mathematics* 6 (February): 310–16.

CHAPTER 6

Clements, Douglas H., and Julie Sarama. 2007. Early Childhood Mathematics Learning. In *Second Handbook of Research on Mathematics Teaching and Learning: A Project of the National Council of Teachers of Mathematics,* ed. Frank K. Lester Jr. Charlotte, NC: Information Age Publishing.

Morrow, L. 1997. *Shoe and Meter: Children and Measurement.* Reggio Emilia, Italy: Reggio Children.

National Council of Teachers of Mathematics (NCTM). 2006. *Curriculum Focal Points for Prekindergarten through Grade 8 Mathematics.* Reston, VA: NCTM.

Piaget, Jean. 1952. *The Child's Conception of Number.* London: Routledge and Kegan Paul.

CHAPTER 8

Edwards, Carolyn, Lella Gandini, and George Forman, eds. 1998. *The Hundred Languages of Children: The Reggio Emilia Approach—Advanced Reflections.* 2nd ed. Westport, CT: Ablex Publishing.

Gelman, Rochel, and C. R. Gallistel. 1978. *The Child's Understanding of Number.* Cambridge, MA: Harvard University Press.

Kamii, Constance. 1982. *Number in Preschool and Kindergarten: Educational Implications of Piaget's Theory.* Washington, DC: National Association for the Education of Young Children.

Kamii, Constance, with Leslie Baker Housman. 2000. *Young Children Reinvent Arithmetic: Implications of Piaget's Theory.* 2nd ed. New York: Teachers College Press.

National Council of Teachers of Mathematics (NCTM). 2000. *Principles and Standards for School Mathematics.* 4th ed. Reston, VA: NCTM.

Salend, Spencer J. 2008. *Creating Inclusive Classrooms: Effective and Reflective Practices.* 6th ed. Upper Saddle River, NJ: Pearson Merrill Prentice Hall.

Shinn, Mark R., and Suzanne Bamonto. 1998. Advanced Applications of Curriculum-Based Measurement: "Big Ideas" and Avoiding Confusion. In *Advanced Applications of Curriculum-Based Measurement,* Mark R. Shinn, ed. New York: Guilford Press.

van Hiele, Pierre M. 1999. Developing Geometric Thinking through Activities That Begin with Play. *Teaching Children Mathematics* 6 (February): 310–16.